DARK
& D

DARK BREAD
& Dancing

⤳

The Diaries of Sue Rawson
1906–2006

Rosemary Rawson

Dark Bread and Dancing:
The Diaries of Sue Rawson

Rawson, Rosemary
Dark Bread and Dancing:
The Diaries of Sue Rawson / Rosemary Rawson

ISBN 978-1480299153
1. Memoir, 2. Women, 3. Family, 4. North Dakota

Book and cover design © 2013
All Rights Reserved by Rosemary Rawson
Cover and interior design and composition by Carol White
Illustrations by Shannon McBride

First Edition 2013

20 19 18 17 16 15 14 13   8 7 6 5 4 3 2

Printed in the United States of America

Dedicated to

The Families

The Lenits
The Gores
The Rawsons
The Letofskys
The Leones
The Flanders

We are all richer for being in her gene pool

TABLE OF CONTENTS

INTRODUCTION

*B*efore my mother died in 2006 she left me with about a bushel and a half of her diaries, hand-written journals she had kept in fits and starts, recording the minutia of her life – who visited, who won at bridge or Scrabble, what she used for cleaning the paneling, when she got her last perm and almost always, what they had for supper. In between she revealed her hopes and dreams and frustrations. Over time she developed a philosophy of "living in love" and a strong Christian faith; she wrestled with disappointment, betrayal and grief. She lived a hundred years, so the well she drew from was deep.

In her will she left $3,000 to publish them. No caveats, no instructions. There were four small notebooks in which she recorded her teenage diaries; four 8½"x5" travel journals, two one-year diaries, one thick loose leaf binder that covered September 1965 to December 1969. Then there were nineteen 8½"x11" spiral notebooks, plus letters, clippings and some taped interviews about her early life. In 2005 I plunged in, arranged them in chronological order and began to transcribe the earliest and smallest, hoping an organization would emerge. When I started on the travel diaries, my eyes glazed over and I put them back in the closet. Over the next few years stuff happened – I was diagnosed with Parkinson's disease and my husband died. My life changed. The diaries languished in the closet waiting for lightning to strike.

It was my daughter Polly who provided the way forward. We took a road trip together to Bryce Canyon and while we rode and hiked and took pictures, we talked about Mom's diaries. Polly had been through a similar process with her own book, *3MPH*, the story of her five-year walk around the world for breast cancer. She, too, worked from the daily journals she kept on the walk and came up with a travel memoir that won awards. She self-published and in the process gained invaluable experience she was willing to share.

But how to get continuity, a "story" line? What about the great gaps of time – decades sometimes – when there were no diaries? "Forget about individual journal entries," she advised, "do it as narrative; you can still maintain her 'voice' and tell her story. The gaps in the thirties, forties and fifties – that's *your* story and in a way it was still her story only from your point of view." I thought it just might work.

I began again with new resolve. This new approach freed me in other ways. While it gave me permission to add my perspective, I tried not to interpret too much, to let her own words speak for her. Some parts are not very flattering; I included them because I think they give the story grit and context and authenticity. Sometimes I felt like she still lived around the corner. I laughed, I cried, I wrote. The volume of material was so great that choices had to be made constantly – whether to include this part or not, to trim here and elaborate there. In the end the book probably contains only five to ten percent of all that she wrote. Someone else going through the same material might come up with a different story. This is mine. I hope Sue would recognize it as hers as well.

Rosemary
January, 2013

CHAPTER 1

The Homestead

...chokecherry picnics

In 1905 a young shipping clerk named Albert Einstein, who fancied himself a scientist, had managed to publish his paper on a radical new theory he called the Theory of Relativity or $E=mc^2$. Whatever that meant. In North Carolina the Wright boys were still fiddling with their flying machine and managed on their second try to keep it in the air for thirty-nine minutes. They were quite excited, of course, but really, what difference could it possibly make in the long run? Neither of those events caused much stir in North Dakota.

Teddy Roosevelt was President of the United States and already annoying the conservative Democrats with his trust-busting ways and really set their ears smoking when he invited that black, Booker T. Washington, right into the White House. North Dakotans were more apt to look fondly on Teddy Roosevelt ever since he declared, "I never would have been President if it had not been for my experiences in North Dakota." His years as a sportsman and rancher in the Badlands "took the snob out of him," he said, and taught him to judge folks on their character and accomplishments, not on how rich and famous they were. That set their heads nodding in agreement.

North Dakota was wide open prairie in 1905. It had only been a state for sixteen years and had fewer people in the whole state than a midsized city holds today. There were no midsized cities here, only small ones, and hundreds of smaller towns whose only purpose was to service homesteaders and get their crops and cattle to market. The Homestead Act of 1862 brought many immigrants to the plains, but North Dakota wasn't the first choice for most of them. They would have preferred somewhere with a longer growing season and shorter, milder winters. Somewhere with a creek or a tree. To make it here you had to be 'tougher than a boiled owl.'

In Kensal, North Dakota, fifty miles north of Jamestown, the town barber, Butch Maynard, and his wife Lena were making plans for the birth of their second child. It was best, they decided, for Lena to take their toddler Margaret and go to stay with Lena's sister Mary in Willmar, Minnesota, until the baby was born. It was January, and a blizzard could come swooping out of Canada at any time with little warning. Better to plan ahead. So bags were packed and Lena and little Margaret rode the train to Valley City and on to Fargo and Willmar. The baby was born on January 27, 1906. They named her – God knows why – Izora Minerva.

"Look, Margaret," said Lena, by way of introduction. "This is your baby sister, Izora."

"Zuzu," said fifteen-month-old Margaret, giving her a poke (the first of many). And so she became and remained, "Sue."

Sue was my Mom. This is her story and mine as well.

Any history of Sue's parents is fragmentary at best. There is a picture of Lena's family, four sons and four daughters, looking quite Edwardian and handsome at the peak of their young adult attractiveness. The parents in the picture look formal and austerely buttoned-up. They had emigrated from Denmark in the mid 1800s.

Butch (Walter) Maynard grew up in Wisconsin. His mother died young and Butch and his four siblings were raised – and as quickly as possible – by their grandmother. Lena and Butch, as was common for young singles at the time, worked their way west as jobs and opportunity presented themselves. How they met or how they landed in Kensal no one knows.

And so they were married, and before long they had baby Margaret, who was not yet two when Lena went off to Willmar to stay with Mary until Sue was born.

The lure of free land was still strong (certainly stronger than the prospects of barbering). By 1909 the free land was pretty picked over. It sounded simple enough: Find an unclaimed parcel of land (typically 160 acres), file a claim, provide some evidence that you intended to stay, live on it for five years and it was yours. They found a homestead in northern Kidder County that had been filed by a guy known as Big-lipped Jim, and now he wanted out of it. They might have picked the least promising spot in Kidder County, near a stretch of rough stony hills known as "the gulches" with deep ravines dotted with sparse growths of box elder, thorn apple and scrub oak along with the more promising bushes of plum, chokecherry and wild grapes. There was plenty of game available – deer, ducks, grouse and pheasants.

The holding had a two-room tarpaper shack and sort of a barn that was dug back into the side of a hill and supported by poles and wires and straw.

In the spring of 1909, the Maynards left Kensal for the forty-some mile trip to their future. They hitched a team of horses to the new hayrack piled with a few household essentials, a Majestic cooking range, a walking plow and one cow, which followed behind. And two little girls. The best of the roads were dirt and gravel, but for the last twenty miles or more there were no roads at all, just a barely worn pair of ruts leading into a rocky, hilly stretch of prairie.

The nearest towns were Sykeston to the north and Dawson to the south, both about twenty miles, where Butch could go with horse and wagon to get the basics: salt, sugar, flour, yeast, coffee and maybe kerosene or nails. It was an overnight trip, and with North Dakota's infamous weather, not to be undertaken often or lightly.

And so they settled into their two-room home. The toilet barely qualified as an outhouse. The well, though a good long stone's throw from the house, was already there. The bedroom took up almost half the house. The girls slept on a feather tick on the floor beside the folks' bed.

Daily life on the kitchen side of the house was royally overseen by the Majestic range, a cast iron and chrome beast that took up a good chunk of the available floor space. The stove had a reservoir on one end that held a supply of hot water for washing dishes and body parts as needed. It was the girls' job to keep the reservoir full, carrying water from the well several times a day.

In a taped interview, Sue described that early life:

> The Majestic cooked our meals, heated the water for baths and laundry and kept us warm, all with our own home-grown fuel – cow chips. Gathering cow chips was a job for Margaret and me. We would head for the pasture with gunny sacks to collect fuel for the ever voracious Majestic. It was important to find the dry ones; the ones that were still a little moist didn't burn, so we had to be very discriminating.
>
> Washing clothes was an all day affair and it took considerable preparation. We didn't have a lot of clothes, nor did we change them daily, so the signal that washday was imminent seemed to come from the cream separator. It was an absolute must to have a clean, white cotton towel to strain the milk into the big bowl of the cream separator, so when all these strainers were soiled, it was time to wash.
>
> Two big galvanized tubs were retrieved from some now forgotten hiding place and set onto sawhorses. Mom would put the big copper boiler on the stove and fill it with water.

When it was sufficiently hot and steaming she would dip it out with a big dipper into the first tub where she rubbed the clothes on the washboard with bar soap until they were clean. Separator cloths, sheets and towels by turns would be put in the boiler with more soap and boiled. When they had been boiled and scrubbed to a fare-thee-well she would take a big stick and pull them out of the boiler and into the second tub for a final rinsing. Eventually everything was wrung by hand and hung outside to dry. It was an all day affair.

While Lena scrubbed, Sue and Margaret played among the piles of sorted clothes, stuffing the pillowslips with dirty laundry and tying them in the middle to make dolls of them.

As brisk fall turned to frigid north plains winter, they counted on the indomitable Majestic range to keep the little house warm — or warm enough.

In fall Pop put layers of sod, a foot wide and maybe three inches thick and stacked them in layers up beside the house up as far as the windows to insulate it from the cold. It seemed like a good idea at the time, but one day, when spring was about to break forth, we got out of our feather tick bed and found it was swarming with brownish wire worms that must have come out of the sod and worked their way up through the floor of the shack. Margaret and I were horrified to think we'd been sleeping with WORMS, but Mom just got the broom and dustpan and swept them up and tossed them out the door.

Of course we had a dog, every farm family did. Tiger was a medium-sized yellowish dog with medium length coat, and he was an important part of the family. He always went to get the cows. On cold nights he would go up on the roof and sleep near the chimney, the warmest place in the whole area.

Uncle Harry (Pop's brother) took a homestead about a mile east of us and built a new house – it even had an attic in it. He was a bachelor well into his forties when he married Hilda, a little Norwegian girl he found waiting on tables at the hotel. She was only eighteen. She once told us, "Harry is twice as old as I am. Just think, when I'm forty, he'll be eighty."

Tilsons lived about two and a half miles away in what seemed to us quite a grand house because it was made of stone. They were older than most of the neighbors; they had three grown children. He had been a jeweler in Carrington, but that wasn't working out for him and they took a chance on the homestead. But he was never cut out to be a farmer.

To the south of us were Paulsons. They had seven children one right after the other. They lived beside the slough which attracted a lot of ducks. We called it Deer Lake, but really, it was just a slough. Mr. Paulson was the game warden, but and he and Pop used to shoot ducks out of season. There was an island in the middle of their slough and in late summer we would pick chokecherries out there.

Henry Brown was our bachelor neighbor and he always seemed to visit on baking day and Mom would give him a loaf of bread to take home. I was about five years old and he loved to tease me. He would ask me, "You want to come home with me?" And I would say, "Sure." But then he'd get on his horse and go home. I thought he just forgot me. He pulled that trick several times. One time I was so determined to go, I started walking through the snow hollering, "Brown, wait for me." Finally Pop came and got me and brought me back. He must have got word to Brown after that, because it never happened again.

Our favorite and closest neighbors were the Hopkins' who lived about a mile from us. Elvie always loved a good joke and no one enjoyed a good joke more than my mother. Once in a while Pop had to go to Sykeston north of us or to Dawson to the south, and stayed all night because he couldn't make it there and back with the horses in one day. We loved it, because then Mom, Margaret and I would walk over to Hopkins's and stay overnight with them just for the fun of it. On one such occasion Mom prepared a beef roast to take with us, and when we got there they were twisting hay and putting it in a stove to keep warm. It was all they had for fuel, and all they had for food was some frozen potatoes. So they boiled up some of the frozen potatoes and made gravy from the roast beef and we all had a good hearty supper.

Even though the neighbors were scattered about the rocky hills, there were times of community gathering together. Every year in early August, when the chokecherries were ready to be picked, we would have a big picnic. Everybody came and the women brought their choicest food. They spread a blanket on the ground with a sheet or tablecloth over the top and spread out our picnic. Then everybody picked chokecherries – the kids stripped the lower branches and the men got the highest with ladders, and the women took what was in between. Everyone brought bushel baskets and wash tubs full of food for the picnic and carried home washtubs full of dark, ripe chokecherries. It was a great time. This insured a supply of chokecherry jelly that would last until they were ripe again. Once Mrs. Tilson made a special dessert with the juice, sweetened with sugar and thickened with cornstarch with a dollop of whipped cream on it. We all agreed she had taken chokecherries to a whole new level.

One year Pop tried to make chokecherry wine. He mixed it up in a wooden keg that he put out in the sun to ferment.

This particular day, Aunt Hannah and Uncle Mike drove out from Carrington to visit us and the grownups were having a nice conversation in the house, when all of a sudden we heard a big explosion in the front yard. The plug had blown out of the keg and the wine and seeds and foam were shooting straight up in the air. We gathered the sweet foam in our hands and licked it off. It was quite delicious, but that was the last time he tried making chokecherry wine.

Every summer we made a trip to the gulches, north of our place. The land is quite rough and hilly up there. We found wild raspberries and wild strawberries in the prairie grass. They never got much bigger than the end of a finger but they were the most delicious thing I'd ever tasted. We always brought cream along and usually it would sour before the day was over, becoming all thick and glossy and tangy, and we put it on our raspberries at the picnics.

Sometimes we hunted prairie chickens along the way. Uncle Harry was a very good shot, so all we had to do was find them. Then the women would tear the feathers off and fry them over a campfire when we got to the gulches. Of course they were fresh and delicious.

At least once a year we visited the Navens who came from Denmark. Mrs. Naven spoke hardly any English but my mother spoke fluent Danish so they would sit and talk Danish all day long.

Eventually we had to go to school. I was seven years old and Margaret was almost eight. We had learned our ABCs. On summer evenings it was still light out way past our bedtime. We were able to pick out letters and then familiar words on the magazines that insulated the walls in our little shack. For a while we walked over to Tilson's and Hazel helped us with our beginnings.

Pop taught school in his early years but he was disinclined to teach his own kids. He loved to read, so his evenings were mostly given over to reading the *Saturday Evening Post*. So he understood how important reading was, and he agreed to haul the kids of the area to the school six miles away. There were no roads, just the ruts that indicated the way. But very soon the North Dakota winter was on us; the snow was deep and the weather was cold. He put a canvas cover over the buggy, like the Conestoga wagons, to at least keep the wind off. We picked up other kids along the way. There was Adolph Morlock and Waltz's two boys, Christ and Jake, who were about the same age as Margaret and I. Christ had been to school a year; Margaret hadn't been to school at all. We were really looking forward to having kids we could talk to, but none of them could speak English so at first they just sat and watched us.

By the middle of the winter the weather got desperately cold. I never before or since had such cold feet. But Pop would get us there. The horses plowed through the deep snowdrifts and when we finally got to the schoolhouse the lunch we had in our bucket was frozen. We put it under the wood burner and hoped it would be thawed out by lunchtime, but the peanut butter was usually melted into the bread by then.

I loved school. Our first teacher was Effie Simmons. I loved her. We went to school about three months that year. As soon as spring had sprung and the roads opened up, the German Russian families wanted their kids at home to help with the chickens, tend the garden and slop the hogs, so the men could get out in the field. By that time Pop had enough of hauling kids to school, and started looking for a way to get us closer to a proper school. So plans were made and we left the homestead and moved into town.

One year at Christmas when Sue and Margaret were about four and five, they went with their mother to visit the aunts in Willmar. Margaret was a cute, curly headed outgoing little girl and Aunt Mary suggested that Margaret sing a song for their church Christmas program. Lena agreed. Margaret quickly learned the song. Sue did too, all three verses.

As time for the program drew near Sue believed that she would be singing the song with Margaret as they had been doing all along. Then there was the matter of the dress. Aunt Mary said that Margaret would need a new dress for the performance. A new dress! In her four-year-old's mind Sue could see them — she and Margaret were the same — in new dresses. The material was selected, and with a snip snip of scissors and a hum of the treadle sewing machine, the material — a tiny lime green check — was transformed into a Christmas dress. One dress. For Margaret. The evening of the program arrived and Aunt Mary took Margaret's hand and marched off, leaving Sue clutching her mother's hand, a tsunami of disappointment welling up within her. She knew that song. She sang it as well as Margaret did!

Twenty some years later Sue still remembered the song and the hurt. She had two little girls of her own. She reconstructed the song with piano accompaniment and taught it to the girls. She made them identical dresses to wear for the program. But in one of life's ironies, Bonnie, the oldest, refused at the last minute to sing for the program. The younger, Keeny, sang it alone — all three verses.

They moved to a little two room house in Pettibone, not much better than the one they had on the homestead. Pettibone was just three years old then, but already it had a pool hall, a depot, a hotel, a lumber yard, a hardware store, a Congregational Church, a newspaper and a few houses. The big two-story white clapboard schoolhouse with six classrooms was almost finished.

Pettibone was one of eight towns platted out by the Dakota Land and Townsite Company along the still-under-construction Pingree-Wilton Branch line of the Northern Pacific Railroad. The towns – Pingree, Woodworth, Pettibone, Robinson, Tuttle, Wing, Regan and Wilton – were all named for officials of the Townsite Company, and plotted about twelve miles apart. Every town had a depot, a water tank (for the trains), and very soon a grain elevator for shipping grain harvest and a stockyard for holding cattle overnight to be shipped for sale. There would be two trains a day, freight and a one-car passenger train known as The Goose.

> We didn't get settled to start school until October and really didn't know what grade we should be in, so we just went with kids our own age. There were a few desks with double seats and Lucille Worley coaxed me to come and sit with her. Margaret sat with someone else. The teacher asked us what grade we were in, and I was horrified at the thought of saying that I only had three months of school, so Lucille stuck her elbow into my ribs and said, "She's in the third grade." I held my breath and didn't say a word. So we were put in the third grade, to our delight, and I don't remember we ever had any trouble keeping up. From then on we were promoted along with the rest of the kids. The school had just been built, a lovely, big school with 1914 engraved over the door. It had two classrooms on the main floor for the primary grades and two upstairs for the future. There was no high school when we started school there, but eventually the

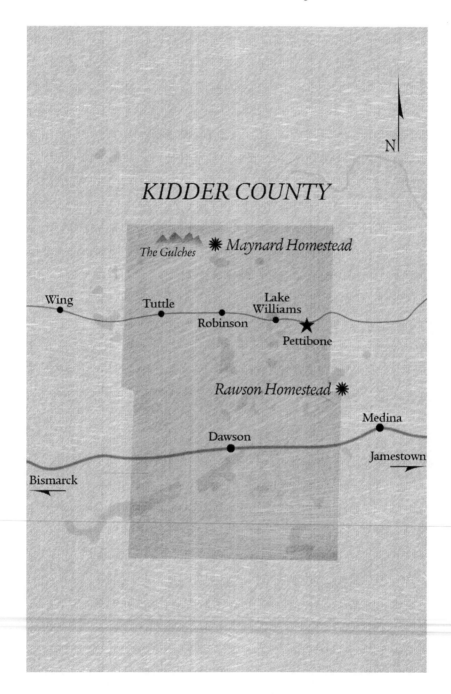

fourth room became a high school, starting out with two years and then expanding to four years.

That first summer our mother became very, very sick (I learned much later that she had a tubal pregnancy and almost died). Margaret and I (we were like seven and eight) were trying to run the house. Mrs. Dethloff came to the house maybe once a week or so and always brought a loaf of homemade bread. She gathered up our dirty clothes, took them home and brought them back all washed, ironed and neatly folded in piles. Then she would clean up the house and give Mom a bath. I don't know how she did it. She had three children herself and she did her work the same hard way Mom did, and she had a bigger, nicer house. Her husband ran the general store. They sold groceries and general sundries like needles and lamp chimneys – things everybody needed.

After the homestead was sold the folks bought some property about three quarters of a mile west of Pettibone – just land, it had no buildings on it – so Pop started by building the barn and the next summer they built the house. It was quite a nice house for its time. It had a dining room and living room with hardwood maple floors and pillars to set off the dining room. The woodwork was all painted white enamel. There was just one small bedroom (without a closet), and, of course, the bedroom was for the folks. It held a bed and a dresser, that's all. Margaret and I slept on the daybed in the dining room (later upstairs in the attic area); at night the sides pulled up to make a full-size bed. During the day the sides folded down to make a couch.

When I was about eight years old, the store ran a special: with every purchase we got coupons to use toward buying a phonograph. The phonograph was still a pretty new invention, and these were little square affairs with a hand crank we wound up to get it going and when it ran down, we had to wind it up again. When we finally got coupons enough for our phonograph they gave us some records to start, and then with trade we could earn new ones. The music it produced was squeaky and veered eerily in tone from high and fast to low and slow, but I thought it was wonderful. Over the years I think we collected almost a hundred records. Some of them were pretty good, some of them pretty bad. Mrs. Tilson gave us some classical music records and I took a special liking to those. I loved it when Mom would play the phonograph after we went to bed and we could go to sleep listening to Beethoven on our couch in the dining room while the folks sat up and read.

Mom had a nice singing voice and she sang a lot — standing over the ironing board and singing, shelling peas and singing, kneading bread and singing. Mostly she sang old Methodist hymns. When I was about ten years old a salesman came through town with a brochure showing the pianos he wanted to sell. He and Pop spent a lot of time with their heads together, and when he left Pop announced that he had ordered a piano for us. He paid a little down and signed a contract promising the rest at harvest. This was monumental in our house! To lay out money for anything as non-utilitarian as a piano was unheard of. The piano, an enormous upright Kimball, was carefully placed — and never strayed from — beneath the long window in the living room. There was one close call. Pop apparently had trouble making the payments and the salesman came back and threatened to repossess the piano. Pop threw up his hands and said, "All right, take it!" And Margaret and I put up a big fuss and cried, and I don't know how, but we got to keep the piano. We went looking for a teacher.

We knew that the depot agent's wife could play, so we went to see if she would give us music lessons. She said she would, for a dollar and fifty cents per lesson. This was very expensive, but since it was the only one available, Pop agreed. She only gave us a couple of lessons when they were transferred to another station. Teachers appeared and disappeared and by the time we'd had a couple of dozen lessons we'd been through half a dozen teachers. But this was enough to whet my appetite and to get me started. I practiced on every

Sue, age 9

piece of printed music I could find in magazines, scrapbooks or sheet music. Aunt Mary had taken music lessons, but by now she had four children and anybody as particular as Aunt Mary would never take time to play the piano, so she rolled up a great stack of music and mailed it to me and Margaret in Pettibone. She had a friend whose son was a band leader and he got all the new pop music for his band. As soon as it got a few months old, or if he didn't like it, he sent it on. Good old Sears Roebuck and Montgomery Ward sold everything, including sheet music. Their after-Christmas sale catalog included a great long list of music that we could get for a pittance — six cents for some, up to maybe twenty-nine cents tops. I would go through this list and come up with quite an assortment for a dollar or less.

I was without a teacher from the time I was twelve until I started high school at fourteen. Then the Bucks came to town. Mr. Buck was principal of the new high school and was there for the three years I was in high school. His wife was a well educated lady and an accomplished musician. She was into classical music and had a record player with these great disks of Wagner's classical operas — most of it over my head. She and I formed a close friendship, more than the usual teacher-student. She staged annual recitals and I was the one she chose to play duets with her. She got music on approval and if it was something her other students couldn't handle, she would give it to me. Of course that really lit a fire under me and I vowed to get it or die trying.

In 1920, the summer after we finished the eighth grade, we were invited to go to Green Lake near Willmar with Uncle Carl and Aunt Tommy and Justine. We were there about six weeks and the cousins came from all directions. There was a whole passel of them all about the same age. It was a wonderful place to go for a vacation — we could go swimming any time we wanted to. But my chief interest was the old piano down there; they also had a record player they called the Aeolian Vocalian that delivered beautiful classical music at the touch of my finger. It was a wind-up affair but it was much more sophisticated than the little player we had at home. We went again the next summer for about six weeks. The music, that's what I remember most fondly about those two summers at the lake.

CHAPTER 2

Courtship

. . . things might turn serious

Sue and Margaret graduated from Pettibone High School in 1923. There were four in their class – She and Marg, her best friend, Lou Dahle, and Paul DeKrey. Their career plan was a common one: to attend summer school at Valley City Normal School (later State Teachers College) and be certified to teach in one of the many one-room country schools in the state. Margaret headed for summer school, immediately, but Sue was only seventeen years old and she couldn't teach until she was eighteen. The state had their standards, after all. The solution was also pretty common: go to work in the post office until next summer. (The post office was in the back of Gambs's store, so she worked in both.) It was just as well. She had been weak and puny for some time, and was hoping a summer of relative ease would bring her out of it. It was only many years later that a chest x-ray revealed she'd probably had tuberculosis. Thank goodness she was planted in the good brisk North Dakota air where Teddy Roosevelt himself had come to toughen up. Her first diary from that time sounds like a typical teenager with typical young-girl-about-to-be-grown-up problems – parents, hair, girlfriends, sisters, new responsibilities and boys, boys, boys. (To say nothing of florid writing.)

19

. She says this small three-by-four-inch dime store notebook is "Volume 3" but this is the only one of that era that survived. She met Claude at a local dance and even at seventeen it was clear she had her eye on him. He had come to town to work with his brother, Willard, in the garage he started. By then the automobile was already the transportation of choice, and 'going for a ride' could lead to ANYTHING. It didn't take these young whipper-snappers long to figure that out. In Claude's case, the car was an Overland, probably owned by the garage, and the 'hoopy.' What's a hoopy?

The journal entries that follow contain a lot of names. Most of them are irrelevant to the 'story' and will not show up again. Key players are Claude and Sue, Willard (Claude's brother), Laura (his girlfriend/wife), Marg (Sue's sister Margaret), Lou (Sue's best friend, married Les).

SUNDAY, AUGUST 1, 1923   Yes, Dear Diary, I have completed Vol II for July. This is the August number. They come as often as the *Women's Home Companion*.

MONDAY   I started work at Gambs's. I like it just fine so far. Not much business though — it's too cold and windy. Claude took me home at seven and took my bicycle back to fix. Sadie Thomas came then and wanted us to go swimming, so Marg and I went along. We had a swell time. Sadie and I dived oodles until we were so full of water we nearly wept. The water was quite cold and the suckers were not biting. I came home starved.

TUESDAY   I had to hustle around and wash my hair and have a little friendly family row over bobbed hair (specifically, mine) and also get dinner before I left. I got to the post office way early and while I waited, Jack came along and asked me if I was going to the dance in Marstonmoor. I hadn't heard about it but supposed I might go. Then Ed came and kidded around for a while. Then Art. Ed treated me to an ice cream just to eat with him. Claude came and asked me to go to Marston.

When I got home the folks hadn't come home yet so I had to hustle. By the time I had milked three cows and gone in to get ready, the folks finally came. Art was going to take Marg to the dance so we both had to hurry. Les and Claude came before I was ready and had to wait a few minutes. I knew as soon as we got started that Claude was crabby and also knew that it meant something was rotten in Denmark. We just got down to Rice's when we had a flat tire, so we went over to the garage to fix it. Finally got down to Marston about 10:30. Talk about a wild ride! Claude sure drove. Lou and Les were agreeably peeved at each other and they still weren't through when we got home. Then we started in.

Sue: I'm so darned mad at you!!!

Claude: All right, then beat it!

Bang Bang Chug Chug Chug chug. And so ended a perfect day! (It's 12:45 and I see a rather cute gent parading back and forth – acts like he might even come in.)

WEDNESDAY Woke up this morning with a funny feeling round about my gizzard – I wonder what it was. Would I see Claude today? Did it mean quits or just a relief? Should I be sorry? Never. Would he be sorry? That was the main proposition.

I came to work as usual at one and Art came in and chatted. Then the Goose pulled in and also Claude, just as I was unpacking bakery goods. I don't know what he wanted, but he asked if I was still mad. I got little satisfaction (nor gave any) so I'm still quite at sea.

I have a dreadfully sore pimple on my nose and a dose of dropsy on the eyelid.

FRIDAY   I didn't see "him" all day. Walked up with Lou after work and we went over to Clara's to see the new baby. I held the wee infant — said I was getting in practice. Lou and I insisted that he should be called Lester Claude because we were the first girls to hold him.

SATURDAY   Claude brought down my bicycle today and ran off like a streak of lightning. Maybe because I told him to charge it. Art came in and offered to take me home, but I assured him I could do very nicely on my bike. I stopped over at the creamery to get weighed. I weigh 127. Tonight we meandered downtown. Laura and I got some ice cream and popcorn at Gambs's and sat in the car and talked. Pretty soon George and Floyd came along and wanted us to go riding which we did. We got back to town about 11:45. I went home with Laura. Stanley [Laura's brother] was pretty put out because she hadn't told him she was going. Then I learned what Laura had to contend with. Not with Stanley but with her dad and having no mother. I could hit myself for what I have complained about, when what she has to take is about sixteen times worse. It gave me something to think about. We tried to sleep but we gave it up and talked. Laura was trying to map out her future, but alas — it seems a question mark. I urged her to try to stick it out two more years — then comes graduation and sweet, sweet seventeen and also, probably, Willard. So her sun is shining at the end of two more years of struggle.

SUNDAY   We got breakfast and did up the work and got ready to go picking chokecherries. We first went to Danielson's and then went on ahead because they weren't ready. We went to Paulson's, but there weren't many cherries so we took care of the kids. We each had a "little one" under our arm – I hinted to Laura that it might be a vision of the future – but I hope not. They were all white curly hair and dirt. We came home about 5:30 just as it began to pour. Laura and I sat out in the car during the worst and talked about funerals. (We just heard that President Harding died.)

When Laura and I came in Mr. Kaczmarski wanted me to play so I sat down at the old organ and played about an hour and a half. He sure was pleased. Laura was sick and didn't sleep all night. I couldn't either so we lay and renewed our everlasting talk. Laura was sick this morning so I did up most of the work for her before I left. I brought Mom a bunch of chokecherries.

Grandpa came today. I was so surprised to see him.

I got the craze to have my hair bobbed again. Pop says "I don't give a damn but I won't touch it." Well he's not the only barber I know. Guess I'll go down to Frieze tomorrow. Will I regret it? That's the question. I hope not. I certainly have a problem with my goose fuzz. I know Claude will be mad and probably Willard, Hurley and Ed too. But puke. I don't care about the boys. I'm looking out for my own welfare.

TUESDAY Dear diary: I'm miserable again. I have the worst canker in my lower gum I ever witnessed. Then to cap to climax I am sick unto death with my stomach. Last night Claude was out – please witness, diary, it's been five days since I've seen him. He didn't come until 9:30. We went down to the park and watched the deer for awhile. Then we came home. I didn't take time to look at the clock because Grandfather was downstairs and there was no light. It must have been near midnight though. I didn't sleep well all night. This morning Mom called us at seven o'clock and of course

I had to roll out. I was afraid I wouldn't be able to work today, but I'd just as soon be down there sick as at home. Claude is going out threshing tomorrow for probably three weeks and I'll be left all alone — sniff. But Pop began to rave about what time I got in. Holy crap — Marg and I have gone stepping four times (at the same time) since she got home and I've beat her in every darned time. I was scared fartless until I got in the house and found that Marg wasn't home yet, so of course everything was peaceful. As long as I get in before Marg it's a small matter what time it is. Guess I'll have to get into partnership with Art and manage to get our dates at the same time. Of course when Marg goes, all will be peace again like it was last summer. Maybe.

THURSDAY   I got my Kodak and have taken about four pictures already. I just got ready when Lou, Les and Claude came. I told Claude I was going to bob my hair and he nearly had fits. He told me that if I expected to go with him that I hadn't better risk it. I told him then he'd better start to look for a new woman right away. I was so mad.

FRIDAY   Well the kids went out threshing today so the coast is clear. Francis *[Claude's sister]* came in and I told her I was going to get my hair bobbed while he was gone. She just loved it. Then Marg and Edythe came in — Marg wanted me to have my hair bobbed so she gave me a check for it. I was busy working up courage when Frieze came in.

> So I made the date.
> That decided my fate.
> To have it done I might hate.
> But to change my mind,
> It was much too late.

So he put his bait
At the barbershop gate,
which I immediately ate,
and lost my mate.
At any rate He'll have to wait
a long long time
before he'll find
another pal so good and kind.
The deed is done
and my regrets
have failed to come.

I went home to see what my mater and pater had in store for me — nothing! Then I went to the lecture. Everybody gawked at my shorn locks. Mama had curled it out and parted it on the side.

FRIDAY   Ike closed the post office for an hour in honor of President Harding's funeral. I got a ride home with Mrs. Daniels because I didn't ride my bike today. I was just finishing a dish of peaches and cream when a car drove in. "Gee look at the bobbed hair" was the first thing I heard in Les's cheery voice. I said to Clauder boy "don't you like me any more?" I guess he did a little bit because we went riding. Claude really likes my hair like this. We had such fun. I felt so happy all evening I simply couldn't be crabby. Claudy thought there must be something wrong because it had been a long time since I was crabby. He called me some names, and even then I didn't get mad, Oh diary, I had such a good time. I was teasing Claude because he was so little and telling him jokes when I got him mad. And yet — and yet — things might turn serious if such continues. Oh diary, what is to be my fate — my future? I don't know myself how I want it to turn out.

SATURDAY   Marg went to work at Morrison's today so it left me to help milk and help Mom with the washing. I got to town early so I rode around on my bike. I wore Marg's red flannel jumper and waist so I was quite 'inconspicuous' riding down the street. Horrors! Such a scandal. All the boys of the neighborhood started in with their esteemed opinions of my hair. Art came and said he would take us to a campout at Lake Williams. So I hastened home and put on my knickers and then discovered I didn't have any film, so I rode back on the bike to get some.

When we got to Lake Williams, Lou and Sadie came up over the hill like a couple of shipwrecked mariners in their bathing suits. Art went into Lake Williams and got some coffee candy and crackerjack. We sang for about two hours until we were entirely assured that we had the coyotes scared away — then we went to sleep. We woke about 6:30 and tried to fix our bed, but by that time we were fully awake. Marg and Sadie got breakfast while Lou and I went for a pre-breakfast dip. When we got cleaned up Lou and I hiked up to Lake Williams and got some pop, candy and oranges. I took some pictures on the way back. I do hope they're good.

We stayed all day and had wieners and sauerkraut for supper besides beans, rock cookies and other stuff. Then we packed up and came home. Farewell, O haunts of the conifer and coyote.

We lost the tent twice on the way home. Sadie stayed with us. We lay out in the yard on our blankets enjoying the fresh air and mosquitoes when we discovered a mysterious looking light in town like a fire, and we went downtown to see what the excitement was. We just got down to the corner when the guys came by, so we went riding. Or was it "parking"? They say if you do all your parking at home (even if it does amount to an hour or two) that you're perfectly irreproachable. And so we are still lily white angels (but oh diary, we aren't). Wouldn't anyone reading this think I was perfectly awful? But listen, diary, I'm not awful, am I? You know that I'm perfectly okay. Just like to make believe is all.

When I got home, Marg and Sadie were sweetly reposing in bed, but even sweeter, they left me the cherished place in the middle.

Margaret and Sue, high school graduation, class of 1923

TUESDAY   Mom is making my blue percale dress. It has white linen collar and cuffs. Otherwise just plain. It's kind of cute, and my hair looks quite good today too. I wish it would always look like this.

WEDNESDAY   Mom was aroused at five this morning by Carl Lydeen. August died last night and he wanted her to come to help. Tonight Pop was hollering at Mom that Marg should be in.

THURSDAY   We went to August's funeral today. It was awfully sad. The mourners took it so hard. We went up to McCumbers to dinner afterwards.

It's been an hour and a half and Marg and Art were still out in the yard talking. Pop hollered until he was sore and then Mom stuck her head out of the door and hollered. Finally Marg came in at last, big as life, and Pop was as meek as a lamb – hasn't said a word. Mom says she knew that neither Marg nor Art realized what time it was. CRAP!!!! When I came home Sunday night Pop blew his head off. I said I didn't realize what time it was, and he told me to shut up, he wasn't talking to me. Claude says he doesn't think the folks are very good to me. I told him Mom and I got along like old pals. When Marg's gone Pop acts pretty decent too.

SUNDAY   My goodness, diary! Pray excuse my unseemly neglect…it's only when Marg's still out that I can sit down and scribe. I just got in, but dear sister isn't home yet so I'm sitting on the upstairs floor as usual writing on my night-gowned knee.

Aunt Hannah was out today and of course I was delighted – (Just got that far when Marg hailed in, so I landed in bed and was sound asleep when Marg stuck her head over the stairs about two seconds later.)

MONDAY   And now, diary, I'm blue – oh so blue. My own Lou – is gone, gone. She came down to say goodbye and believe me we both had tears in our eyes. I was awfully blue all day.

Started work at 8:30 helping distribute mail. I had a swell time finding all the Hingers and Flemmers and Guthmillers by the dozens. I don't mind the work. I'm going to get thirty-five dollars a month this winter. I think it's pretty good, but if it were about fifty I could go to Normal next winter. I'm living in hopes. I really get ambitious occasionally and want to get a real education, but I'll be so stagnant by the time the winter is over I'll be a vacuum mentally. What a dark future. I feel like I was struck with a brick bat, all because Lou is gone and Claudie is going. I can almost say it without even sighing now.

Got paid up tonight. Have only nine dollars and something left I had so many bills. Well my lamp is dying, so goodbye, diary – be good.

FRIDAY   Got a letter from Lou and also from little Clauder. I was pleased of course. When I got home I read it to Marg and Mom because it wasn't a bit mushy and I knew that's what they expected. I wrote to Claude after I got upstairs. It was very short but simple. I hope he answers real speedily. He's only been gone four days.

SATURDAY   Marg, Alice, Laura, Beth, Willard and Ed all went to Woodworth tonight. I'm a lonesome mama but I don't know of anyone (else) I care to a dance with. It seems to me like they're getting pretty stale, all but one. It wouldn't take much to change my mind regarding this matter and that's the hell of it. I wish I were a little more stable and knew my own mind. Heard from Lou today. Same old kid. Wish she were here.

Marg leaves tomorrow. Goodbye. Here's your hat, what's your hurry.

SUNDAY   Mr. Worley, Sadie and Laura came to take Marg to her school. She'll start teaching on Monday. I went along to keep Laura company on the way back. We drove around quite a bit and finally landed at Marg's school to eat our lunch. Laura and I gassed (talked) so much our lips were chapped. When we got home I found that Claude had been here twice and had just left. I knew he would be disappointed. I know I was.

Ed, Willard, Les and Art were here and they wanted us to go riding so we did. We finally decided to go to Medina. We found Claude and Les downtown. They seemed awfully surprised but not especially pleased to see us. Claude looked so grouchy I asked him if he was mad because I came. He said no, he was glad, but I know something was wrong. I guess he was unreasonable enough to be mad because I wasn't home. Willard nearly went to sleep on the way home so I drove a ways. Didn't get home until 1:30, so now there is something else to settle for. We snuck in as quietly as possible, but of course Mom woke up.

I wrote another letter to him Monday. He hadn't gotten my first one yet. That was returned Monday. Gee I was sore. Tonight it's trying to storm. I hope it rains enough so I can wash my hair in soft water. I got a letter from Sadie and one from Marg today and answered them this evening. I started to read *Nancy Stair* today. It's almost moral enough to give me an inspiration. Maybe that's why I was kind-hearted enough to bring home a piece of pineapple pie for supper. O diary, if those feelings of kindness and ambition would only last, I'd be a better "woman" there's no doubt. Nothing special happens when I get this so-called inspiration, but it gives me such a happy feeling it's great.

I got so many compliments on my hair today. Three different people remarked about it. It probably did look a little better than usual. Some of them really flattered me. Don't worry, diary, I'll never never never never get vain. I have too good judgment and reasoning to ever do such a thing. Well, grandfather is lying on the bed trying to rest while I scribe, so goodnight, I'm bedward bound.

WEDNESDAY   Well I've gone into soulful things. Got a most excellent inspiration so before it fled I sent an order for sheet music for "The Rosary," "Sing me to Sleep," "Our Yesterdays," "His Lullaby," "O Promise Me," "Melody of Love." I guess Pop doesn't enjoy listening while I pick and poke along trying to learn new songs. He asked, kind of sarcastic, what they were supposed to do when I practiced, and I answered cheerfully that I hoped it might drive them out and I'd be rid of them for a few days.

FRIDAY   Got a letter from Claude. He is still just mine. There's a little spark of love still burning. The letter sort of fanned it for a minute or so. I felt punk all day today. We all sat around like dizzy flies. All but the flies. They swarmed on everything else.

Last night I was just finishing milking, had on my knickers over my dress — when Willard came. They wanted me to go to a dance in Tuttle. Mom insisted that it would be base, idiotic, foolish and show lack of respect etc if I went, but I could suit myself — so I did and I went. Had a pretty good

time, too. Quite a bunch of the kids were there. Laura stayed
with me. We took off our shoes and got in quietly.

SUNDAY   Marg came home on Saturday – thrill, thrill! She
went to a dance in Robinson with Bill. Mom and I were
home alone. It seemed delightful for a change. We do enjoy
each other's company.

Looking back on those early years from the perspective of seventy some years, Sue remembered the music more than the boys.

I took lessons from Mrs. Buck for four years. I made high
school in three years, but I was too young to teach so I
worked in the post office for two years and continued to
take music lessons from Mrs. Buck. That was the last year
they were at Pettibone, but I got quite a ways in music by
then and could play music at about the fifth grade level.
Later, when I went to summer school in Valley City, I took
piano lessons. I picked the highest paid teacher because
I thought she was probably the best, and since I was only
going to be there a few weeks it wasn't going to make much
difference on the cost. She had me playing sonatinas and I
took a real liking to that type of music and worked on it a
lot after I had finished in Valley City.

I also took a few violin lessons, but I never got to playing
anything on the violin. As it turned out, I was recovering
from tuberculosis, which I didn't know I had. I was very weak
and to hold up the violin and play was almost too much for
me, so I soon gave up. It also dawned on me that I couldn't
make any progress trying to learn both of them, and that I'd
better settle on one.

When the Bucks left there was no piano teacher in
Pettibone, so Morrisons and Leoppkes asked me to give

lessons to their kids. So I started teaching those three or four kids, and soon I had a class of about twenty, maybe. I got fifty cents a lesson.

Sue spent the winter working at the Gambs's store, which also held the post office, and if she continued her diaries, they did not survive. The next summer, 1924, she went off to Valley City to get the credentials she needed to teach. Happily, that diary did survive in a four by six inch notebook. It begins in April, 1924, two months before she left for summer school.

> **THURSDAY** Dear Diary: I haven't written for nearly a month, firstly because I ran out of diary and couldn't remember to get one except when I was all wrapped up in the Post Office and secondly because I was too busy. I just casually strolled down to Dethloff's last night and discovered these notebooks on the bargain counter.
>
> Mom was in pain all last week. She got word Sunday noon that Uncle Fred was dead so Jack Crawford took her to Carrington. She and Aunt Hannah left from there that evening. Margaret came home Saturday and Pop bobbed her hair. Holy fright such a catastrophe! Bill is going to take her home to Wing Sunday evening. We went down to Knobels for supper — six of us. Pop got Mikey to help him milk so I could go to Wing with the kids. Talk about fun! It was threatening rain and everything, but I couldn't let a perfectly good Sunday evening go to ruin, so I went. They had fur robes in the back and six of us in the old hoopy. Ed drove and drive he did! We went over in less than two hours *[about thirty-five miles west]* and came home in an hour and a half. Claude was scared but I wasn't.
>
> With Mom gone, the house, of course, was getting terribly dirty. There were two beds to make, separator, milk pails

and dishes to wash and supper to get, besides milking the cows and the once-over job of sweeping. Tuesday night I was all set to do Hurley's ironing *[Lena took in ironing for extra money]* and go to bed, but Claude and Bill and Ed came out just as I got nicely started so I kept right on. I got all the shirts ironed and then we went for a little ride to cool off. I was feeling blue that night for some reason. If Claude doesn't baby me with my little griefs, I'm not feeling at home. But he did, of course, so all was not so bad.

I hated to think about batching it for two weeks with Pop. The work didn't bother me, but, oh, the companionship. Pop always acts like I am an eight-year-old servant. He hardly speaks at all unless it it's to bawl me out for trivial matters. But what a break! He was swell-ish, so sociable and good-natured. I didn't mind the work at all.

Alice is here. It's Thursday night and we're going to stay home. Pop went downtown early so we pinned blankets over the kitchen windows and shut off the living room. We heard the hoopy go by, but all was in darkness within. Then we put a chair under the door and we took a bath (I mean two baths. Ha!) and got into bed at a really respectable hour.

FRIDAY   Alice went to Heaton, so Pop and I were alone. He churned and had a kettle of water on for me with a good fire under it. Well we tied into it and did up all our work. Most of the kids went to Woodworth, Marston or Heaton, but Claude came up home for a while. He was terribly tired so didn't stay long. Pop and I were up to Lydeen's to supper. She gave us a loaf of fresh bread and then Mr. Knobel brought us a loaf of rye.

SATURDAY   The high school kids had a basket social. I felt it my duty to go, and Mrs. Lydeen offered to pack my lunch for me. Mrs. Gambs sent down meat for sandwiches, rocks, doughnuts and chocolate, cheese, dofunnies and some divinity. I made a bunch of fudge for the kids and me, of course. Claude couldn't stay for the social. Paul got my basket and he took me home, but he got rather cavemanish, so we had rather a struggling time of it. I like Paul best at least two feet away and then he is just fine. So I went in and wanted Claude and played the piano until Pop came home about one. Then I expired.

We were invited out to three places to Sunday dinner. Lydeens, Knobels and Monks, but we went to Monks as Pop had to go after some horses. We had a fine time and a big turkey dinner. Bessie gave me a book of German composers. I was so tickled.

Claude came up about seven to help us milk. Willard came in half an hour, so we all went out and each milked two cows and then we went out to see Soup *[Laura Kaczmarski]* (well mostly to see Soup. Ha!).

TUESDAY   Mom came home and I fell all over her I was so tickled, but I was sorry she couldn't have stayed longer for her sake. We would have managed. I broke myself entirely to give her money to get there ($13.50). It sure seemed good to come home and see a clean floor and supper all ready. She brought me a pair of sport stockings and some music, "Dream Daddy" and "That Old Gang of Mine."

Mrs. Buck is going to give her recital soon. I took my lesson and now all I have to do is practice up on my classics and give her a demonstration. I want to play about four pieces because I can't decide. Mrs. Buck is going to play a duet with me. I ordered "Poet and Peasant" and several others. Do hope they come today.

I wish that Claude appreciated music. I am afraid that is a trait that is sadly missing in him. I miss it too when he doesn't even listen when a person plays. Well, he and I got into a serious argument last night, so that accounts for my attitude. Claude has acted so odd lately.

About ten Claude got the Overland and we went for a ride. He said that he might have known better than to come tonight etc. etc. until I really got disgusted. Then we started to talk of other things. Something very important. We sat out in the yard and talked and argued about everything else. He said that he could argue with me for a couple of weeks and never get any place, so he gave up. He really acted terrible and I guess I wasn't very sweet either. But I am happy I opted for "bad to better" instead of "bad to worse."

FRIDAY Took my music lesson this morning. It wasn't a lesson — more of a practice recital. Played our "If I were a Bird," a Paderewski's Minuet, "Prelude," "Serenata Makowski" and "Song of the Nightingale." I'm going to play the Minuet and Nightingale and also a piano duet. I am too sleepy to write now.

SATURDAY . . . It was still raining Friday. Sure was sloppy. The kids were planning a little spree at the hotel, but there wasn't much stirring; we hung around until about ten anyway. Willard wanted to take Soup home and as she was going to stay with me, we beat it up to the garage. There was so much confusion about who was going with who and Claude and I ended up spending an hour or so in the garage waiting for the ride that never came. So you see the circumstances that led up to the catastrophe!! We waited and waited and finally I said, "Let's go home!" and Claude says, "We'll have to find a way first." So he looked outside and everything was dark so he came to the conclusion that everything was locked up and Bill had gone home. So we cranked up the hoopy and went home. The first thing we heard when we got in was "Where have you been 'til this hour?" Just to quiet things down I said "We were up to Cahill's." In the morning I told Mom all about it. Darn I was sore. Ed and Bill had come to our house and blabbed it and asked the folks if we had been home etc etc. By golly, we always stick up for them and help them out of all the scrapes we can. Of course we couldn't get around it at all. I could have killed those guys. I don't give a darn except that it would be all over town how we were up in the garage. It isn't that we couldn't behave while we were up there, but what we MIGHT have done. I am afraid the old hens will get a hold of it make something of it. Oh well.

CHAPTER 3

Valley City Normal

...full of enthusiasm

Sue spent the month of May biding her time until she left for Valley City Normal. She practiced the music for high school graduation and baccalaureate services, she attended the official going away of the Bucks, She sewed her summer school wardrobe. Claude was out of town. Finally the day arrived and she took the train.

JUNE 10, 1924 VALLEY CITY   Well, here I am at 211 9th Avenue with Laura *[Smith]* and so is Lou. We're having a heck of a time – not stepping out or spending wildly, just doing our duty. There were fifty-five teachers on the train from Jamestown to Valley, but we managed quite well and found Olsbys without any trouble. I just got through registering – what a tedious job! I signed up for twelve weeks taking violin twice a week. I hope I will like it. Lord help me, a violin is hard to play unless a person gives his whole attention to it and that is what I intend to do. Tonight I'm full of enthusiasm even after a hard day of registration. I hope it lasts. I will be dejected at times, of course. I have to expect that. I got a letter from Claude and he is spurring me on too.

He is so good to me that it's almost painful. Valley City is beautiful – everything is green and bright. Well Diary, I must roll in. It's been a strenuous day.

WEDNESDAY   We just got back from the show – Tom Moore in *Big Brother*. It was awfully good. We are having a regular time down here. Not lonesome yet!! I took my violin lesson this morning, but all he gave me was a few position exercises. I have to go back again tomorrow. I saw Catherine Betzina and her sister yesterday and didn't have the nerve enough to speak to them. Nut!! We went down to the barber shop today and I got a Dutch bob. Laura got a shingle and it looks keen on her.

THURSDAY   Got a sweet letter from Claude this afternoon. The more they come the better they get. I saw Catherine Betzina up at the Normal today and introduced myself.
    I said, "Hello."
    "Hello."
    "You're Catherine."
    "Yes. But I'm sure I don't know you."
    "I don't suppose you know anyone from Pettibone."
    "Sue?"
    "Yes." (smiling)
    "Oh, I'm so glad. Why didn't you tell me you were coming? How did you happen to know I was here?" Etc. etc.

   Sue fit naturally into the college scene and liked all her teachers. She lived with other girls that were cookie-cutter images of herself, away from home for the first time, experiencing the novel attractions of the "city." Her friendship with Catherine Betzina blossomed and her family provided a glimpse into a whole other lifestyle. Then one of the girls took ill.

SATURDAY   Flag day. Erma Dotsan and Hulda nearly knocked me over when I came in to Chapel. They told me they saw Pat carrying Alice into the clinic last night. I just withered. I was kind of blue anyway so it just about finished me. I would rather take a beating than go to class, but I got through my Elementary Education class fine, even the recitation. When I got out I found Laura. She had been to the clinic to see Alice. Alice got sick just out of Jamestown and by Friday night she couldn't move or anything, so they brought her down and had her tonsils out on Saturday morning. When we got there, she couldn't talk to us. Her tonsils had poisoned her and her whole body was full of rheumatism so she couldn't move.

Saturday afternoon I went back up to school to practice my violin for a while. I got up in the balcony and was sawing off until Mr. Frayson came down and wanted to know where the violin music came from. I finally came out of my hiding place and he told me I could take the room off the stage to practice, so I locked up the doors and practiced for a whole hour.

Then it began to rain so we wrapped our hats in our scarves and ran home. We went down to see Alice about eight and stayed until we were afraid of getting kicked out.

SUNDAY   We went to see Alice for a while and then we hiked out to the camp and took about six rolls of film. It's so nice out there. We climbed a "mighty mountain" and took some pictures of the city and got some more popcorn. It was fun — especially curling up in the culvert and feeling cars pass over our heads. My poor nose and the back of my neck are sunburned. We had supper there and came back to town. Had a swell time.

We picked up Alice and took her up to our room and went to get her a malted milk (and of course some for ourselves). Didn't get to bed until nearly eleven. She stayed with us and Laura slept on the floor.

TUESDAY Catherine walked down from Normal with me this noon and then she asked me to go to an ice cream social with her tonight. I think Catherine is awfully nice.

Laura and I went down to the violin concert in the evening. They put us up in the balcony and we nearly died *[of the heat]*. We finally discovered a window where a fire escape went down so we sat in the window and when the last number was over we went down the fire escape and downtown for some grape juice.

WEDNESDAY Alice is leaving today. She is still in bad shape. We got some liniment to rub her wrists, but it didn't seem to do much good. I took her down to the barbershop and then to get her some malted milk. It was pretty extravagant, but she is sick and needs attention. Took my music lesson. I've been practicing an hour a day at least, and my fingers are blistered on the ends. Tonight we went to see *The White Sister* with Lillian Gish. It certainly was a wonderful play.

FRIDAY We had dinner up in the room this noon — soup and crackers, then I hopped up to Normal to practice. I began to realize that I wouldn't get along very well with so little practice and so much to do, so when the next period rolled around a great inspiration seized me and I decided to drop Music Appreciation. Miss Amidon is too hard-boiled anyway. Now I am happy as a lark.

SATURDAY Got up at 6:15 to finish my psychology. Not a half bad day in school. I took my music lesson and got my new book. Mr. Frayson said that I could get Beriot's because it advanced more rapidly. I tried to practice but someone was always using the room, so I had to stand in the hall to practice. It's the weeds, but I'll have to make the best of it. Tonight we went to see *Women, Don't Doubt Your Husbands*. It was about a young married couple that always quarreled. It reminded me so much of Claude that I got lonesome for just one little quarrel. Got in about ten and talked until eleven, and then I sat up until twelve writing to Claude.

SUNDAY   Catherine invited me over to supper. We took a picnic lunch and went down to the woods to eat. Had a dandy time and nice talk. It was mostly on friends, high ambitions and last but not least – matrimony! Catherine is interesting and interested in me too, I guess. She is one I would like to know better. She has high ideals. I hope nothing happens to her like it did me to keep her from realizing them. I came back to her place with her and stayed a few minutes before I came home. Mrs. Betzina seems awfully nice. Catherine and I have each made a new friend.

MONDAY   We had very good intentions of going to school early and getting our studying done, but we didn't get up there until 10:30 and I practiced music for about an hour and came home. Then we loafed around until four and I didn't do a bit of studying. Catherine called me up about 5:30 and wanted me to go to *Rosita* with her. It was a swell show and I had a fine time. We're planning on going to *The Lullaby* next Friday night. I treat!

TUESDAY   Catherine invited me over to play for her this afternoon and kept me playing until five o'clock. We sent for some yarn for sweaters this evening. We're going to make them all ourselves.

I tried to study a little but then we just got silly. First I hollered for my notebook, and as no one got it for me I rolled head over toenails and scraped a square inch of hide off my wrist. We wrapped it up in a towel and it stopped bleeding. Then we played kid tricks. We nearly asphyxiated each other with our feet. Laura pulled off my socks and threw one on each corner. Then she tried to sew my shirttail to my blouse. But I objected so strenuously that she finally withdrew, returning with a pillow and stuffing it in my pants. All this 'effort' strained our mental capacity so we delivered ourselves to our respective beds.

SATURDAY Laura had rheumatism and couldn't go to school. It rained everything from pickled pigs' feet to angleworms. Had a test in El Ed. I got four wrong out of seventeen, but that was a little above the average anyway.

The Chautauqua movement of adult education programs was very popular at the time; it brought culture and entertainment to rural areas that didn't have much of either one. The Chautauqua company performed plays and concerts and solo performances under the big tent. Sue and her student friends went to Chautauqua often that summer. They saw the *Barber of Seville* and *The Calling of Dan Matthews*.

SATURDAY I haven't written for a whole week because I have been so busy with Chautauqua and everything. It's been one swell time. Monday we saw Mildred Wilmer. She gave a long play reading on the adventure of youth — with a strong moral of course. All of us girls walked out there together. We took our yarn along and got a lot of crocheting done. Catherine and I came home together. Of course we had all kinds of things to talk about. The clear cool evening served as an inspiration.

THURSDAY   I took my music lesson today and he said it
was very good. Imagine that!

It's the last day of school this week so we took our lunch
and went out to see *Is Marriage a Failure?* It isn't. By the
time it was over we were starved. It was awfully good. Only
sentimental plays make me want my old man. I am always so
happy coming home from Chautauqua. I told Catherine and
she squeezed my arm and said, "I am so glad." I am too. I
went down to Betzinas to curl my hair. We were talking about
personalities and she said, "I like someone who has a winning
personality and is still very unconscious of it – that's just the
way you are (accompanied by a squeeze around the neck)."

THE FOURTH OF JULY   The others were awakened by the
roar of a cannon but I slumbered on. I got up about ten and
got down to breakfast-dinner at 11:15. We had just pulled
out of The Liberty when Orville, Marg, Sadie and Mike
Miller drove in. I had been ranting all night about her letter,
it made me so sore. And here they come. Well we went out
to Chautauqua and had dinner – chicken, fruit jello and ice
cream – and then roamed around looking at other main
attractions and finally went home. Later we went to the
dance at the bowery and had a good time.

The kids left and Laura and I have been celebrating by
eating ourselves silly and crocheting. We ran all the way
downtown to be in time for *Start to Train Your Wife* and found
out it can't be done. So we got some popcorn and came
home and made some lemonade.

THURSDAY   I got word that I couldn't get my credit in high
school geography from Mr. Buck. It so completely upset me
that I missed my methods class. I was a nervous wreck. Then
to cap it off, I bought a violin and paid thirty dollars for

it (only it isn't paid for yet), and between the two I nearly worried myself to death.

FRIDAY   I couldn't sleep so I got up at five o'clock and studied, soaking my feet while I read my geography. Then I ran up to Betzinas. They had company which included a baby, so Catherine gave me a little course on child training. Then we went up to the fair and I went in to have my fortune told. This was it:

I'm going to live to a ripe old age with my man. I'm going to be married in 1924 or 5 early in the year and have three children — boy-girl-boy, the first one being born in '26. The folks will object strongly to my wedding but it will be for the best. I'm going to travel a lot and run my own car. My man will love me all through my life and never turn his back on me. I am very musical but especially in vocal music. Although I take great interest in instrumental music, I will never specialize in it; however I will give lessons and I'm going to be an instructor next winter. My best life is before me. I will make many friends and no one will ever be able to say that I wasn't a fine moral person. I will overcome

Sue circa 1924

my present weakness, which is hastiness. I shouldn't trust humankind too much because they will prove faithless to me and break their promises. I went home and told Laura EVERYTHING.

SATURDAY   A good day. Got letters from Claude and Soup. We are now sitting around in our nightgowns acting ridiculous. Lois cleaned up the dresser and wouldn't let us put anything on it. She said she didn't care what we put in the drawers so Laura began piling up shoes and old clothes and stuffing them in the drawer. Finally she grabbed me around neck and stuffed me in drawer. And so ends a perfect day.

...and a journal. I assume she continued the journal and others, but they are lost. Some seventy years later Sue remembered that time:

In Valley City I earned enough credits to enable me to teach second grade elementary for one term. Then with a second year of summer school I got my first grade elementary. I took a school in Horning Township out by the Waltzes and Morlocks, not too far from where I started school as a seven or eight-year-old. I rode a horse out there that first winter and luckily it was a mild winter or I might have run into more difficulty than I did. It paid seventy-five dollars a month, which didn't reach very far even though I stayed home.

The next year they asked me to take the school in Marstonmoor. They had five eighth graders that had failed the state examinations [which would enable them to enter high school] the year before and they wanted me to get all of them through the eighth grade. I also had two first graders and most of the grades in between. Another first grader, who didn't speak English, came six weeks late. About that time I threw up my hands and said, "She will learn whatever she's able to pick up, but I can't take the responsibility of getting her through the first grade." The two boys were no great shakes as students (and I was no great shakes as a teacher), so they weren't doing too well. By spring the little girl knew more than both of the boys put together. And the five eighth graders passed their state exams.

It was a very hard winter that year with lots of snow. I stayed with the Slossons most of the winter. They had four kids in school, and they always hitched up the horses to the sled and took us all to school.

I was teaching piano on Saturdays and after school for as long as I was able to get into town. When the snow got too deep, I didn't get back and forth very often and that, of course, was not too good for my *[piano]* students. Since I planned on getting married I decided I'd better have a piano before I took the step or I probably would never get one, and I couldn't conceive of getting along without a piano. So I contacted a dealer in Bismarck who came out with a list of pianos available, and then I made a trip into Bismarck to handpick it. I picked out a medium-sized Kimball. Since the first one we had was a Kimball, it was the only one I knew very much about. I paid twenty-five dollars a month on the piano. By then I was getting ninety-five dollars a month for teaching. After I paid my board and room there wasn't very much left.

By the spring of 1927 when she was twenty-one, Sue had taught for three years and gone out with Claude for four. It was time to get married, and that did not go over well at home. The reasons are unclear. Certainly they must have known it was serious. Sue was apparently given the choice: Marry Claude and never come home again, or give him up. Of course she'd made her choice long ago. It broke her heart. It was never mentioned in our family and I was shocked to hear about it when I was well into my fifties. As far as I know she never saw her "Pop" again *[after her marriage]* and he never saw his granddaughters, Bonnie and Colleen, even though they continued to live in the same small community. She continued to have a warm relationship with her mother and the sisterly love-hate relationship with Marg.

JUNE 22, 1927   Dear Diary: I started to write Oh so long ago, but I've been too busy to write. I owe so many letters. I am sacrificing a lot for you, don't you see.

I went back to the old home about the middle of May at Mrs. Rawson's request. I wasn't homesick nor did I need help – I was made more than welcome wherever I went and was invited to stay at six different places for the summer. I had a bad case of bronchitis and rheumatism and she mistook it for grieving. Well, foolish or not, I went home. "Forgive us our trespasses as we forgive those who trespass against us." I thought perhaps if I made the first move that apologies would follow, but, of course, they didn't. There is still a barrier. I could overlook it, but I can't ask Claude to. He has taken more than his share already. So I have been staying here and there since my home isn't at home any more. Of course I am blue – how can I help it? Nature has bestowed us with a love of home, parents (and also a pride of such) so that a break like this cuts to the core. For months I have asked God in my prayers to guide me the right way. I am not capable of such a choice. Whichever way I choose my heartstrings will be strained. Lead Thou My Feet.

That next week I gave exams all week. We had our picnic

the previous Friday – it rained of course – but we had a good lunch. Laura was my guest. I stayed with her two nights that week and with Florence Danielson one. They really like to have me out there, I think. I must have love or I don't care to live.

All my eighth grade pupils and the two algebra students passed their state exams I'm happy to say. The Monday after school was out I went out to Marg and Orville's to paint and stayed three days. I came in on Thursday for a party for the teachers and Friday I drove to Tuttle with Florence and Mom to the N.P.L. *[Non-Partisan League]* convention. Then we went to the high school graduation. After that I felt like celebrating so Claude and I went to a barn dance outside of Medina. The roads were a nightmare. We got stuck once but finally got out without chains. It was almost light out by the time we got back to Rawson's.

They planned to get married at the end of June – just stop at Reverend Mielke's in Medina on their way out of town, pick up the tent they ordered and then to the Black Hills of South Dakota. But before that there was a month of frenzied activity and a lot of thinking. Sue and her students gave a piano recital, Claude borrowed the '26 Chevy coupe from Willard's garage and got it all spiffed up. They visited Willard and Laura who were married by then and Lou and Les Larson who would be their witnesses at the wedding. Sue went on the train to Valley City and Cooperstown to surprise her college friends and have one last fling with the girls.

...and yesterday we made nightgowns for our trousseaus – white with rows of lace and dabs of colored embroidery. I think they will be cute though they're not quite finished. Last night we were at Gertie's sewing. Gertie was sewing lace on a tiny dress. I'll bet she is happy. I would be. Maybe you, dear diary, will reflect me doing the same thing. It is my fondest dream just now. Only God grant that my babes don't take things to heart as I do, or that I may help them overcome it if they do. Time will fill these blank pages with history. I can't plan the future with any amount of accuracy. Perhaps it is best I can't see it.

SUNDAY, JUNE 26, 1927   "O precious time how swiftly art thou gliding past."

Erma and I drove into town and when we got back Claude had arrived. We finally went to bed and then, of course, we talked half the night. It was so hard to part.

Earl *[Erma's brother]* had given me a little dissertation the night before as to the whereabouts of his heart. Only you, diary, know that — you are my confidante. Mary B. tried to scare me about this one-man life. I held my ground and put up my weak argument — the usual one. It is a powerful one, just weak as it comes from me. I have no regrets that my life has been comparatively untarnished. What my life shall be henceforward only God may know. With his help it will be as He intends. May He never forsake our home.

We are all packed up and ready for the Black Hills — all our clothes in one grip. My spirit sort of rebelled like a spoiled child at the sight. But now my better side has manifested itself and I feel that those belongings are in my trust and it's my duty to protect and keep them presentable. Awhile back I feared that, although I knew what the outcome would be, when the crisis was reached I'd lose courage. Now the crisis has been reached. Have I slunk away? With God's help I braved it with courage and now I have a real job in life — one with an honorable goal needing a responsible person to make it a success. "We have crossed the bay, the ocean lies before us." I have fought practically alone the last several years, becoming more and more alone day after day, until my thoughts were heavy enough to crush me. I usually "thought" myself to sleep and woke up irritable and nervous. I have reached this conclusion: "With a companion in misery, half the load is lost." I am now feeling well and happy and strong. I weight 122 again — off three pounds over two weeks ago.

I just wrote to Marion and Erma and now I must make a few notes of things to get in Bismarck before we start our journey. Tonight is my last of maidenhood. At least I am, I feel, a clean woman and carry no bad scars from my youth. So au revoir, diary. Wish me luck!

CHAPTER 4

The Honeymoon

...I've found love at last

MONDAY, JUNE 27, 1927 Well, diary, greet Mrs. Rawson! My new husband is in the bathroom and I have just discarded my rose dress for a lighter, shorter sleeved one. My wedding dress is two shades of rose with medium waist.

(Claude interfered so I had to quit and humor him a bit.) Then I took a bath and we went to the show. It was Corinne Griffith in *Three Hours*. Awfully sad. When she cried I had a hard time checking the tears. We had some cheese sandwiches, ice cream and strawberries before coming up to the room. Our room is No. 427 with a bath at the Lewis and Clark Hotel in Mandan. We went to the show at 7:30, forgetting that Mandan time was an hour earlier than Bismarck. It was a good joke on us. Here I am raving on when I haven't said a word about the preliminaries.

We left Rawson's about nine o'clock and as Rev. Mielke wasn't home we had to go to Rev. Peterson. He was very good though — preached a nice sermon. Lou and Les were with us. Then we went to the drug store and had malted milks. I gave Lou a box of candy. Our tent came on the noon train, so as soon as we got it we hit the trail. We arrived here

at three. Tomorrow we expect to get way into South Dakota.
We will start our camping out and initiate our new tent and
camp stove and last, but not least, the feather tick. Well
goodnight, diary, pleasant dreams!

WEDNESDAY   Still in bed. I didn't write last night as it
was raining bullets and they came right through the tent,
so we made our bed and tried to sleep in it. The rain ran
down under it and we finally gave up and got in the coupe.
We made kind of a bed with bumps and wrinkles in it and
wedged ourselves in. Guess we shrunk in the night, however,
because it was almost room enough to be comfortable this
morning. Here I sit writing on the old ledge where I used to
park my hat when we went stepping. Claude got up to start
the fire. He is combing his hair and grunting like a day-old
piglet. I was going to step on the starter to see if all the juice
leaked out when the lights were on all night. Claude said,
"No. It's in gear, and if you start it, it will run away with the
tent." I said, "What difference will that make?" and he said,
"I'll be dressed, without any tent and you'll be riding around
in your nightgown." Clever boy.
    Yesterday we went about two hundred miles. Got up at
5:30 and hit the trail. The roads were pretty bad, so we made
only about fifty miles by 9:30 when we stopped and got
breakfast. There was a mound with a little pool about sixty
feet below with clear soft water in it. A great big tree almost
hid the pool and wild roses grew just thick in the solid mass
around it. So we stopped on top of the mound and had
breakfast. Claude got some bread at a neighboring farm
house while I got dinner. A little kid hollered at him from
upstairs and told him to help himself. We had bacon, eggs,
potatoes, bread and butter, coffee and olives for breakfast.
It surely tasted good. Then we drove, taking turns, until we

reached McLaughlin where we stopped and had ice cream. We came through the Fort Yates Reservation and for about twenty miles all we could see was Indians – little ones, big ones, fat and skinny ones, all riding ponies or rounding them up. From Dupree we went on to Lanfry and heard that further on the bridge had washed out, so we had to return to Dupree. We arrived here at Faith last night about eight, I guess. We pitched our good-for-nothing tent and got supper. Our stove is ideal – cooks like "only mother can cook." We had fried sausage balls smothered in onions, fried potatoes, tea and bread and butter and olives – the trusty old lasting olives. Well my hubby has everything ready to get breakfast and guess he is lonesome and hungry, so I'll close and join him.

THURSDAY   Here we sit by the camp fire trying to "lubricate" our joints a little. It rained hard from eleven this morning to four this afternoon so we were driven to a cottage.

We left Faith early Wednesday morning to get to our destination without losing another day. The roads were bad for ten or fifteen miles when we struck a state highway that was much better. We got into Rapid City quite late. Claude unpacked our bedding and hung our still-wet blanket on the fence to dry. We nearly drowned the night before and the bedding was still suffering the consequences. We had cheese sandwiches, tea, peaches, cake – and olives. Claude was worrying that we might have to buy more before we got back!! When we got to Wasta we hit the highway where President Coolidge drives on the way to his lodge. The road was perfect. In Rapid City we got a few provisions and walked around awhile. We saw a couple who were hiking around the world. The man's back had "Around the World" on it and the girl's had "Me 2." They were a cute couple.

Claude and Sue circa 1925

There were signs along the road reading "Hidden City" so we drove out of town seven miles to see it. It was a mysterious structure – straight walls made of uniform stones – even had a corner where the walls intersected. An archway had been there but someone had removed the stones for building purposes not realizing what they revealed. A little further on a stone floor eight inches deep was unearthed. It apparently ran the whole area of the hill, but that was as far as the work had gone. They've been working only since April 1, 1927. I'm anxious to hear of the developments. It was estimated to be over eight thousand years old – before civilization was supposed to have begun. But of course all the time estimates are only estimates. A few still contend that it is natural, but I don't believe that's possible.

We drove on to Hermosa and stayed there overnight. A storm came up but it didn't amount to much so we were comfortable all night. A family going to Iowa from Wyoming camped next to us. We borrowed some cream from them for our coffee. They had a tent and a stove like ours and lastly a car like ours "used to was."

We drove down to the trail to see President Coolidge go through, but didn't see him until later on the road to Sylvan Lake. The scenery was beautiful all the way although not so very astounding until we reached the Needles. The road was mostly uphill and we had to drive in low (gear) most of the way. The hills were very steep and covered with pine and spruce and a few birches. Little streams ran through the hills. Fantastic heaps of rock broke the monotony of the hills. We drove about fifteen miles before we reached points of greatest interest.

Then we drove on to the President's Lodge where armed guards met us at the gate. We passed several small stores, filling stations and cottages and continued up and up until we reached the Needles, Harney Peak and a few other wonders. Pictures can only suggest what it was like. Even the road was hewn out of solid rock with hundreds of feet of tower shapes above and below us. Some of the needles formed part of the wall beside the road. We had to look straight up above our heads to the top. Some of them were balancing rocks that looked liked they could drop down on us any minute.

We saw Harney Peak from the distance through a field glass. There is a lookout tower nearby and we could see the American flag through the glasses. The house was just a tiny speck with the naked eye. As we drove on, the needles became closer and weirder. Several times we stopped to get a better and bigger view – one that will last in our memories and we can recall when the monotony of our rolling prairies begins to weigh on us. We passed through several arches and tunnels hewn out of solid rock. The roads were narrow in places and we could see several hundred feet into the canyon below.

After many miles of this we reached Sylvan Lake – a dark, deep-looking pool with solid rock walls on two sides. It made me think of the pictures of the high rocky coasts of Maine. A thunderstorm came up just then. It sounded about a hundred times worse than at home as it re-echoed through those rocky hills. However our time was so precious we kept on going. The road to Hill City was a series of hairpin curves ever downward, back and forth and around. The rain roared as it fell on the steep slopes and formed little waterfalls some of which fell into the channel at the side of the road. We were extremely thankful that the road was only rock and gravel – and not like Woodworth's gumbo. The rain was still coming in torrents when we finally reached Hill City and we managed to rent a little unfinished cottage up on a high hill, surrounded by funny rock heaps and overlooking the town. Claude went down and got some steak, milk and bread for our dinner. We were so exhausted that we napped for an hour and a half after dinner.

We just returned from a trip downtown where we bought some souvenirs of our visit – a cute album and sweetheart plaque. Also got some postals and a Sunday paper. Now I must go in and make some soup before we go to bed. All is going well, diary, I'm almost too afraid to say it: I am very happy. I am. I believe I have found love at last.

SATURDAY   Well, I made some tomato soup and it curdled horribly but we ate it anyway and it wasn't bad. We didn't even wash the dishes we were so tired. The next morning the carpenters came before we were ready to leave – two nice old fellows who told us all about the Hills. One told us of Wild Bill and Calamity Jane. Wild Bill was a dirty tough crook who took advantage of greenhorns – his gun was his law. Calamity Jane was tough too, I guess, but she was better known for what she did for the sick. He showed us a good route with some good scenery. Just before we left I went back to take a picture of our "love nest." The old carpenter must have been having trouble as he let off a long string of cuss words that would shock a horse. So we snapped a picture of one end of the hut and beat it.

Out of Hill City we found one canyon after another in a series – Ice Box, Spearfish, Boulder and Elk Creek (the last two out of Deadwood). We first went to Lead. It was much larger than we expected and the home of the Homestake Gold Mine, the largest gold mine in the world producing about $6,000,000 yearly. They make the bullion into gold bricks valued at $250 each. The guide that took us through told us that they make about 1,000 of those bricks a day.

The car wasn't working very well when we got there so we took it to a garage. The long ascents and descents had worn both the brake bands and the low gear so they hardly worked at all. Claude had to stop and tighten the low gear just before we got to Lead. Meantime, I got out and straddled the fence and took some pictures.

We got the car and made a tour through the two canyons, Ice Box and Spearfish. We were a little disappointed going up but coming down again we got a wonderful view. We then went on to Deadwood about five miles entirely downhill. There we saw the graves of Wild Bill and Calamity Jane. The garage man pointed above his head where a steep cliff of rock projected and told us it was right there. We began to wonder if the old hootenanny would make it, but by making series of hairpin curves we managed fine. The car is shaking so I can scarcely write. We also saw Mt. Rushmore. Then we descended and passed thru Boulder Canyon to Sturgis where we spent the night in the tourist park. They had a dance in the pavilion close to us, but being tired old married folks, we went to bed.

At first glance we might think they gave Mt. Rushmore pretty short shrift, but what we know as Mt. Rushmore was still just a mountain when Sue wrote this. President Coolidge dedicated the memorial that year (1927), but none of the carvings had even been started. The Washington head was formally dedicated in 1930, Jefferson in 1936, Lincoln in 1937 and Roosevelt in 1939.

We slept quite late the next morning so we got rather a late start. We hated to leave the Hills. There were so many things we would like to see. We didn't even get a decent look at the President. From Sturgis we went to Crystal Cave. We had to be pushed up a hill and finally had to hitch a horse on to get us up the last part. The roads were rotten, but the scenery good; a little creek ran parallel to the road all the way. We saw a small waterfall. A young man took us through the cave. We took pails with candles to light our way. They showed us all kinds of rooms. One was called the President's room, then there was the meat market, butcher's parlor, eagle room, zoo, bridal veil falls etc. There were 1,500 rooms already explored and many others they hadn't even found. One place there was a canyon over a hundred feet deep. At the place where we were standing it was impossible to stand erect. The cave was noted for its many crystals. Almost the entire cavern was lined with crystal. In one spot we went down step after step for a hundred feet. Below that were tiny clear lakes of sweet spring water of which several of us drank. Then those who were tired went back, but we went on to the finish. I bumped my head and cut a gash in it. I can still feel the effects of it.

We stopped in Rapid City on our way home. We got to Wall (South Dakota) that night and pitched our tent early as it looked like a storm. It was our intention to go through the badlands, but a fellow at one of the stations told us the roads were pretty rough and we were afraid of not getting back before the rain.

So we pitched our tent in the brambles, ate supper and made a hurried bed in the car as a storm seemed to be approaching. Before we were in bed half an hour the whole outfit was shaking like a ship in a hurricane. I hardly slept a wink, and towards morning Claude got up and took the whole business down and bound it around the car. The tent leaked like a sieve. We were feeling a little owly and wretched the morning after. I was just getting some bacon in to fry when Claude said, "Do you know this guy?" and there was Harold Adams. They were camped right across the road from us. Both Mrs. Adams and John came over and congratulated us. We had a flat tire so Claude fixed that and also fixed the generator before we went on.

A little jockey and bronco buster asked for a ride to Quinn so we took him along. The roads were pretty rough and slippery from the rain, so we didn't make very good time. We headed for Belle Fourche when we were possessed with a wild desire to turn back and take in the rodeo. Claude finally decided that we could go back for the rodeo and then drive early and late to get home on the fifth. So with light hearts we began to retrace our steps.

We had four flat tires before we reached Spearfish. Stopped at Rapid City and got some milk and hamburgers and a pint of ice cream for dinner. We stopped and ate it in a little squirt of a place – Center City, I think it was. We just got nicely started when a pin came out of a valve so we drove back about a mile to get it fixed. The garage man there didn't know anything about it so Claude had to fix it himself after all. Then we went on again. While we fixed one of our numerous flat tires I counted forty-nine cars that passed us, most of them headed for Belle Fourche. When we got to Spearfish it was growing late and we were afraid we wouldn't find a place to camp at Belle Fourche, so we decided to stay at Spearfish and take a trip up the canyon. It was a beautiful drive, the most picturesque canyon of our trip. Six miles out was the bridal veil falls – just a long dash of spray – we could see clear through them. We watched and drank the cold sweet water (just like an ice spring), filled our jug, took a couple of pictures and returned. We camped under a big tree and didn't get started for Belle Fourche as soon as we expected. The road was alive with cars and the dust so thick the driving was dangerous. The place turned out to be quite a little burg with lots of life – cowboys and girls, Indians and even an old '76 stage coach. The Indians were dressed in feathers, beads and skins. Even the paint wasn't left out.

We ate dinner beside the fence of the rodeo and then got reserved seats in front of the grand stand. The [rodeo] was surely good, but, to our disappointment, the President didn't come.

We left for good old North Dakota early, and with a few flats we finally reached Faith. We just stayed in the car as we were too tired to put up the tent. We hit straight for Medina next morning and had one flat after another — sometimes two at a time. Even the spare went flat on the back end of the car. I would fall asleep and be awakened with, "Wake up Suzie and help fix the tire." We finally just took it like the joke it was. There were TEN flats before we got home. We bought three inner tubes and a casing in Streeter, stopped in Hague, Wishek, Mobridge, Mound City and Isobell. Nearly every town was a refuge for us poor "tire-tired." We ate sandwiches and drank milk all the way home. We reached home at 1:00 A.M. about as dragged out and tired as we could be. No one heard us arrive. The folks were all ready to go on their trip, so they got up at five ready to leave. We got home just in time. I guess our honeymoon hasn't quite ended yet. I hope it endures eternally.

That diary/journal continued in fits and starts through that first year of marriage. Claude's parents had persuaded them they needed help on their homestead in the Chase Lake hills southeast of Pettibone. The crops had been good enough the last few years to support two families, they thought. So Claude and Sue, somewhat reluctantly, began their marriage sharing a tiny homestead house that they divided down the middle to make two homes. Claude's older sister, Nellie, had married Christ Eisinger and they lived on a farm nearby. His younger sister, Frances (Frank) taught school. Marg married Orville Larson. Sue's friends, Lou and Les Larson were married and lived near Pettibone. Willard and Laura were married and lived across the alley from the garage that played a role in Claude and Sue's early courtship. Sue drove to Pettibone once or twice a week to give piano lessons, shop and visit friends. There was never a want for company or entertainment, and now with cars, distance was not much of an impediment.

FRIDAY   Soup and Willard came out and stayed until midnight. The next day I ironed almost all day and didn't even get the bed made. I went to town in the evening and got a haircut and some groceries. Came back by way of Lou and Les's but found nobody home. Claude says, "Come to bed old sweetheart." So I will finish later.

SATURDAY   I went to town to give lessons and take in some cream. I gave only two lessons – to the Leoppkes. Then I took the cream to McCumber at the creamery. He shook hands and bawled me out for not letting him know of our coming marriage, then he insisted I write up the particulars for the paper. So I went home and did that. Got my dishes and few other little articles. Loeppkes gave me a darling kitten. We had a hard time catching him, but he lay in my lap all the way home. He is such a bright little nut too. He knows his sandbox – learned it in one day. I named him Felix.

In the evening we went in to the show and Claude got a haircut. Got home about one, I guess. This newlywed life is the weeds for late hours. One would think that married life meant staying home, but I haven't seen much of it yet.

SUNDAY   Got up early and tore into things so we could go on a fishing party with Nellies and Geislers and Reardons.

Got a late start but finally got there in time for dinner (lunch) and fished until suppertime. We had rotten luck until we got some minnows and then we women caught nine swell perch. We didn't leave Crystal Lake until 10:30 and then we had to milk when we got home. Also cleaned two bullheads before we went to bed. One stung me at the lake and I went through agonies for about two hours with it. It bled quite a bit for such tiny hole.

MONDAY   Home all day for a relief. Hot as sin. I pepped up enough to clean the house a bit but that was about all. Carl is here helping with chores etc.

We got a wedding present from John and Dora – a little teapot. Also a box of candy and disheartening letter from Earl. I feel sorry for him but I imagine he'll recover. Claude has gone to bed to recuperate. Guess I'll have to join him.

WEDNESDAY   Letter from the folks saying they would be back on Thursday. We picked up Monk's trailer and loaded up our furniture. It seemed good to have it "home" at last.

THURSDAY   The folks arrived before I had dishes done. Dirty house of course. Fish for dinner. We went to Johnson's to Ladies' Aid, had a good time and met lots of new people. Reverend Mielke took us home.

FRIDAY   I painted all day and it rained for accompaniment. I'm fixing dresser, bed, and chair for the bedroom.

MONDAY   I haven't written for over a week as time seems scarcer than ever. Time happily filled! Sunday we went fishing to Lake Williams. Lou, Les, Laura, Willard, Claude and I went out in Monk's boat. Claude caught three and I

caught two. Then we went up to Willard's to fry them. Lou
and Les came over about eleven just in time to get in on our
sparse fish feed. I had a nice time and got home about one.
Washed and ironed Monday. I painted most of the week
and finally got the last of it done on Thursday afternoon. I
made some little doilies for my dresser. Saturday I gave six
lessons in town and got home just in time for the "surprise"
party. There was a big crowd and a good time with lots of
nice gifts: three mixing bowls, a silver butter knife, cake and
sandwich plate, water set, Turkish towel, two sheets, two
Pyrex baking dishes, rag rug, dish pan, coffee pot, berry set,
spoon case, broom.

 That same day I got a silver butter knife and sugar shell
from Aunt Margaret and Uncle Will and a beautiful set
of salt and peppers from Alice. I also got a letter from
Catherine which I must answer at once.

 Sunday we went to Lake Bill (Williams) again with Laura
and Willard and the Vans. I told Lou my holy secret and
she could scarcely believe it. I am becoming happier daily
because of it. We are going on a fishing trip to Lake Williams
again Saturday night – we three pair. Hope to have a grand
time providing we get a boat.

Sue was pregnant. She couldn't have been happier. They were
settling into their half of the house. The major purchase was a
kitchen cabinet. It covered a lot needs. One upper door concealed
a flour sifter that would hold maybe twenty pounds of flour. The
middle section held essential seasonings and baking ingredients.
The upper right probably held the dishes. The counter slid in and
out and featured an easy-to-clean enamel surface; the space below
held the cookware. Most kitchens of the era had something similar.

 They had to return the coupe to Willard at the garage in Pettibone. That must have trimmed their sails considerably. "No more

spreees for us till daddy jars loose with another hoopy. I miss it frightfully."

She went back to teaching that fall, but there was no time for keeping diaries.

MARCH, 1928   I quit teaching on February 10 and set to work on my layette. I got three rooms papered before my time ripened and the house is pretty well cleaned.

TRINITY HOSPITAL, JAMESTOWN, NORTH DAKOTA   Baby was born Friday, March 30, at 9:01 A.M. after two and a half hours illness. With God's help I came through with little real suffering and was much relieved that the nine-month vigil was broken. Bonnie Lou weighed just five pounds ten ounces. She didn't feed well the first several days, but outdoes herself now. She weighs six pounds five ounces this morning, a gain of fifteen ounces since she quit losing. She's getting fat and dimply, much to my delight. The doctor says I may leave this afternoon. I don't doubt that I can give her as good care as she gets here, but babies are so fragile. I sometimes feel like a helpless idiot.

I've had so much company. There were sixteen here Thursday, and on Easter there were fourteen including Reverend Mielke. Only one day passed without some company and none without mail. I received twenty-one letters and three parcels besides fruit, candy and gum — much more than I could consume. I am going home on Wednesday. Home Sweet Home once more. Daddy is so proud of his little family and lonesome too, I guess. I wonder what next big event I will set down in these pages.

CHAPTER 5

Hard Times

...we never went hungry

Sue's diary ends there, but not because nothing was happening. Much of what did happen was not good. The next year settled into somewhat uneasy routines. Baby Bonnie Lou thrived in a fussy fits and starts kind of way. The crop was not too bad, considering. By the time Bonnie was eight months old, Sue was pregnant again, and on July 22, 1929, Colleen Carol (to be called Keeny, mostly) was born, a happy, contented baby, to everyone's relief. But it was a hot, dry summer and a scanty crop. With two babies, the small half of a small house was getting to be a tight fit. Money was tight, too. Grandma Rawson complained – and not too privately – that Sue was taking the car to town too often to give piano lessons. The next obvious question was going to be, "Why did they need that piano, anyway?"

The crash on Wall Street in October 1929 barely registered in the Chase Lake Hills of North Dakota, but by 1931 the Depression was catching up with them. There had not been a good crop since 1928, only wind, grasshoppers, and no rain to speak of. Claude applied for the Standard Oil agency in Medina and it looked like he would get it. Plans were made. But that job went to the brother-in-law of the guy who ran the garage. Then they heard that the agency in Pettibone might be available, and in desperation Claude applied. And got it. But he needed a truck and there was no money. Ike Leoppke ran a Ford dealership in Pettibone and he happened to have a used truck he couldn't sell and he offered it to Claude for nothing down and five dollars a month. So in early spring, 1931, Claude drove the truck out to the farm and loaded up the kitchen cabinet, the bed and dresser, the piano with the rest of their meager household essentials and their two little girls and drove through snow and slush to an uncertain future. At least the farm was behind them.

They moved into the Lydeen house and soon discovered that bedbugs had moved in ahead of them. But it was theirs and Sue bought a bolt of cloth and made curtains for the kitchen and pinafores for the girls and soon it was warm enough to plant the garden. They decided they could make do with one bedroom and rented the second to Rupert Rohde. The room and board he paid helped out with the rent.

It was about the bottom of the barrel as jobs go – trying to selling fuel oil to farmers who hadn't had a crop in three years. But he sold a little, some on credit, plus some kerosene, floor wax and harness oil. In the spring of 1931 Claude managed to collect a substantial sum – I heard $200, but that seems too high for those times – from a farmer to whom he had sold fuel oil on credit. He was late getting back to town that day and he wasn't able to make the deposit in the bank. The next day the Bank of Pettibone failed never to open again. Everyone who had their money there lost it.

One by one, farmers mortgaged their farms to buy seed in hopes that this year, this year, there would be a crop. But this year, like last year and the year before, the wind came without the rain, and by mid-summer the dust had piled up around the houses and barns and the Russian thistles stacked up at the fences. Bankers began to foreclose on one farm and then the next. Sometimes a farmer managed to elude the bankers for a while. Sometimes he just threw up his hands, got off his horse and walked off.

Claude was no longer farming, but his business depended entirely upon the farmers' success; they were tethered together running a three-legged race. Grandpa Charlie, suffering the formidable triple threats of drought, Depression and old age, eventually lost the Rawson homestead to the bank and moved into Pettibone to run the creamery. My parents never spoke of those days once they were past. When asked, Sue said, "We never went hungry, there was always plenty of food, and everyone else was in the same situation."

Bonnie and Keeny, so close in age, were raised like Tweedle Dum and Tweedle Dee, much like Marg and Sue. Sue taught them to help with chores as she had done, and exposed them early to music and poetry. But your children are never really yours, they are their own, and Bonnie and Keeny arrived with their own wants and expectations. Their memories of those days were not exactly nostalgic and sepia-toned. They remembered Claude flying into rages and smacking them until their teeth rattled. Bonnie was admittedly an "active" child. When she was little more than a toddler, she climbed to the roof of the outhouse and fell off, breaking her arm. She was smart and, even she admitted, contrary. She remembered being sent frequently to stay with Grandma and Grandpa Rawson or Aunt Nellie. It may have been for her own protection, but she felt it was to get rid of her. Keeny felt like she was born in the wrong family. She wanted Sears Roebuck dresses and matching anklets. She wanted a pretty bedroom with a real bedspread. She hated music lessons. What she got was homemade hand-me-downs, patchwork quilts and thankless chores.

Claude and Sue still had a social life, but instead of dancing they had people over to play cards – whist and pinochle. There was Homemaker's Club, Ladies Aid for the church ladies, church suppers. They joined the Lutheran Church because Grandma Butch had been raised Lutheran, and somewhere along the way Sue became the church organist – only it was a piano. And she played for the Congregationalists, too, when they needed her. She always had a few piano students.

Sue's 'Pop,' Butch Maynard, died of a stroke in 1931. He was only fifty-four. The next spring Wally was born at home on April 5, 1932, and named Charles Wallace after his grandfathers – sort of. When Doc Meltzer finally got there he hoisted him up on his hand scale and declared him to be over ten pounds. Two stories survive: One afternoon Sue lay down with him, hoping he would nap. She did. He didn't. She woke with a start when he managed to clip a clothespin to her nose. The other, as a bedtime inducement Sue was reciting poetry to him. "Where's my wandering boy tonight?" she began. "Here I are," he replied.

Wally and his cousin Tom, Marg's son, were the same age and fellow adventurers. They got tricycles for Christmas the same year, and one spring day got the notion to ride their tricycles to the gravel pit about a half mile south of town. They were four. They were past the railroad tracks, about halfway there when they were discovered missing, quickly found and retrieved.

The Drought and the Depression roared on. The homesteaders who had been barbers (like Butch Maynard) and tinsmiths (like Charlie Rawson) were the first to pack it in and move – some, like these, to town, some headed west to California or Oregon. After a few years of no crops even the heartiest were rethinking their options, which were fading. The population of Kidder County dropped about seventeen percent from 1930 to 1940. Not as bad as Kansas and Oklahoma, but the tight knit communities of their childhood homesteading days were shrinking. Their friends from teenage years, Lou and Les Larson, gave up and moved near family in Minnesota. Margaret's family moved west and took Grandma Butch with them. But enough stayed so Claude's Standard Oil Agency survived. Those who stayed he referred to as "good managers."

Sunday, April 15, 1934, produced the worst, most spectacular dust storm ever. It all started with an enormous front that started in Alberta, Canada, swooping down across North Dakota and points south and east. A great wall of black dirt rolled over the plains, gathered up the rich topsoil laid bare with plows and dried by the relentless sun, and continued east. Even cities in the Midwest and East saw black residue falling from the sky. It became known as Black Sunday. The dust sifted into closed cupboards leaving a dusting of grit on just-washed plates and permeated the seams of the clothes that hung in closets. Those who had cars left them in the garage for fear of ruining the motors. Visibility was such that anyone brave or foolish enough to venture out had to stay within feet of the fence so as not to get lost.

By late summer farmers were already feeding the winter's supply of hay to the cattle because there was no grass left even along the roadside ditches. They sold off livestock for pennies – herds they had worked years to develop – just to prevent them from starving to death. It began to look like the smart money was on those who were cutting their losses and heading west.

1936 was the coldest, snowiest winter anyone could remember, followed by the hottest, driest summer. Temperatures soared above 110 degrees. The wind blew and blew the dirt with it. Sue took to pulling the couch out on the front step at night in an attempt to get some slightly cooler air and maybe some sleep. She was pregnant again, the third of their four children to be born since the Depression and Drought began. But a neighbor told her, "This baby must be wanted, you look so happy."

I was born on August 6. Sue went to Carrington to stay with her Aunt Hannah and Uncle Mike until my arrival was imminent and then she went to the maternity home. I was named Rosemary (or Rosie, which was apt because everyone remarked on my rosy cheeks) and in a surprising gesture of modernity, Jill as a middle name. By that time the family had moved to what we always called "the little house" kitty-corner from the Congregational Church. It had two bedrooms upstairs. Bonnie and Keeny had one that I remember most because it had stars on the ceiling. My parents had the other one which also had a three-quarter size bed that I shared with Wally until we moved from there when I was seven.

Downstairs were a small living room and dining room and a tiny kitchen with a gas range, the kitchen cabinet and a stand which held the water pail with a dipper, which everybody drank from. Clothes were still ironed with flatirons, heated on the stove, until they got one that stayed heated with gasoline, flames visible out the sides. And yes, Keeny did set her clothes on fire with it one frightening day and carried a scar on her tummy for years. The closest thing to an icebox was a box inside the Fagering's well where we got our drinking water. We did have electric lights. Ray Grimm started Pettibone Light and Power Company with a gasoline engine which generated electric power for forty-nine users – surely all the residences and business in town and a few nearby farms. Ray soon

Keeny, Baby Rosie and Wally, Winter of 1937

found it was uneconomical to run a gas engine twenty-four hours a day and converted his operation to five wind-powered generators that could work individually as needed.

Bonnie remembered me as a whiny child which was no doubt true. I do remember that Mom, in exasperation when I was whining underfoot while she was trying to get supper, would point and say, "Go to the bawl room!" And I would. The bawl room was actually the entrance to the second floor, but it had a door, and I would go in, shut the door and carry on for a while until I was over it, whatever it was, and then let myself out.

Being the fourth was an enviable position, I found. I got all the advantages of being the baby (no chores), but mostly I got to tag along with the big kids and do big kid stuff. We played Kick the Can in the alley between Fagerings and us. We played Ante-I-Over which involved throwing a ball over the garage, and if someone could catch it he would run around and tag the team on the other side. On one memorable occasion I even got to play Run Sheep Run with the big kids. As I remember it, Run Sheep Run was a team version of hide and seek played after dark. One team would head out to find a hiding place somewhere in town – maybe behind Dethloff's chicken coop or Danielson's shed – and send one member back to the other team to lead or mislead them in their search. When he got the opposing team far enough away he would yell, "Run Sheep Run!" and everyone would streak back to home base, hoping to be there first for the win. With the first one back and the win secured, the leader would yell, "Ollie, Ollie Ox in Free!" so no one would be left out there hiding in the dark all night. I'd never been part of something so dangerously exciting in all my six years.

Sometimes my cousin Butch (Duane, Willard's son) would come over to play and Mom would make us brown sugar sandwiches, which I remember because Butch always ate his sandwiches upside down and he lost a lot of brown sugar until we persuaded him to fold it in half. Or sometimes I went over to his house to play.

Bonnie and Keeny standing, Wally and Rosie seated. Summer 1937

Aunt Laura had a pair of wicker rocking chairs which when turned upside down made splendid caves. Butch and I were playing caves one day when he apparently did something extremely annoying and I reached over and yanked out a good fistful of his hair. Aunt Laura carried on quite a bit about that and I never got to play caves with the wicker chairs again.

My best girlfriend was Arlene Leoppke. She was my age and we played dolls and paper dolls and Chinese checkers, and went wading in the ditch in front of the house when spring came and the snow melted. I was heart-broken when her family moved to Heaton before we could start first grade together.

I wanted to go to school in the worst way. And I did. One crisp fall day when I was only two or three, I took off on my own to make it so, heading for the schoolhouse a block and a half away. I got there and caused such a ruckus that the Principal (the Principal!) pulled Keeny out of class and ordered her to take me home. I bawled all the way, she reports, and then, stating the obvious, declared, "Sosy cay cay" (Rosie cry). Keeny was mortified. I had to content myself with 'home schooling,' eventually practicing writing my name backwards in the back of my baby book where it lives in infamy.

Rosie at three

Grandma Butch, now in California, lived near Aunt Hannah's daughter Dorothy who, it happened, had girls. So once in a while we would get a big box from the post office that included store bought (!!!) dresses that might fit me or my sisters. Mom made virtually all of our clothes, including coats, and they were fine. But Grandma Butch's boxes were a combination shopping spree and Christmas. The one I remember best was dusty rose with little buttoned tabs detailed in front. It's the one I'm wearing in my three-year-old picture.

Saturday night was bath night. Water was heated on the gas range and filled the round galvanized tubs in the basement where they were also used for laundry. One after the other the six of us got the weekly scrubbing. I can only guess what the water looked like by the time Dad got his bath at the end. For the rest, the order was not written in stone. I remember asking, "Can I has a bas' assa you?" (Can I have a bath after you) and being teased for it.

Sunday we went to Lutheran Sunday School, sang "Jesus Loves Me" and "What a Friend We Have in Jesus," listened to the stories of Lazarus, Mary and Martha, and at Christmas about the baby Jesus. I was three when I stood on the piano bench beside Mom and sang "Away in the Manger" for the Christmas program the first time.

My parents were rather shadowy figures in my early memory. Dad sometimes sat with me in the rocker and sang the poor little friskies song. It was the story about a hunter who went out and shot some squirrels leaving the baby squirrels motherless "and the poor little friskies they cried and they cried, and no one came near them and soon they all died," he would wail plaintively, and I would say, "sing it again." Mom, in her turn, would recite poetry from memory, most memorably, "The Leak in the Dike," a long and mournful tale of the little Dutch boy who saved all of Holland by holding his finger in the dike where it had sprung a leak, thus holding back the sea. About halfway through we got to the scary bit:

But hark! Through the noise of the waters
Comes a low, clear, trickling sound;
And the child's face pales with terror,
And his blossoms drop to the ground.
He is up the bank in a moment,
And stealing through the sand,
He sees a stream not yet so large
As his slender, childish hand.
'Tis a leak in the dike! He is but a boy,
Unused to fearful scenes;
But, young as he is, he has learned to know
The dreadful thing that means.
A leak in the dike! The stoutest heart
Grows faint that cry to hear,
And the bravest man in all the land
Turns white with mortal fear.
For he knows the smallest leak may grow
To a flood in a single night,
And he knows the strength of the cruel sea
When loosed in its angry might.

Just to hear the opening line, "The good dame looks from her cottage at the close of a summer's day..." I automatically snuggled down for a long, satisfyingly scary tale, grateful that I lived where there were no dikes and no sea. I loved it. Often we would fall asleep to Mom playing the piano – something classical from her dog-eared copy of *Piano Pieces the Whole World Plays*. So whatever others suffered in that time, I sailed through it blissfully unaware.

Things started improving about fall of 1938, and Sue started agitating for a little getaway. I imagine it was a hard sell. Where to? With all the kids!!! Who would mind the truck? Where would the money come from? Bert Nieswaag had helped out in the past. He could take over the truck route for a week. Sue had saved a little money from piano lessons.

This picture was taken at Grandma Rawson's birthday (the day before mine) in 1939. Pictured from the left and around back: Nellie, Sue, Grandpa Charlie, Claude, Grandma Winnie, Willard holding Duane, Christ, Joy (half hidden), Ben holding baby Winnifred. The clutch of kids in the front are Rosie, Wally, Bonnie (half hidden), Nellie's son Dick, Aunt Frank behind Keeny.

And so, in the summer of 1940 the family took their first road trip to Yellowstone Park, driving a blue 1936 Chevrolet sedan. Bonny was twelve, Keeny was almost eleven, Wally was eight. I was only four and I stayed home with the Fagering family across the alley, sufficient adventure for me since I'd never been away from home overnight before. The trip is recorded in an odd diary, ostensibly written by Bonnie. Bonnie says she never wrote it and, indeed the handwriting is Sue's. I'm guessing that she wanted the whole experience to be recorded from the point of view of the kids, but Bonnie refused, so Mom wrote it channeling her own twelve-year-old self. Her fingerprints are on it – her penchant for long descriptions of the scenery and recording every meal and expense.

(This proved useful for future planning and lends a whole layer of understanding now.)

FRIDAY, JULY 7, 1940 We started out at 7:15 and it poured rain until we hit *[highway]* number 10. Our wash job on the car went in a hurry. Stopped in Bismarck and Mom got a babushka and some peanut butter kisses and we kids all got glasses. We *[the kids]* saw the Missouri *[River]* for the first time. Signs of buttes and Badlands began to show up around Glen Ullin. We picked up cherries and apples and a quart of milk and stopped outside of Hebron at the dam and ate our first meal out: buns with cheese and cookies, milk and cherries. Three boys were catching fish in gunnysacks at the dam.

We drove through Richardton and Taylor — both nice little towns. Richardton has a lovely big Catholic Church and seminary. Dickinson is a nice place with a nice new college building. The kids were taking a snooze (Wally on the floor and Keeny on the seat) when we crossed the Montana line. We ate our supper at Terry (a historical point) in the trailer camp. We had table and chairs and could see the buttes off across the river as we ate our bacon and eggs. Then we struck out again and went to Custer, about 110 miles I guess, where we got a two-room cabin that Walt Kaczmarskis *[from Pettibone]* had the night before.

SATURDAY Started out again before eight. We passed beet fields with irrigation ditches and Mexican workers. We came to a little place called Pompeys Pillar and just out a ways we could see the pillar itself. Captain Clark of Lewis and Clark expedition has carved his name on it and the railroad company has protected it with a steel screen.

Billings, Montana. This is where we saw Sacrifice Cliff. They say that during a smallpox epidemic the Indians leapt off the cliff to appease the wrath of the gods. There are very picturesque rocks and cliffs almost surrounding the city. We stocked up on groceries ($1.25 worth) to take us into the park at least.

A couple of miles out of Billings we began to see the Bear Tooth Mountains, their silvery heads looking like floating clouds. They were fifty miles away but they kept getting more distinct as we approached. At Red Lodge we caught the beginning of Cooke County Highway. At the foot of the mountains we stopped for early dinner. It was nice and cool and we stopped at a tourist park beside a babbling creek with the cleanest, softest, coolest water we found on the whole trip. It was melted snow directly out of the mountains. We kids took off our shoes and socks and went wading while Mom and Dad got dinner. We managed to get thoroughly wet slipping around on the rocks and almost floated our anklets down the creek. We had bacon, lettuce and tomato sandwiches for dinner. We washed towels, and washcloths and things. The water was so nice we wanted to play in it all day.

After dinner we went through the zoo and saw every kind of animal and bird found in the mountain and park. About three we started again and went right into the mountains on the Cooke City Highway. We climbed mountains for about thirty miles by a series of switchbacks that were hair-raising to say the least. We reached the summit at 11,000 feet and made snowballs on the eighth of July! Only no one felt frolicsome enough at that height to have a snowball fight. Little chipmunks darted across the road and numberless rills, creeks and falls lined the road all the way up. The summit was flat with no trees. It looked a lot like our North Dakota prairies. The trail down was less startling and very beautiful. We finally reached Cooke City, which was about the strangest city we'd ever seen — a combination of mining camp, old west, with everything to cater to tourist trade, all in a tiny compact mass called Cooke City. All the buildings were made of logs. We went on shortly, aiming to reach Mammoth by night.

We made it to Mammoth over bumpy roads mostly narrow and under construction. We saw Tower Falls from a footbridge we got to by taking a narrow trail around the base of a cliff. Then we drove about a mile down a winding road past the overhanging cliffs near the falls to see the petrified tree. We got up there by climbing a LOT of steps. Wally nearly fell headlong coming down too fast. The petrified tree was bigger than any of the living ones in the park.

We finally reached Mammoth Hot Springs tired and hungry and a little more than half frightened. We got a little cabin across the creek from towering mountains ($1.50) and made our supper of meat and potatoes. The folks slept in the cabin and we kids slept in the car. It was so cold we nearly froze by morning.

There were cars from all over the U.S. there: cars from Utah, Pennsylvania, and Missouri were our closest neighbors. Everybody was friendly and we had interesting visits with many of them. They had a water pail in every cabin and water faucets every four or five cabins so we could carry in water for our own use. Each cabin had a little wood-burning stove with a teakettle, a wash dish and pitchers. But they weren't as nice as the other cabins we had — or as cheap.

SUNDAY This morning we went up to Mammoth Hot Springs with a party and a guide. The springs were very interesting — terraced and many-colored and very hot. One little spring was smaller than a gopher hole and it emitted hot water. The guide told us that when they put in a new road a new spring started up right in the middle of the road. We climbed so many terraces that by the time our excursion was over our legs ached and we were very warm.

Then we started out for Norris. We picked up two boys
going fishing. They were from Nebraska and Pennsylvania. We
missed Norris, but finally reached Madison Junction. On the
way we saw the Golden Gate (a pile of yellow rocks forming
an entry), a spring with water that tasted like unflavored pop,
the Obsidian Cliff which was like black glass and Roaring
Mountain, a white ashy-looking mountain with smoke rising
from every crease and crevice and making a humming sound.
Below it was an absolutely green lake with a bunch of dark
dead pine trees standing upright without a branch.

We were hungry and ready to eat when we left Madison
Junction (we went to a museum there), but before we found
a place to eat, the pools and geysers started showing up.
The first big basin we saw was very interesting. A geyser was
continually spouting up out of an odd-shaped base. Nearby
was a very beautiful pool, crystal clear on top but blue down
in. It looked very deep. Other geysers were more or less
active, some spurting and some just steaming. Nearest the
road were the Paint Pots. The largest and most spectacular
was the large pool of white gas that looked as thick as house
paint. It bubbled and boiled like porridge, making a great
noise. It was amazing.

Then we came to a bridge – a foot bridge where we all got
out and clambered up to a boardwalk that led us around a
beautiful pool, the crater of an extinct volcano now filled with
hot water from the hot springs above. The walk led us through
various hot springs and pools of the most beautiful turquoise,
blue and crystal clear. They all had names like Sapphire,
Turquoise, Opal, Morning Glory, Gem and many others.

Later we got to another geyser basin where the Grotto
Geyser was steaming like it was about to take off. So we
backed into the woods a few feet and opened our tomato
juice and had bacon and egg sandwiches. Mom and Keeny

went to rinse the washrag in a hot pool, and while they were there they saw the Riverside Geyser erupting so they ran down to the river to see it. It only erupts every five and a half to eight hours so they were lucky.

By the time they got back the next one started erupting, so we rested while we watched it. The Giant Geyser was also in that basin, but it erupts only every three to ninety days. It shoots up two hundred feet and is the largest in the park – largest in world in fact. Eventually we came to Old Faithful. There was a large building there where three girls and a man were running their legs off trying to serve the tourists demanding cold drinks. We were very dry and tired ourselves by that time and the day had turned very hot. After we had our drinks we went to watch Old Faithful do his stuff. In about ten minutes, right on schedule, it started bubbling and slopping over and finally up she went, higher and higher till it reached its full seventy-five feet. Very thrilling.

We went back and bought some souvenirs – some little dolly moccasins for Rosemary and I got some too. Dad got a knife and Wally got a gun and holster. We went through the museum and drank gallons of water and soon it was time for Old Faithful again so we went and sat in the car to watch this time.

We went on to Yellowstone Lake. The day had cooled off some so we felt better. It was a pretty drive around the lake, very cool and refreshing. The lake is three hundred feet deep in spots and looked like a dandy place to swim, except that it was very cold. We came out by the fish hatchery and an immense hotel for big shots at the lake. We saw bears in the woods along the way. We saw thousands of trout on their way out to the lake from the hatchery. Then we drove up the canyon expecting to view Artist's Point and Inspiration Point and get a cabin for the night. It was getting late when

we arrived at Artist's Point, and it was the most thrilling view
we have had. It was almost dusk when we got to the Grand
Canyon of the Yellowstone. The rocks were yellow and gray
with pinnacles sticking up in the canyon below us. We went
up the narrow path to the lookout. The folks were at the end,
of course, and the creek was deep down in the gorge, so it
was a little scary. Then we got to a platform where we could
stop and just look. The gorge shaded into pale pink, yellows
and light greens – things you see on picture post cards and
think they are exaggerated.

Then we drove down and watched the wild bears come
out of the woods to eat. We counted fifteen at one time.
By the time we got back to the camp there were no cabins
left so we had to drive back to Yellowstone Lake with about
the same results. We had to take a three dollar cabin or go
without. So we took it, ate a potluck supper and rolled in.

MONDAY   This morning we drove out the east entrance and
into the most exquisite mountain scenery we've ever seen –
Shoshone Park. There were fantastic rocks, mountains
and buttes together with the creeks, falls and cascades.
Eventually we came out at the Shoshone Dam where we
went through three tunnels. Altogether it was thrilling and
we agreed it outrivaled even the Yellowstone Park in beautiful
drives. We stopped at Cody and got drinks and looked
around a bit and then went on toward Greybull.

Dad got sick just out of Cody and rode in the back and
Mom drove. By the time we reached Greybull, Dad thought
he was going to die, so we took a cabin and put him to bed
and gave him sleep pills. A young man at the filling station
was very kind to us and let us wash out some clothes and
iron them. There was a hose running on the lawn and we
had lots of fun getting thoroughly soaked. There were also

showers there and we had two each before we left. The
weather was very hot and we made about six quarts of
lemonade, which made Dad feel better, so in the evening we
all went up town and got ice cream.

TUESDAY   We got up and had breakfast and started out
early, hoping to make good time before it got hot. The
roads were fine until we got up into the Big Horn Mountains
and then Dad took the wheel. It was ninety-seven miles to
Buffalo through winding mountain roads, but after Buffalo
the roads and the country were smoother. The whole
country as far as the eye could see was nothing but buttes
and hills until we got near the Black Hills.

WEDNESDAY   We got a cabin on the crest of a hill in Hot
Springs with showers and a gas plate. We just dropped
down over the precipice and were at the corner store for
groceries. This morning we went down to look over the
town. We saw the Evans Plunge and the Old Soldiers and
then drove to the Wind Cave. It was awfully hot and a fire
was raging in the hills near Hill City. We went on at least to
see Mount Rushmore where they have carved four figures
of Washington, Lincoln, Roosevelt and Jefferson. We saw
it from several different heights and from three tunnels. We
skipped Needles Highway because of the fire. We could smell
it and the smoke was thick
    We left the Black Hills at Rapid City armed with a gallon
of lemonade, a quart of milk and a cantaloupe besides our
bread etc. We sat under a tree near the highway and had
our dinner outside of Rapid City. We hit out about two and
really made good time till we got to Pierre toward evening.
We watched the Black Hills disappear and our own prairies
begin to unroll before our eyes. At Pierre we got a little old

cabin with a bum electric plate for a dollar. We grabbed a quick lunch and went to the show, *A Farewell to Arms*, which was good. It tried to rain all night but didn't succeed.

THURSDAY   We picked up some little presents for Rosemary *[I asked for, and got, a little hammer. I've no idea why]* and got on our way again about nine. I think we got a little more homesick as we drew nearer North Dakota. We stopped at Selby and got two big cans of tomato juice, bread and meat for dinner – and then left it there! We drove across the state line and stopped by a big tree to eat before we discovered it. So we drove into Temvick, got more bread and meat, parked by the road with a quart of cold milk and bag of popcorn. We stopped again at Hazelton to quench our thirst at the town pump.

Well, we're almost home now and I haven't even mentioned the Badlands of North Dakota. We took a seven-mile drive over a Federal Project road and saw all the different shapes and sizes of buttes. We saw one lone buffalo standing forlornly on a hilltop.

If my math is correct, the whole trip – a family of five for a week to a tourist destination – cost under $50, but that was a tidy sum then. There were other road trips, but none so far or so exotic that involved the whole family.

Claude's illness on that trip was typical of the ill health that dogged him over two decades and was never diagnosed or cured. He had surgery to remove his appendix and gall bladder, and later he had all his teeth removed, all without specific symptoms, in hopes his health would return. There were indications that some of it was mental – anxiety, depression. He didn't get better, he didn't get worse. But through it all he always worked, driving the big red truck to the surrounding farms.

CHAPTER 6

The War Years

...the back roads of the home front

Soon rumbles of what was going on in Europe began reaching North Dakota by way of the clipped and measured cadences of H.V. Kaltenborn coming through our little crackling box of a radio. Anyone uttering a peep during his suppertime broadcast was severely "shushed!" Then one Sunday in December came the news that the Japanese had bombed Pearl Harbor.

Pettibone, North Dakota, could hardly have been further from either the war in Europe or the islands of the Pacific, but even here in the furthest back roads of the home front, there was a sense of urgency and patriotism. Our small towns competed with each other to have bigger scrap metal and paper drives. Mom saved bacon grease that was sent off to be made into explosives. Our garden didn't change, only now it was a Victory Garden. The rationing books with their little red and blue and green stamps were husbanded and doled out carefully. As a six-year-old I was drafted to play the patient as the local women learned some basic nursing skills like making a bed with the corners squared and sheets taut even with someone in it (me). Sugar was rationed, but sometimes, on rare, reckless occasions, Mom used it to make a batch of fudge and then it was doubly sweet. Mom played the piano for bond rallies and we kids sometimes sang. By the time I was six or seven I knew all the words to most of the war songs: "I'll Get By," "White Cliffs of Dover," "When the Lights Go on Again," "I'll Walk Alone" and "Mairzy Doats." I suppose I learned them from my big sisters.

By that time I could go to school. I started first grade with Marla DeKrey, Ahmed Kamoni, Sherwin Rohde, Vernon Herman and Marlow Flanders. Marlow was my first crush, a blond, curly headed dreamboat. We made our way through *Dick and Jane* the first year and by the middle of second grade Marla and I were moved up to third grade leaving the boys behind. Actually we only moved to the far side of the room. First, Second and Third Grades were all in the same classroom. It was a seamless transition except for the challenge of long division.

One late summer day I was downtown with half the townsfolk, watching them dig the basement and lay the foundation for a building. The German Lutherans had bought the old Marstonmoor Hall (where Claude and Sue had danced their way into marriage) and were moving it into Pettibone to be their new church. Someone came by and said, "Your folks just got a refrigerator." A refrigerator! Never mind that there was no electricity yet and no room in the kitchen to park it. REA (Rural Electrification Authority) was coming and the Philco refrigerator fit snuggly into the dining room. Keeny ceremoniously put the Sears Roebuck catalog in it so it would serve some useful purpose until the power arrived.

We moved to the Thorstness house in the spring of 1943. It was about the biggest house in town. It had three bedrooms upstairs and one down. It also had a room with plumbing fixtures (or at least a bathtub) in it, which makes me think it was a Sears Roebuck House or another of the kit houses common in those days, but it was never plumbed and never used. The house also had an open staircase with a banister and colonnades between the dining and living room and a built in oak bench. There were other houses, farmhouses that I believe now were kit houses, though I never heard it then. There was also a barn/garage out back with a walk-up haymow and a chute to slide down, and a windmill – so we had our own water at last. Bonnie, Keeny and Wally each had their own bedroom. I got shunted between Bonnie and Keeny, but I still occasionally had "accidents" of bedwetting and was not very welcome as a bedmate. Bonnie and Keeny made vanities for their rooms: two orange crates with a board across the top, and then fitted with a flouncy skirt of the cotton print of their choice. Keeny's was the prettiest. She had (and still has) the best taste in the family.

Wally got the room with the staircase that led to the attic, which made it scary at night. But during the day the attic was a big wide room with nooks and gables and it was pretty much mine. It was vast enough for several 'houses,' so when my girlfriends were over we could visit each other with our baby dolls and play at being our mothers.

Even at seven I was a singularly incurious child. I never noticed my mother getting fat and I don't remember that anyone told me about it, though they must have. But suddenly it was announced: I had a baby sister! I went off to stay with Grandma Rawson for a few days in October, 1943, and then Mom returned with Claudia Lind wrapped in a flannel bundle. Dad would have preferred that she be a boy to even things out a bit, but naming her after him must have been a consolation. And indeed, he doted on her. After a week or so, with much preparatory fanfare, I was allowed to hold her. Unfortunately, she wiggled and slipped off my lap and onto the floor and that was the end of that.

Bonnie was fifteen by then and was working out as a 'hired girl' at Vellengas when school was not in session. But Keeny, at fourteen, was still home and she took over much of the day-to-day care of Baby Claudia.

My days were filled with adventures. David Hobbs and I hiked out to the dump at Johnny's Lake looking for good stuff and carved our initials in the spindly trees by the lake. We played in the hayloft and slid down the chute until someone broke an arm – I forget who. Inside, the family penchant for games blossomed in earnest. There was usually a jigsaw puzzle in process and when the new card game, Canasta, showed up there were marathon pickup games. In between were Rummy, Sorry and Monopoly, which could go on for days.

My education continued in realms outside of school. A couple of the Big Kids, not my siblings, reported the news that there was no Santa Claus, it was my parents that filled my brown cotton stocking with an orange, a popcorn ball or candy and new socks and left a doll with my name on it. What!? I felt quite betrayed. Lied to. (This despite the fact that I was terrified of the Santa in the beat-up starched mask that gave out the candy bags at the Christmas Program.) What else might grownups be keeping secrets about? I suspected they might be lying about Jesus, too, but they did seem to be carrying that to extremes what with the churches and all. And then Ardella told me where babies came from and how, which I found unlikely in the extreme. It never crossed my mind to ask my parents about any of this. Never.

Once a month or so we would make the fifty-some mile trip to Jamestown to buy what we couldn't get in Pettibone or order from the Sears Roebuck & Company catalog, like yard goods and underwear and, for the start of school, new Buster Brown shoes. Most of the shopping centered around the J.C. Penney and Pred's department stores where the clerk would write up the purchase, take Mom's cash and put it in an empty cartridge that was then whisked up to the office area on the mezzanine on an elaborate wired system. For lunch we went to the Palace Café for hot pork sandwiches with deliciously glutinous gravy and the special white bread we never got at home. If I didn't go along, Mom usually brought me a coloring book or paper dolls from the Woolworth store for staying home without whining.

For all my vivid memories of the Thorstness house, we lived there less than two years. The folks were planning to buy it and had put money down, but there was nothing in writing and when the owners got a better offer, they took it. The real estate market in Pettibone, about fifty houses, all occupied, offered few choices. Happily, the Schmitt house was available. It was a one story, three bedroom bungalow (possibly another kit house), with two porches and a lovely yard with caragana trees and lilacs, a pansy bed and a vine house (a small chicken wire room covered with climbing vines). The lot to the west, as large as the one the house sat on, was all garden. The house was on Main Street across the street from Uncle Willard's garage and kitty-corner from their house. Mom said it was the nicest house in town. It cost more than the Thorstness house, but the war was winding down, things were looking up and they thought, with luck, they could swing it. They bought it for $3,000.

They did considerable remodeling as well, making archways in the living area where square doorways had been, filling in the trapdoor to the basement in the kitchen pantry and making it into a breakfast nook, which became a centerpiece of my teenage years. REA had come to Pettibone and the Philco refrigerator was a working appliance. With the war over, household goods were becoming available again and the kitchen was outfitted with white metal cupboards all around and a metal sink with running water. The old gas range was replaced with an electric one. We even had a bathroom with a tub, a flush toilet and running water, the first for our family. Where he learned how, I have no idea, but Claude (and maybe Willard) wired and plumbed the house and many of the other houses in town as well.

Mom was delighted to discover that, at last, she had a kid who liked to read. It started with the Bobbsey Twins books that my teacher read to us a chapter at a time to start the school day. I soon read my way through the meager library at school. Then Mom wrote the State Library in Bismarck asking for books appropriate for a nine-year-old and a stack of four or five would arrive at the post office strapped together. And so I read my way through Laura Ingalls Wilder's Little House books, one by one. Then there was *Lassie Come Home* and the other dog books and then the horse books, Nancy Drew and other mysteries, and eventually *Little Women* and all the Louisa Mae Alcott books. Like thousands of other girls of the era, I wanted to be Jo. Reading sometimes got me out of washing the supper dishes. "Oh, I'll do them," Mom would say, "She's *reading*."

I also got piano lessons, of course. I liked playing well enough, but I had to work in the half hour of practice every day around what by now was a very busy household, plus Mom's piano students in the after school hours. I resented that, unlike them, I didn't have a regular lesson time. "Come on, Rosie," she would say out of the blue, "I've got time to give you a lesson." And often as not it would involve her counting along loudly from the kitchen (ONE, two, three, four, ONE two, three, four) as she was getting supper started. I got so I could play a respectable Mozart, but was totally incapable of playing in public. My hands shook so I could scarcely make it through my recital piece and I never learned to play the simplest of hymns for group singing, all of which Mom could do effortlessly. It must have been a great disappointment to her.

Wally, being a boy, was excused from piano lessons. He got the violin (the violin Mom splurged to buy in Valley City in 1924). Nobody quite remembers how and when he learned, but he was a natural. He explained, "Oh, Mom showed me a few things and I picked it up." Few things indeed. She never had more than the few lessons she had that summer at Normal School. I never saw her play the violin. But Wally fiddled like a pro and went on to be very accomplished on the harmonica and mandolin as well. Of all her children, Wally was the one who got her music gene and he got the least instruction.

Wally got other perks. He got time with Dad. He learned how cars work and how to fix them when they didn't. He got a gun. First a .22 rifle, then a 12 gauge and then I lost all interest in guns, but in our house there was a gun rack just inside the back door. It was preached and well understood that there were to be no loaded guns in the house. So one day when Wally carelessly left his rifle in the dining room, I picked it up to put it on the gun rack. For some reason I chose to test the trigger and shot a hole clean through the back door and into the floor of the porch. In the great silence that followed I looked around the corner at Mom who was working at the sewing machine. She sat there with her eyes squeezed shut and her hands over her face, so afraid to see what she might see.

Guns were for hunting. While the girls didn't get to shoot, the family would spend Sunday afternoons in the fall riding around looking for pheasants (which comprised a good part of our winter meat supply). Wally and Dad sat in the front seat with guns (carefully unloaded), girls in the back with eagle eyes. Duck hunting they did on their own, thank goodness, because it involved getting up before dawn and going out to sit on the edge of a slough just about the time fall was turning to winter. Dad acquired a black lab/spaniel mix that was to be his hunting dog and he would race into the slough to retrieve the kill.

Mac arrived as a puppy on the train, crated. His first act was to pee on the kitchen floor. His second was to chew a thumb off my new cherished red leather mittens. I never liked him. He apparently had some training as a retriever. He became Dad's companion on those long days bouncing along the country roads in the truck. If a pheasant or a rabbit happened to cross the road, Mac was beside himself, barking and demanding to be set loose to track and retrieve. Dad came back to the truck one day, after he completed a delivery, and found half a dozen eggs on the seat in the truck. Mac had found a nest and reverted to one of his training drills

This was taken about the time Bonnie left home for nurses training, 1946 or '47. Bonnie, Wally and Keeny standing; Rosemary and Claudia in front.

to develop a 'soft mouth' – to retrieve without damaging the kill. There was not a crack in any of them.

We had a whole lineage of cats. There was Dewey – Thomas

Agnes Dewey – that I found nearly dead in the post office in 1948, who rewarded me with years of devotion. Prissy and Petunia followed along with regular batches of kittens. We never had trouble finding homes for them; they were beautiful and well socialized. "Mother cats will teach you most of what you need to know about parenting," Mom observed. Prissy once brought a mouse home to her half-grown kittens. She dropped it in front of them, and it ran away! The kittens just watched, curious but unsure of what was expected of them. So Prissy caught the mouse again and brought it back to them. Eventually they got the message: "This is a mouse. It's your job to catch it. Watch and learn."

Wally had a paper route. The bundle of fat, Sunday papers, The Chicago *Herald American*, I think, would arrive from Chicago almost a week ahead of time and thus was devoid of real news, but it had a big colored comic section – the "funny papers" – featuring Dagwood, Snuffy Smith, Dick Tracy, The Katzenjammer Kids, Little King and others that were past being funny even then. There must have been enough feature news to keep twenty or so of the townsfolk interested enough to pay fifteen cents a week to get it delivered to their homes. By the time he was thirteen Wally was ready to move on to more grown-up jobs and I inherited the paper route. It was always an ordeal to get me to do it, Mom spending her Saturday mornings nudging, "Rosie, did you do the route?" She made a bag out of some tough upholstery material to help tote the papers, and it was very heavy at the beginning of the route. I was sure I would grow up lopsided, one shoulder inches lower than the other. Winter was worst, sometimes tromping through deep snow and maneuvering the bag of papers. Some of those on my route always had to scrounge through their junk drawers and couches to come up with fifteen cents; my appearance at their door seemed to come as a complete surprise. Some couldn't come up with the change and I would have to remember from week to week if they owed fifteen cents or thirty. My favorite customer was Zana

Kaczmarski, who always had wonderfully funny, gossipy stories to tell about her kids and irreverent things to say about the Ladies Aid. One day she invited me in, flung open her broom closet to show me the painting of a frog – tall as a grown man, greener than new grass – she had painted on the inside of the door. (Zana went on to become one of North Dakota's most illustrious artists with art shows as far away as Oklahoma and Montana.)

Most of the money I earned on the paper route went to my college fund, but I got enough to go to the show (movie) on Saturday night and roller skating on Wednesday. All of this and more took place in The Hall downtown. Since the school had no gymnasium, all the school events were held at The Hall – class plays, school Christmas programs, basketball practice and games, graduation and sometimes on Fridays, a dance. It was, even then, a dreary, ramshackle building with no redeeming features, but many of the defining events of my childhood took place there, and I remember it with affection.

Our tiny towns were too small to field football teams. But we all had basketball teams, boys and girls. With fewer than thirty kids in the whole high school everybody had a chance to make the team, athletic or not. I was a lousy player, uncoordinated and too short, but quick, and I spent time after our regular practice to shoot free throws, where athletic skill wasn't so necessary. Keeny was the only one in our family who qualified as a good player. Dad even went to her games and more than once I saw him tear up in pride when she swished a long shot.

Often Sunday afternoons were spent visiting the Rawson relatives in Medina. Aunt Nellie and Uncle Christ lived on a farm and he was always trying to teach me how to milk a cow. It never worked. In Medina, Aunt Frank and Uncle Ben had my five cousins a notch younger than I, but close enough to make games. Sometimes late in the year, we would drive home in the dark as the northern lights swung in luminous curtains across the sky.

They all came to our house for Thanksgiving – busy chaotic affairs with mountains of food. The main course was always roast pork, not turkey, but the rest was classic – mashed potatoes, gravy, dressing, squash, cranberries and pumpkin pies – none of which I liked (okay, the potatoes and gravy) until I was older and discovered taste buds. The kids were always relegated to the card tables a safe distance away and only gradually did we make our way to the main spread by way of the piano bench which sat at one end of the dining room table and could hold two almost grown kids.

These were busy years for Claude and Sue. One morning before the flurry of kids leaving for school and Claude on deliveries, Sue looked around the clutter that awaited her day and, ignoring it, sat down and wrote a parody of the "Night before Christmas" that gives a pretty good picture of what her life was like in those days.

Mother's Daze

'Twas the day after washday and all through the house,
Everything was upset as the nest of a mouse.
The stockings were flung here and yon without care,
In hopes Mom would retrieve them, I swear.
The children still nestled all snug in their beds,
While thoughts of the school day slipped through their heads.
And Dad in his nightshirt and I in a wrap,
Had just roused ourselves from what seemed like a nap.
When what to my still bleary eyes should appear,
But all of yesterday's mess with additions, I fear.
With a little of everything piled up so thick,
You would think at first glance it was stirred with a stick.
There on the end table in wild disarray,
Various magazines and catalogues lay,
Where our teen-aged daughter attempted to find
A pattern just suiting her teeny-bop mind.

And under it all, as I shifted my look,
Was Rosemary's latest Bobbsey Twin book,
Place marked with a comb and, as I expect,
Her arithmetic paper I forgot to correct.
Hardly shifting my gaze I soon got an eyeful
Of the rag Wally used for cleaning his rifle.
What's that on the bookcase in a crumpled brown sack?
Oh yes, it's those gloves that I have to send back.
Two bushels of ironing insult my gaze
As I head for the kitchen, still lost in a daze.
Ye Gods, what is this, on buffet, rough and oily?
Oh yes, just a cookie tucked under a doily.
And out in the hall, what have we here?
Needle, thread and a button on the seat of a chair,
Where our four-year-old daughter attempted to sew
On a button – just how I don't know.
Still forging ahead in the kitchen I find
Dregs of tea, crusts of bread and some shriveled orange rind.
I waste not a sec but go straight to my work,
Light the fire, fill the kettle, set the coffee to perk.
But I can't help exclaim as I set things to right,
"Does anyone else's house get such a fright?"

                                                   Sue, circa 1947

Farm kids were expected to work at home, and we town kids were expected to get jobs early. Bonnie and Keeny spent the summer working in Jamestown when they were fifteen and sixteen. Bonnie got a job working in the laundry of Jamestown Hospital since she was too young to be a nurse's aide. Keeny worked in a café, the Donette. They lived in a big grey stone rooming house on Main Street where the landlady kept half an eye on them. Sometimes, if they had a few days to come home, they hitchhiked to Medina and Dad picked them up at Aunt Frank's.

Bonnie graduated in 1946. True to form, she defied the expectation that she would summer school in Valley City and teach in a country school; she insisted on being a nurse and applied to the Sisters of St. Joseph School of Nursing in Jamestown. They accepted her despite the fact she had no high school credit in chemistry, because she had graduated as salutatorian of her class (never mind it was a class of five). The next year Keeny graduated in the largest class Pettibone High School produced – an even dozen. She went on to the AC (North Dakota Agricultural College) in Fargo to major in Home Economics. Both of them were happy to get out of Pettibone. But me? I couldn't imagine a life outside of Pettibone.

The winters of 1947 and 1948 were particularly harsh. Howling blizzards roared out of Canada so thick we couldn't see the bottom step. We listened intently to KFYR radio out of Bismarck as they read the school closings, hoping to hear ours. Meanwhile huge, solid snow banks accumulated in the schoolyard providing a perfect hill for sledding. Sometimes the roads and even the train were blocked and we would be isolated. In those days before snowmobiles, Fred Walz, who owned the implement shop, built what amounted to a snowmobile out of an airplane chassis and skis from an old farm sled, and with that they got mail and essentials in and out of town. We were probably never stranded for more than a few days. One day word came that the rotary plow was coming through. It was an enormous machine that cut through the solid snow banks and spewed snow up and over the top. The cut through the road past the school must have been twelve feet deep. However trying that winter was for the grown-ups in town, I thought it was wonderful. I was eleven.

We went to Bonnie's graduation from nurses training in the spring of 1949. Mom dabbed at her eyes with her handkerchief when they announced that Bonnie had graduated with honors.

That summer Dad went on a fishing trip to Canada with small group of the guys. We got word that there had been an accident, an explosion and fire, and Claude was on his way to the hospital in Jamestown. It was the only time I remember seeing my mom flustered and about the only time I noticed a concern for his welfare, but she shot off to Jamestown to be at his bedside. He was in the hospital for three weeks and when he got home he was grizzled (he couldn't shave), the right side of his face still pink and raw-looking and the ruffled edge of his right ear gone. His face eventually healed without scarring, but his ear remained a constant reminder of how close a call that was. He was the only one of the group injured. The fire happened because a kerosene can was stashed too close to the wood burning stove. A very odd mistake for the gas man to make.

CHAPTER 7

Years of Change

... the cloud of unknowing

I entered high school in the fall of 1949 so naturally I began casting around for a boyfriend, and my gaze landed on Jim DeKrey. The way such relationships began was the boy asked the girl if he could "take you home" after a school party or roller skating or whatever. Jim returned the gaze and took me home after a school party. What's more, he kissed me! My first real kiss. It was fairly modest, as I remember, a simple quick pressing of the lips and the noses did not collide. I levitated for days. Apparently it worked for him too, and we quickly progressed from "take you home" to "going together" which meant we went together to roller skating, finagled to ride in the same car to away basketball games, and weather permitting, we parked in his green Chevy pickup at the ballpark for some congenial smooching.

When winter set in in earnest, the kids who drove ten miles or so to get to school began boarding in town during the school week, and ours was one of the homes they stayed in. So in the heart of winter there were four teenage boys staying in Wally's room in the basement sleeping in wall-to-wall makeshift beds. Jim was one of them, along with his brother Ted and his cousin Kenny and Wally. Upstairs were Kenny's sisters, Jeanne and Carol and I.

101

This all seemed perfectly natural. For me it was one long sleep-over. For Mom, however, it meant work. Feeding seven teenagers for supper every night is not for the faint of heart. We had a lot of chile and baked potatoes, macaroni and hamburger goulash, meatballs with sour cream gravy, canned vegetables from last summer's garden, home canned fruit for dessert.

When we were not away practicing or playing basketball, roller skating, or gathered in the breakfast nook doing homework, we regularly had card parties, with yet more kids, three or four tables of teenagers playing whist. Mom supplied the popcorn. We never saw her get up in the morning, we never saw her go to bed at night. And we never thought about it. But the money she earned from these winter boarders and giving piano lessons provided the money for my sisters and eventually me to go to college.

Eventually spring arrived as it always did, the meadowlarks warbled and the lilacs bloomed. As usual, one of Dad's customers would show up one day with his tractor and plow and half a load of manure to get the garden ready for planting. First we got radishes, leaf lettuce and chard, then beans and peas, then carrots and beets, which all grew by the bushel, and by my birthday there was sweet corn and tomatoes. Our summer meals were dictated by what was peaking in the garden with plenty to can and freeze for winter. In fall there would be a final harvest of carrots which wintered in a box of sand in the basement pantry, and red potatoes which sat next to them in gunny sacks. The acorn squash had to wait for the first frost. It made them sweeter, she said. The popcorn, which warmed our winter evenings, was picked last. It needed to be good and dry or it was hard to shuck and didn't pop well.

Years later, Claudia wrote a paper for her college English class that recalls Mom and the garden:

My mother had five children, starting around the time of the Depression and ending along with the war. Times were hard, of course. Not hard to the point that you thought you wouldn't survive, but hard to the point where you were tired of times being hard. I was born seven years after my youngest sister. My mother loved me and was happy to have me, but I had arrived at the time in her life when she'd had enough of raising children, and had decided that they didn't have to be raised anyway — they just grew, and I did.

We lived in a tiny, tiny town in North Dakota. It was quiet, stable, and entirely safe. You could see for miles and miles around because of the flatness of the land. Although I knew there were hills around because people used to say, "Oh, you know, up in the hills north of town." There was great expansiveness of sky and land. You could just fill up your soul with all that expanse of sky and land, wind and endless vast numbers of stars. In the spring everything was irre-pressibly green, just pushing, and bursting with enormous energy to life. In August the fields were shockingly golden. Not like grass that kind of turns brown and lackluster, but beautifully, undeniably golden. No one ever goes to North Dakota for the scenery. They don't go there for anything.

The day I was thinking about when I started to write this was late in the fall one year when I was nine or ten. My mother had a big garden out behind our house where she raised vegetables enough to last through the winter. All summer long, when I'd get up in the morning, I'd look out my bedroom window and she'd be sitting out there on a three legged stool next to the garden hose with big dishpans full of vegetables, and she'd be washing them, snipping the ends off the green beans and cutting them into inch-long pieces, shucking the peas.

The corn she'd pull the husks off and then she'd stand the cobs up on end and run a sharp knife down each side, slicing off the kernels. Then she'd scrape down each side of the cob so all the juice would squish out. Lots of times it would squirt in her face, and she'd have corn pieces in her eyebrows. Then she'd put all those things in plastic cartons and freeze them.

But anyway, on this one day, my mother wasn't home and for some reason my sister decided that we had to go and dig up all the potatoes. She must have thought it was going to freeze or something. It was pretty chilly out, and the wind was blowing real hard. When it's chilly in North Dakota it isn't really chilly. It's cold. The air is very dry and doesn't make you feel "chilly." It hits you and stops on the outside. It doesn't seep in and shake your bones.

So we were out there digging potatoes — at least a hundred feet apart. We'd pull out a plant and then dig in the dirt underneath for the big round, red potatoes and all of a sudden I was filled with such joy. It seemed to me that being there at that moment was the most thrilling, wonderful thing that could happen to a person. I was thrilled with the dirt and the sky, the wind and crisp fall smells and I started to sing at the top of my lungs — old hymns — the wind blew the sound right back on me, so no one ever knew but God and me.

She got an A.

After Reverend Bosworth retired as pastor of the Congregational Churches in the mid-forties, a series of student pastors came from the Hartford Seminary in Connecticut to fill in during the summers. By this time I was more Congregationalist than Lutheran. That's where my friends were, I went to their camp at Lake Metigoshe, and they definitely had better music. (The DeKreys all had wonderful, booming voices and their little Malcolm Church in Weiser Township fairly rocked on its foundation when they held forth with "How Great Thou Art.") The student pastors brought a new level of east coast sophistication and intellectual stimulation to the prairie. The first, Neil Zabriskie, introduced me to the Winnie the Pooh books and others the state library had somehow overlooked. The second, Art McGill came back and married a local girl.

The third, Dexter Marsh, led a philosophic bible study, a small group of half a dozen ladies who met at the home of Helen Vogel. Helen had been one of Mom's high school teachers and went on to become her best friend. Mom was one of the group. Soon she was reading Evelyn Underhill, *Cloud of Unknowing*, St. Augustine and even Soren Kierkegaard. She was spending more time at Helen Vogel's and Dexter Marsh spent afternoons on our front porch in deep philosophical discussion. Sue, unshackled from the dawn to dusk work of raising a family, was changing. But the town tongues began to wag and clack. "Young pastor seems to be spending a lot of time at your place, Claude." It was preposterous. She was in her mid-forties, he in his twenties. I was around then and saw no hint of anything improper. But it hurt her. I think for the first time she entertained thoughts of leaving Pettibone.

Wally went the Valley City route and got a provisional teaching certificate and began teaching in a little school northwest of town. He had four students. Around that time he announced he wanted to bring a girl home for Sunday dinner to meet us. Well, didn't our ears perk up! This was serious. This was Wally who had once declared, "I can't dance so good, but boy, can I intermission!" This was Wally whose high jinks with Pete and Jimmy had been a constant source of worry to the folks. A wait and see attitude hung in the air. He arrived with Luella, shy, blue-eyed, slightly freckled, and the blondest hair I'd ever seen. By the end of the afternoon we wondered if *we* had measured up.

I got my first 'real' job that summer. I heard that Marvin and Ethel Vogel were having their fifth baby in about as many years, and the girl who had worked for them summers was graduating and leaving town. When I saw Marvin in town one day that spring, I asked if they would be needing a girl and told him I was available. I was not quite fifteen. He looked dubious. Mom was certainly dubious, pointing out that I couldn't even keep my room clean and my cooking repertoire consisted of baked potatoes and cream of tomato soup. But they took me up on it.

It was a perfect first job for me. Ethel was my kind of house-keeper. My first day there she got on her sun hat and handed me the red checkered *Better Homes and Gardens Cookbook*. "Make this frosting for that cake," she said, pointing to the open book. "I have to get at the garden." I barely had time to register a "but, but…" "It's easy. You won't have any trouble." And she was gone, four little boys trailing after her. Indeed it was called, "No Fail Chocolate Frosting" and it didn't.

I gained a great deal of confidence that summer, just because Ethel foolishly or in desperation, assumed I could do whatever task she set me on. One day she surveyed a stack of printed flour sacks, washed and saved, and handed me a pattern. "You sew, don't you? Here make these up into shirts for the boys." And I did. It was a simple pattern, but involved sleeves and a collar. If some were a bit askew, it didn't matter, and some of them turned out well enough that they could wear them to town.

By the end of the summer I could point with authority and say, "Outside!" And the boys – Tommy 5, Clifford 4, Clyde 3, and Russell 2, along with Obadiah the dog would scurry off to find entertainment that was not under my feet.

One day I went to gather them in for dinner (lunch) and they were nowhere to be seen. "They said they were going gopher hunting," said the hired man, pointing over the hill toward the slough. In panic, with thoughts of a rifle and the boys being sucked into the mud, I raced up the hill. There they were near the bottom, carrying a big stick and a bucket of water in search of big game. The idea was to find a gopher hole (not a huge challenge), pour the water in it and then hit the escaping gopher with the stick. So far they'd had no success.

Even though their baby was due the end of June, the Vogels allowed me go on the trip to San Diego with my family. We were to go through the Black Hills and Yellowstone National Park so Claudia and I could see what the older kids saw in 1940.

SAN DIEGO TRIP – JUNE 16, 1951

(Sue writes): The alarm went off forty-five minutes late getting us up at 5:45 A.M. We got into our jeans and shirts, had coffee, made a jug of lemonade, threw in last night's sandwiches and woke up Keeny and Vern to tell them goodbye, then got Wally up – precious kids all of 'em. With many a departing glance, took off.

Cool and cloudy. Spirits are good, the country green and lush looking – all nature out for its morning constitutional – rabbits, ducks, a snake, badger and myriads of birds. Have my little "gold guide" and Concordia from which there is no vacation. By eight o'clock clouds were forming, lightning flashing and wind rising.

We went through the Black Hills of South Dakota, planning to stop in Spearfish to see the Passion Play, and Mom was disappointed to find it didn't start for another two weeks. We settled for a stop at Mount Rushmore, but it was fogged in. A batch of young travelers had put a dime in the telescope that instructed, "turn to clear view." It got a laugh anyway. We mostly ate at roadside stops and slept in the car and traded off driving. (I could drive by then, thanks to Jim and his green Chevy pickup.)

Dad was driving after dark through the switchbacks of Tensleep Canyon when around one bend we came upon two elk, their antlers tangled in mortal combat trying to push each other over the precipice. We pulled into the next row of cabins we found. We drove through the Shoshone Canyon with its rushing river and high cliffs and tunnels and stopped at the Grand Canyon of the Yellowstone with its white and coral spikes and peaks, and the bubbling pools. Mom marveled at the sights as though she were seeing them for the first time. Dad drove, Claudia read and I was fourteen. Fourteen-year-olds are un-WOW-able. Mom was coming down with a doozy of a cold.

> We got a rough cabin unfurnished except for a few pieces of furniture and a wood-burning stove. They sold wood in bundles with a sack of kerosened sawdust for starter. We rented sheets, two for a quarter. Got supper (soup and melon), wrote to the kids at home and went to bed about half sick. I got cold in the night and Dad got up and made more fire. We gave up about 6:00 A.M., but Claudie was set to sleep on for hours. She has a "reader" along and just glances at the geysers and pool and goes back to her reading.
>
> Finally we reached Old Faithful and, as always, it erupted on schedule. Then we ate in a big park with tables. At the lodge there was still snow piled on the steps. Now we are off again toward the south entrance driving through pine forest again with the floor a continuous blanket of snow.
>
> I feel rough. My cold has settled in my left eye (if indeed it has settled). My throat is scratchy and my nose a continual blow. I hope it eases up before too long. We just came onto three more bears — fresh things!

We drove into Jackson, Wyoming and I was feeling rougher all the time. It's going into bronchitis fast – headache, fever, scratchy throat, sore chest and I ache all over. We went to see a doctor but he was locked up. Ten minutes too late. We found a nurse in the grocery store trying to remember the third thing she was to get. I engaged her in conversation and found she could give me a shot of penicillin and she persuaded the druggist to give me nose drops and troches. We went into the park with a milk bottle full of hot salt water so I could gargle. Terrific headache. Made a bed in the back seat with Claudie on the floor and slept a little while Rosie and Dad barreled along. The Tetons were grand and we went miles on flat land beside them before we were actually there. We stopped in a grassy field beside an irrigation ditch and ate our hamburgers, tomato juice and celery served on a wooden gate (laid down, of course). Dad drove until about 1:00 A.M. when we pulled up to sleep.

We stopped in the outskirts of Salt Lake City for breakfast. My head cleared a little after eating and I feel some better. Now we're driving down to the lake for a look-see. We can see it in the distance as a murky expanse. Signs on every little house indicate there is fruit for sale and we saw many trees laden with cherries. Every yard had brilliant fuchsia roses but many are weedy and unkempt.

In San Diego Marg and Grandma Butch were waiting for us with a long list of things to do and see – the zoo at Balboa Park, the beaches and the sailboats, Mt. Helix with its spiral road and iconic cross and a weekend trip to Mt. Palomar Observatory. (Marg was working as a practical nurse since her divorce from Orville in 1948.) We went to a drive-in movie theatre where we SAT IN OUR CAR and watched Mario Lanza in *The Great Caruso*! Wow was becoming a distinct possibility. I got the worst sunburn of my life at La Jolla beach (and learned to say "La Hoya," not La Jawlah"). Marg packed a picnic lunch to take on an outing and she cooked RABBIT. We wanted to buy something called "tacos" from a Mexican street vendor, they smelled so good, but Marg advised not, and promised to make them at home. She did and they were wonderful. Tacos became a whole new food group.

My cousin Bill (who was Keeny's age, about twenty) took me on a "date" to show me San Diego night life which included going out for another culinary first, pizza pie, and to a Jai-alai game, a fast-paced Spanish game, sort of handball with baskets. Very exciting. (And I think perhaps illegal for me to be there since there was betting involved and I was only fourteen. Being illegal made it even more exciting.)

Soon we left for home. We stopped in Los Angeles to visit friends, then continued north through the giant redwoods of Sequoia National Park and past Mt. Shasta. We continued on through Oregon and Washington, stopping to see old friends who had left Pettibone. Sometimes we splurged for a night in a cabin so we could have showers and a decent night's sleep. Otherwise we drove long and slept in the car.

> Dad drove until about 2:30 A.M. and then pulled off in some tall weeds by the railroad tracks to sleep. Several trains went by and scared the bejesus out of us. Claudia had to pee in the morning and Dad suggested that she squat in the weeds. When she objected, he said "Oh, so you don't like the accommodations I provided?"
>
> We cleaned up in a restroom and went out to breakfast. We always have "store-bought" breakfast when we sleep in the car. We ate at Molly's and had cinnamon toast and coffee and big gobs of plum jelly.
>
> (Rosemary writes): We left Tacoma at noon and drove through an irrigated desert that reminded us of Dakota.

We drove all night through Idaho, stopping to doze at half-hour intervals, and got into Butte, Montana, at about nine. It looked like a gold rush town with no new houses since 1890. We drove all day past mountains, but never hit them. When Eleanor got back to Standard Red Crown gasoline she couldn't be slowed down. [*Eleanor was our '47 Chevy named for Eleanor Roosevelt — she got around.*]

We had chicken-in-the-basket for our last dinner out, then drove till midnight and stopped at a hotel in Terry, Montana. We got back to North Dakota for lunch. It never looked quite so good.

We ate lunch at the Chateau De Mores in Medora and I drove from Hebron to Steele where we had supper and then home sweet home.

Upon arriving home we learned that Cara [*Hoersch*] had cut her finger off. Ethel [*Vogel*] and Ruth had their babies, Joe and Ardella were both in the hospital and other items that brought us up to date on the local news. For the first time in four weeks Dad put on his nightshirt to go to bed.

Safely back at Vogels, my duties shifted to changing and bathing the new baby, Patty. I was crazy for babies, so this was a happy turn of events. I'd never had such a new one to play with.

CHAPTER 8

Family Explosions

...our own little boomlet

Other members of the family were at a crossroads. The polio epidemic was reaching frightening proportions, and Bonnie was recruited to work in the Chicago Municipal Contagious Disease Hospital. It was a sit-up-and-take-notice moment. Bonnie? My groundbreaking sister, the nurse? Polio!? Chicago!!! The Korean conflict was flaring into a real conflagration and Wally joined the Marines. Wally? My mellow, fiddle-playing big brother in boot camp? War? Korea!!! Keeny graduated from the AC, and soon she brought home a tall, soft-spoken, teddy-bear of a guy she introduced as Vern Gores – he had a civil engineering degree and now a commission as a pilot and a Lieutenant in the U.S. Air force. They announced they were getting married. Keeny? Who never wanted anything so much as her own place the way she wanted it, was getting married?!

I remember that Christmas as the year we bought three Christmas trees. The first was too scraggily even for us. The second fell off the truck on the way home; the third was a lovelier, taller than usual pine that sat on the floor, not the end table. Bonnie came home from Chicago bearing gifts, all of them wrapped in blue tissue paper with white ribbon and frosted bells. Just like the *Ladies*

Christmas 1951. Clockwise from the top: Claude, Sue, Colleen, Claudia, Bonnie and Wally. Rosemary is off to the left.

Home Journal! (Mom was always wrapping, and sometimes making, our presents at the last minute, sometimes with two different kinds of wrapping paper, no bows.) Vern didn't get leave until just before Christmas and so he and Keeny quickly arranged to be married the day after Christmas in Vern's Catholic Church in Fargo, thus provoking a scurry to find hats for us all. Then Wally appeared in uniform, honed and confident from eight weeks in marine boot camp, to surprise Mom and the rest of us. She cried.

Mom had asked what I wanted for Christmas and I told her I wanted a Siamese cat. "Oh, Rosie," she said, with a slightly dismissive wave, "Where in the world would we find a Siamese cat around here?" But on Christmas Eve, halfway through our traditional gift-opening, Aunt Laura and Uncle Willard appeared at the door bearing this beautiful brown-nosed, blue-eyed, loud-mouthed treasure I named Luke. It was the Best Christmas Ever.

It was inevitable that Wally would be sent to Korea. He came home on leave and persuaded Luella (Lue) that they should get married before he left. It took three days to get married in North Dakota, which required a blood test, but across the border in Minnesota they would give you a license and marry you on the spot. His leave was only ten days. So before dawn on a cold crisp morning in early March, Wally and Lue, her sister Ruby and Kenny DeKrey to act as witnesses and Jim and I representing family, I guess, squeezed into a big sedan they borrowed from someone and headed for Moorhead, Minnesota, to get them married. Mom and Dad had sent them off with their blessing and crossed fingers. They were only nineteen.

All this marrying set off our own family baby boomlet. Keeny and Lue were both pregnant by the time their husbands returned from leave. We made another trip to California that summer, this time with Lue along, to see Wally before he shipped out. Back home we watched the war news with fear and trepidation and welcomed each letter that confirmed he was safe. In September a telegram arrived in its classic yellow envelope. It lay there in my hands a long minute as Mom and I looked at each other, neither of us willing to ask the question or open it. It was from Vern, announcing that the first grandchild, David Scott Gores had arrived in Enid, Oklahoma, and mother and baby were doing fine.

Since you might ask: There was talk, periodically, of getting telephone service in Pettibone, but it hadn't happened yet. In 1952 any long-distance telephone call came through the Northwestern Bell switchboard operated by Georgia Orner, who would walk over to your house to tell you there was a long distance call for you. Needless to say such calls were reserved for life and death situations. When one of Dad's customers needed a delivery of fuel he either told him in person or left a note in the notebook nailed to the door inside our porch. It seemed to work fine. Mom wasn't sure she even wanted a phone. It might be annoying having it ringing all the time. Or it might be someone you didn't want to waste a lot of time talking to.

Claude and his truck

Ricky Lee Rawson was born in Bismarck in December. He would be nine months old before Wally saw his baby boy, but many, many photos traveled over the Pacific before that happened.

My high school days wore on as expected. In turn I was: Editor of the paper, editor of the annual, in plays, on the basketball team, class president, Carnival Queen. None of this was remarkable in the least; the same could be said for a number of my friends. Did I mention it was a very, very small school? It was my enormous good fortune to have Florence Welch for a teacher. She had married a local boy when he was a soldier and ended up in Pettibone. She had a Bachelor's Degree with a major in Biology and minor in English. The school board knew a good thing when they saw it. She taught all four years of English, Biology, Modern Problems, Bookkeeping, Typing, Speech, and, in a first for our school – Spanish! She didn't do it the easy way either. In Biology we made bug collections – finding them, pinning them and identifying them by order and species. In English we read one Shakespeare play each year, and were required to memorize passages that I can still (almost) remember. She thought we (some of us were college bound) needed to learn to write a research paper from note taking to bibliography, and enlisted the state library in Bismarck to send us resources on our chosen subjects. Every week we wrote an essay for the Modern Problems class. She read them, graded them and added comments. On top of that she produced and directed the class plays and served as advisor for our publications. I don't know when she slept. Or what they paid her, but it wasn't nearly enough, not even close to what she gave us.

By this time Jim had graduated and gone off to college, and my attention, given its short span, turned to dancing. Dellwyn Clark was the best dancer in Pettibone High School and we were clicking along pretty well in the dance department. It happened we were cast as the 'romantic interest' in a one-act play for the school Christmas Program that year. I remember almost nothing about the play except that he was to kiss me in one climactic scene. I don't remember how it we handled it in rehearsals, but the night of the performance he clasped me in a long embrace and serious kiss of some length. The audience – our friends, families, classmates, townsfolk – whooped and whistled and stomped their feet. Of course I forgot my lines (prompting more whoops, whistles and stomping), and that pretty much put an end to my budding career on the stage.

Rosemary and Dellwyn at the Christmas Dance,
Jamestown College 1953

I graduated in 1953 and headed for Jamestown College ("North Dakota's only Liberal Arts College"). I squealed when I saw my roommate assignment: I was to spend my freshman year living with Arlene Leoppke, my best friend when I was four – and her sister Betty.

In July Bonnie married Oscar Lenit, a surgical resident she met in Chicago. We were impressed to have a doctor in the family, but she reminded us, "You don't marry a doctor, you marry a medical student." And he was Jewish. In Pettibone, we had barely lowered our eyebrows over Keeny marrying a Catholic and now this. Oscar was wonderfully funny, played the piano and whatever else he was was okay with us. True to form, Bonnie got pregnant on her honeymoon. Bonnie said, "I told Oscar I was going to write Keeny and ask her to send the maternity clothes, and he said, 'All right, but don't tell her what they're for.'"

Stephanie was born in April, at home, so eager was she to get going. She was all dark eyes and hair, a first for our family, which was traditionally more scraggly beige. And so Mom began the round-robin marathon of going to help out when a new grandbaby was born and carrying the maternity clothes back for the next one.

Back home Claudia may have been an only child, but the house was still a magnet for high school kids. Her friend Arlene Witt was one of them. Her mother died when Arlene was only five and she was shunted off to one aunt and her sister to another. It was not a happy arrangement from the start and the situation had become more and more unbearable. Now she was old enough to determine her own future, and Arlene confided to Claudia that she had decided to quit school and find work in Jamestown. She was sixteen, and she couldn't see much of a future where she was. Claudia wouldn't hear of it. Come and live with us, she begged. Claudia made the case to Mom and Dad and must have made it persuasively. Arlene says, "Claudia told them, 'she followed me home, can we keep her?'" For a pair with a history of rescuing drunks and stray cats and hitchhikers it was probably a no-brainer to take in a sixteen-year-old girl. Or Sue might have seen something of her own young self in Arlene. Maybe they were thinking of Claudia. For her last few years at home Claudia got a sister her own age.

To everyone's relief, Wally came back from Korea in one piece and took a teaching job in Weiser Township south of town. He and Lue lived in a trailer on the school grounds with their two babies. (Patty arrived roughly nine months and fifteen minutes after Wally got home.) Dad, now in his mid-fifties, was weary of driving the truck through bad roads and bad weather and sometimes bad crops. Standard Oil had opened a terminal near Eldridge outside Jamestown that offered perhaps an easier segue into retirement. Wally took over the truck in Pettibone.

As I was growing up I thought (and I think everyone else did too) that Dad was never quite "all there." It started in the early diaries when Sue wrote, "Claude was behaving oddly all night." She told me once that way back when they were still on the farm, she looked out the window one day and saw him waving his arms, talking to himself and ranting – all alone. The older girls remember the rages and violence directed at them, but Wally and I and Claudia never saw that side of him. He spanked me twice – over the knee, flat hand on the butt spankings – both of which I had coming. He almost always seemed distracted, absent-minded, doing inexplicable things. His hands trembled and he seemed to accumulate debris around his plate at every meal. He would sweep up crumbs with an old handkerchief and empty it on the floor, his mind somewhere else entirely. For a time – several years in the forties and fifties, he would blurt, "MOM!" in a Tourette's type cry. He wasn't calling her, it was just an involuntary outburst. Or he would emit some short garbled fragment that sounded like he was talking in his sleep. It seemed to come from nowhere. He talked to himself. We got so used to it we scarcely noticed. And then, as mysteriously as it started, it stopped.

Sometimes his missteps made for entertaining stories and he accommodated, sometimes almost relished, being the butt of a joke. Once he got new long johns, a one-piece suit of underwear, in preparation for winter and they needed to be cut down to fit. He grew impatient waiting for Mom to cut them down and replace the cuffs properly, so he set about to cut them down himself – and he cut off one arm and one leg. "Look what I did," he said, holding them up in dismay and wonderment.

Sometimes it almost seemed part of a calculated game he played. My classmate Ted said once, "You can always tell who owes Claude money. He just follows him around town. Wherever the guy goes, he turns around and there's Claude. Never says much, just follows him until the guy is so spooked he just pays him." In later years when we played bridge he would be clumsily trying to manage his cards, distracted by some triviality, making bids that made us shake our heads – only to discover it was a brilliant maneuver. "Hah!" He would exclaim triumphantly, slapping down the king we were sure he didn't have. "Outfoxed you!" He loved to talk to car salesmen. Wearing his shabbiest he would do his dumb hick act and lead them on until they were sure they had really hooked a sucker this time, and then leave with promises to return with a check and never did.

Wally saw the better side of him, the clever, capable problem solver the girls didn't see. Even I could see he was a hard worker, a responsible employee. At the end of the month he would retreat to his "office," a high desk behind the furnace in the basement, to "do the books." He kept a meticulous record of sales and inventory in neat columns of numbers. The auditor from Standard Oil came periodically to check his records and always found them in order. His customers considered him an honest if sometimes peculiar businessman. One thing I always loved about Pettibone was its acceptance of the eccentrics among us. Anyone who put on airs was regarded with suspicion, but the slightly strange were embraced. He had a knack for all things mechanical, and when electricity and plumbing came to Pettibone he was trusted enough to wire and plumb many of the houses in town. He was one of the parents relied upon to drive the kids to basketball games away. He paid his bills and he didn't drink.

It's difficult to piece together just what was happening to Sue and Claude at that time. Their kids are never the best ones to judge their parents' relationship. The whole family dynamic is too close, too intimate, too fraught with emotional pitfalls. I often wondered what brought them together and whether either of them regretted it. They never — we never — had displays of affection, but neither did anyone else that I knew in that time and place. No quick "Love you," no casual goodbye kisses. That was the way it was.

There are hints (in letters from Helen Vogel) that Mom might have been planning to leave him. She took several Piano Teachers Workshops at Jamestown College during the summers. She was tired of his penny-pinching and his seemingly willful embarrassing behavior (capped, perhaps, when he ran naked from the bathroom to the bedroom in front of a guest); she had seen the possibility of a different kind of life in San Diego. Or maybe I misread the clues entirely and they were simply considering a move to Jamestown — together.

In a series of events we can't quite piece together, Dad ended up in the state mental hospital in Jamestown being treated for depression, and Mom took a teaching job in one of the last country schools. Why did none of us seem to know about this? I was in college there at the time, but I had no transportation to get me to the state hospital probably five miles away and I used that as an excuse not to go. I visited him there once, shocked and saddened to see him looking so vulnerable and frail. He clasped both my hands in his and his eyes were pleading, but we didn't say much.

I don't know how long he was there, not long. He returned to driving his truck (Wally took the job at the terminal in Eldridge), and in 1960 he had a heart attack and retired for good.

In Jamestown I got a summer job at *The Jamestown Sun*, the local daily, and shared an apartment with Carol DeKrey, a Pettibone classmate. *The Sun* had an editorial staff of four: Bill Wright, the editor, Sam Lowe, the sports editor, and Marianne and Cookie, two Dickensian ladies who did the "women's" news. Bill and Sam took me under their wings and taught me how to conduct an interview, check the facts and write a lead. They introduced me to the classic ritual of reporters – drinking. I loved the whole romance of the newspaper world. For the first time I could begin to see the faint outlines of myself as a grownup. That fall I returned to the dormitory for my senior year, but I chafed under the rules after my summer of being an "adult." I was sick of school, especially since they offered nothing in journalism. I began to play fast and loose with the curfews and complained loudly. "Why do the girls have to be in at ten o'clock and not the boys?" I whined. "If the girls are in, the boys will have nothing to go out for," someone explained in the logic of the time. "Then keep the girls in Monday, Wednesday and Friday and the boys in Tuesday, Thursday and Saturday," I suggested. "Oh, Rosie," my friends sighed. I was ahead of my time. I was a pain in the ass, and all of this did not sit well with the Presbyterians in charge. There was a new administration that was determined to set strict standards of behavior. After a couple of warning shots across my bow they kicked me out. In a student body of about 350, I was the sixth to be expelled that fall. And I lost my job at the paper to boot. I packed my belongings in a couple of cardboard boxes and took The Goose home to Pettibone. "Don't worry, we'll get you back in," said Mom. "Not the best kid I've got," muttered Dad.

I didn't want back in. But I wanted my degree and quickly applied to the University of North Dakota in Grand Forks where, with some fancy footwork and summer school, I graduated a year later with a major in English and a minor in Journalism.

While I was still at *The Sun* it was their turn to host the fall gathering of the state AP (Associated Press). Irv Letofsky, sports editor of the Bismarck *Tribune*, came for the event. He was an old buddy of Sam's wife and she introduced us. We sat in one of the big round leather booths in the Elk's Club, six of us, Bill and Sam and their wives and Irv and I. The scotch was good and the banter even better. An hour into the evening Irv looked at me and said, "Bet you don't remember my name."

"Sure I do. It's Irv Letofsky."

"Spell it," he said. And I did.

We kept in touch infrequently. At UND I discovered he had been quite a big deal in student journalism circles there and took notice. Meanwhile he moved from sports writing in Bismarck to straight reporting at the *Pioneer Press* in St. Paul. With my degree in hand I set about to find a job and headed for the nearest big city, the Twin Cities of Minneapolis/St. Paul, since I had a contact there. Irv said he'd be happy to help. We were married that summer and true to the family tradition had two babies before I could say, "How do you spell that again?"

Arlene graduated in 1959 and that fall she married Merrill Flanders in a small wedding in the Lutheran Church with a reception at home afterwards. Claudia graduated the next spring, finishing high school in three years. She decided on nursing. Bonnie and Oscar said the best training for a nurse would be Cook County Hospital in Chicago, so in the fall of 1960 Claudia left for Chicago to become a nurse. She was sixteen.

While we weren't entirely responsible for the baby boom, we certainly did our part. This is what the family tree looks like after the Boomlet.

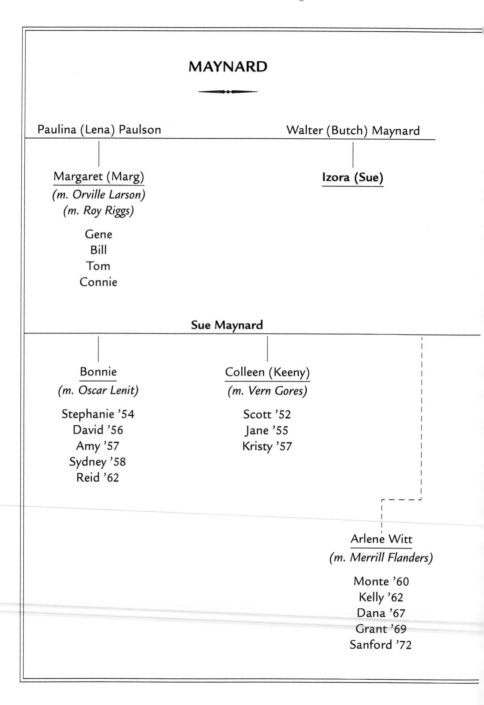

MAYNARD

Paulina (Lena) Paulson	Walter (Butch) Maynard

Margaret (Marg)	Izora (Sue)
(m. Orville Larson)	
(m. Roy Riggs)	

Gene
Bill
Tom
Connie

Sue Maynard

Bonnie	Colleen (Keeny)
(m. Oscar Lenit)	(m. Vern Gores)

Stephanie '54	Scott '52
David '56	Jane '55
Amy '57	Kristy '57
Sydney '58	
Reid '62	

Arlene Witt
(m. Merrill Flanders)

Monte '60
Kelly '62
Dana '67
Grant '69
Sanford '72

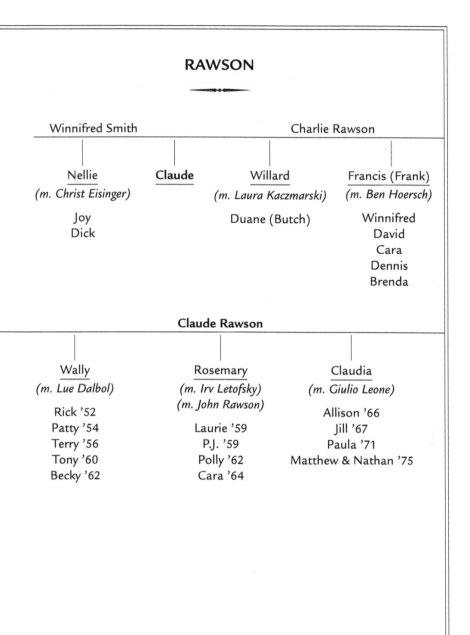

RAWSON

Winnifred Smith   Charlie Rawson

Nellie	**Claude**	Willard	Francis (Frank)
(m. Christ Eisinger)		(m. Laura Kaczmarski)	(m. Ben Hoersch)

Joy   Duane (Butch)   Winnifred
Dick   David
                                   Cara
                                   Dennis
                                   Brenda

Claude Rawson

Wally	Rosemary	Claudia
(m. Lue Dalbol)	(m. Irv Letofsky)	(m. Giulio Leone)
	(m. John Rawson)	

Rick '52   Allison '66
Patty '54   Laurie '59   Jill '67
Terry '56   P.J. '59   Paula '71
Tony '60   Polly '62   Matthew & Nathan '75
Becky '62   Cara '64

CHAPTER 9

The Little Red Trailer

"...a resounding success

On Labor Day 1963, Claude and Sue posed for pictures in front of their car and took off on the first real test of their retirement. The car was packed up to the back seat windows and they were hauling a twelve-foot red travel trailer that looked like an enormous canned ham. It would be their home for a year. They were happy to put the last few years in Pettibone in the rear view mirror.

It took most of the summer to plan and prepare for the trip. They rented their house to one of the teachers, so it had to be cleaned and cleared and cured of a thousand daily injuries. They took some short test trips in the trailer to better determine what they would need on a long trip and what would be just added baggage. Arrangements were made to forward their mail. Friends, family and customers were given notice. Their first stop was Wally and Lue's in Moorhead, Minnesota, where they parked in their driveway, plugged into their electric and settled in for a couple of weeks. Then they hit the road.

SEPTEMBER 18 Just left Moorhead bound for Lake Cormorant with trailer in tow after two and a half good

weeks with Wally's family. I made five dresses for the girls
and a blouse for Lue and played many good games of
Scrabble and bridge. I just came from the dentist who says
I have to have a thirty dollar gold inlay. Dad went fishing at
Lake 15 and caught the limit of walleyes and lots of sun fish.

SEPTEMBER 30   Left at 1:30. We ran over a pheasant, so
we cleaned it and put it in milk carton of ice. We stopped
in Willmar to see Aunt Mary and arrived at Rosie and Irv's
at 1:00 A.M. I finished the last book of Gold Bond stamps,
and used them to get Rosie her pinking shears and a scale
for their Xmas. She was very pleased and so was I. I fried our
fish and made slaw for all of us for supper and we played
Scrabble in the evening. I left my sewing machine and
took Rose's.

It was a symbolic passing of the torch that she left her big con-
sole machine with me as I was just starting my family and took the
little portable featherweight I had bought with my first paycheck.

They had their morning rolls and coffee, took pics and started
out about noon the next day. The first stop was Watersmeet, Wisconsin, to see Uncle Harry and spent a few leisurely days sharing
old memories and meals in the trailer and enjoying the scenery
and the season. "It gets dark early now," Sue wrote, "the sky is a
beautiful opalescent. I love the long nights for reading."

On the road they ran into traffic, on occasion got lost or got the
trailer kinked into a spot they could hardly get out of, bought a
pair of new tires for the trailer when the old ones went bad. They
settled into the learning curve. They headed for Morton Grove
outside of Chicago and found a park to settle the trailer not far
from Bonnie and Oscar and their five kids. They were to stay with
the kids while Bonnie and Oscar went on vacation. But first they
would go to Claudia's graduation from nurses training.

Perhaps tops on the list, they were to meet Giulio Leone, the young medical student who had persuaded Claudia to marry him. Meeting Giulio meant meeting the entire Leone clan: North Dakota, meet Italy.

NOVEMBER 15   Just catching up now. We attended Claudia's graduation October 23, followed by a reception with champagne. She was on the honor roll, graduating fourth in her class. Bon & Os left that Sunday by separate planes *[a security precaution lest a crash would leave their kids orphaned]*. I've engaged the kids in a game to shed their bad habits and they're all doing well. David has even quit wetting the bed.

I shopped for fall sewing materials and sewed all weekend – made two skirts and two dresses (with jackets).

The Leones came to supper on Thursday. I served breaded pork chops, buttered peas, lime jello salad and apple crisp. It was a big experience for us all. The weather has been nice the whole time; we even picked bouquets of flowers on November 9. No killing frost. Even maple trees are still leafed out and we wore just sweaters and rain coats on our trip to the zoo.

B&O returned November 9th. Since then I've made three light flannel nighties for Bonnie's girls (for Christmas) with round yokes and long ruffled sleeves and lace on the collars. On Thursday I shopped for sweaters for the boys.

Mrs. Leone discovered a lump on her breast and had surgery on Thursday. It was cancer and the whole family is much upset. Poor Giulio. Poor Nerina, poor Boppo. Bonnie, Claudia and I sent flowers. We are beginning to feel like relatives – how I do like that boy!

So now we are on the road again. We stopped for soup just out of Joliet, in the trailer of course. It's so like home and we continue to adore it. Bonnie & Os gave us a fourteen-tube transistor radio for our early Christmas.

They headed south, hoping to outrun winter. For the first time they were not staying near family, but they found that if they simply drove into a filling station or similar public business and asked if they could park the trailer for the night they were almost always accommodated. Often the owner would plug them into their electric. Gas, Sue noted, was thirty-one cents a gallon and they were getting fourteen miles to the gallon. Driving through Kentucky and Tennessee, "Nearly every little house has a pile of coal, a washing machine on the open porch and an outhouse of sorts," she wrote. "More old cars and car dumps than we've seen anyplace else. Every porch has a swing, a settee or chairs. Washes hang on fences or lines, tossed over and overlapping. We drove in three states in five minutes – Kentucky, Virginia and Tennessee."

On November 22 they were driving through mountains heading toward Gatlinburg and they stopped to pick up a boy near Marysville.

"Did you hear? The President got shot in Dallas." he said.

Shocked, Sue asked, "Did it kill him?"

"Yes, ma'am," he said.

The terrible news is all that's on the radio. The wind is blowing a gale and roaring through the trees and rocking us like a cradle. Leaves scuttle across road like scared rabbits. Started to rain in the night.

NOVEMBER 23   No miscues today unless it was not stopping before dark as I strongly recommended. Finally we got to a country store and I went in to ask if we might park there for the night. Frank Rose introduced himself and couldn't have been more gracious. As it happened they had prepared a space for their daughter to put a trailer while her husband was deployed overseas. It was 6:30 and completely dark. Dad pulled the trailer across the road and found the spot. In a minute Frank was here, offering to hook us up to his power and said, yes, of course, we were welcome to use the phone. We had supper and at nine I went over to make my call.

Frank was working a jigsaw puzzle and soon I was on my knees finding pieces. So we called Wallys and then visited for some time with these good people. I played some hymns which we sang together. They invited us to go to church with them at their little Baptist church a mile and quarter down a narrow gravel road. The sermon and singing were good. People are the same all over it seems. Only their speech distinguishes them. As soon as we got "home," the Roses asked us over to dinner. We took our pictures and went over. She had slaw and beans with bacon, meat loaf and mashed spuds, brown and serve rolls. After dinner she took us in her old car (an Olds) and showed us the TVA dam. A relative of hers in charge showed us through. This is beautiful country, hilly, and some of the roads are very steep. I got some groceries when we got back and we stayed in the trailer and had oatmeal, toast and bacon for supper.

TV is all details of Kennedy's death and events related to it. It tears your heart out, but these events make you realize how fleeting life is and uncertain, even for those in the highest places. Our best contribution to all of life must be to be kind and trusting of others. No friend could have treated us more kindly than these people. When Edith said grace at lunch, she thanked God for the privilege of making these new friends and prayed that He would protect us on our journey.

They headed west toward friends, the Morrows, in Missouri and stayed there for Thanksgiving. Then, laden with food, they headed for Little Rock, Arkansas. Sue writes:

> We went through the town twice looking for the way to the park and finally stopped and asked. Then it was easy and close. Our fellow trailerites, Richard Ellis and Mrs. Bergman, gave us quite a start! They are traveling together in overalls, rockford socks and tennies. Ellis is probably thirty, she more like sixty-five. Their camper is a Ford bus with camping supplies wherever space affords. You'd have to see it to believe it. Later we drove to an overlook to view the city, walked the promenade lined with magnolia trees and holly. I dipped into a spring, but it was too hot to handle!

They continued west, across flat and treeless plains of Texas and through cotton fields still being harvested in December. "This Texas has a way of lifting the spirit and I've become even more aware of the space up as well as out," she wrote. Texaco was selling gas for twenty-three cents, "but ours (Standard Oil) always costs more." They stopped in Hollywood, New Mexico, to pick up their mail. "While I was reading letters we drove into a lovely evergreen forest on both sides of the road. This, along with news from home, is pure joy. First light snow appears on the slopes."

They drove on through Alamogordo, Lordsburg, Tucson and crossed the Imperial Valley of California, camping at parks, filling stations, beside lemon groves, stopping at roadside markets to buy oranges and grapefruit. They were heading for San Diego to spend a few days with Margaret, long enough to plant a tree on Grandma Butch's grave and have tacos.

Vern was stationed at McClellan Air Force Base so Keeny's family was living in North Highland outside Sacramento and they headed there for Christmas. The fog lifted as they reached Fresno and the radio was playing Christmas music. "Handel's 'I Know that my Redeemer Liveth' and 'Hallelujah Chorus' are so exquisite one can only participate with tears," she wrote.

They celebrated a string of late December events – Dad's birthday on the 22nd, Christmas Eve and Christmas, Vern and Keeny's anniversary and Vern's birthday. The Christmas tree was frosted white with teal balls. The gifts were practical: a wool shirt for Dad, a robe and face cream for Mom. When the holiday was winding down, she went piano shopping with Keeny and bought a Wurlitzer organ instead.

In their mail the Steele *Ozone* contained news that Harry Johnson of Pettibone had been found frozen to death outside of Wing, North Dakota. He got lost trying to walk out of a blizzard when it was twenty-five degrees below zero.

Sue and Claude in San Diego in their early travels

They spent the winter in California, seeking out old family friends who showed them their favorite spots, getting acquainted with the *Woodall's* Directory, the sacred book of RVing, exploring some of the hot spots of tourism. They visited the artichoke capital of the world in Castroville, Fisherman's Wharf in San Francisco, and took the spectacular coastal drive at Monterey with its "surf, seals, bird rock and cypress." And from a cabin for seven they shared with old Pettibone friends, they watched the sun set over the Pacific at Big Sur. "Lovely, lovely, lovely," Sue wrote. "Dad brought a thermos of coffee and ice cream bars to the cabin." And a final note on the hazards of the good life, "I weigh 140 now – ugh."

They spent almost two months in San Diego mostly on the mundane. Dad lost his glasses and spent forty dollars for new ones. Mom had a tooth repaired. A "nice young marine" backed into their car and it cost almost sixty dollars to repair. Sue began looking at neighborhoods and houses wondering if they might find a permanent home here.

Toward the end of February they headed north. In Sacramento again they settled into the trailer court they found at Christmas. They were clearly getting the hang of this trailering business.

"We went to the drive-in to see *Lilies of the Field*. The next night we listened to the Cassius Clay fight. It lasted five rounds." They decided to "do" San Francisco before heading north. The journals reveal a new air of confidence.

> We stopped at Keeny's one more time for baths and the last of the laundry, lunch and mail. Then we hitched on the trailer and left about 1:30. Traffic was heavy with some wind. It's good to be on road again. We drove through beautiful country with lovely homes and turned west off 101 to Los Gatos and a beautiful drive on Blossom Hill Road.
>
> The next day we stopped at AAA and got brochures on San Francisco and points north for the trip ahead, then drove

up 17 to 101, thru Golden Gate Park, across the Golden
Gate bridge and found Lucky Court. And lucky it was – two
dollars a day with everything. We helped folks from L.A. get
their trailer hitched and going – that is Dad did. So we got
a late start. We spent the day in Golden Gate Park taking in
the museum, arboretum and the Japanese tea garden. We
took pictures and had tea. Art museum was wonderful – Van
Dykes, Ruebens, Rembrandts, El Greco, Cellini sculptures. I
never enjoyed painting so much. We had an acoustiguide
(walkie talkie) to explain it all. On Tuesday we went to
Fisherman's Wharf, boarded cable cars and went to China
Town for chop suey, chow mein and egg roll. It was cold and
damp. I wore my deerskin jacket and was still cold. The cable
cars were terribly crowded but I guess that's par. At every
stop some had to get off to let others off, then leap back
quickly so they didn't get left. Tonight we saw the Egyptian
Museum again. Then home to ham, eggs, tomatoes and dark
bread. Nice being home again. It's a beautiful morning and
the park is altogether lovely (I must find some new adjectives).

Heading north again they found more North Dakota friends in
Oregon and Washington and delighted in the reconnection. Then
they stopped at the World's Fair in Seattle where they spent half
a day in the Science Building, went up in the Space Needle and
had apple pie in the revolving restaurant while the needle made
a complete circle.

Then they went in search of Sue's eccentric aunt. (Aunt Tommy
was the widow of Lena's brother Carl. Justine was one of the cousins that came for summers to Green Lake in Minnesota when she
and Sue were about thirteen):

Today we went to see Justine and Aunt Tommy. We had an
awful time finding the place. It seems like all Washington

streets and roads have names that don't match the maps.
Finally a mailbox gave the clue. They have four or five acres
of land and a pretty good house though it's badly run
down – no drapes, shabby shades, and linoleum gummed
to the floor. Justine said that Tommy didn't want her to do
anything. She said the kitchen was "all torn up." and it was
too expensive to do thoroughly, too bad for half measures,
so we got no escorted tour. There were many windows, all
with eight inch panes with wooden dividers, all peeling and
in need of refurbishing. Every room had wallpaper, all badly
soiled. Even Tommy was quite dirty with mounds of dust on
her slippers and a filthy dress hanging in the doorway. 'Tine
was clean and neat with a white blouse and sweater, blue
wool skirt and makeup (albeit a bit crooked and spotted).
Her hair was done somewhat and held in a net. Tommy
excused herself and went to bed where she began to breathe
rapidly and with apparent difficulty, fanning herself as if she
were on the verge of expiring. In two or three minutes she
was up again, talking as if nothing had happened. When I
expressed alarm, 'Tine signaled that it was "all in her head,"
and said later that she'd been doing it for forty years. About
three o'clock Tommy thought we should have coffee. 'Tine
said there was nothing to eat in the house; she'd have
to go to the store. Tommy wondered why she hadn't got
something before this since we were expected. As we left for
town she said, "I'm taking a bill, okay?" But there was no
response from Tommy. I drove her down and she got meat,
bread, cake, cookies and cheeses. Said she didn't bake as
mother ate little and not at all what she should have. She
stood for some time in the store aisle and talked animatedly
about the sad situation at home. Mother was senile,
stubborn and willful, and she needed a medical checkup
and glasses. She would have neither, nor could Justine get

her to change her clothes and clean up. While Justine was
filling me in on the situation Tommy was telling Dad that
Justine shouldn't have gone to Europe, she couldn't afford
it. The house is mortgaged to the hilt. So it appears to be
another case of quiet desperation. I suppose 'Tine *[by going
to Europe]* was grasping at one bit of pleasure lest life leave
her completely bereft of significant experience. We made our
excuses and left early. Friday we trimmed hair, had showers,
washed underwear, shopped for apples, ice and bottle gas
($2 here) and were grateful.

By then, North Dakota was calling. At a leisurely pace they made
their way south and east across Oregon, Idaho and Montana. Back
in North Dakota they stopped for visits with Willard and Laura in
Steele and the Aunts in Medina before heading home.

MAY 5   Back in Pettibone and it all appears as we left it.
We're happy to note that many seem glad to see us. Sarah
[their renter] and I plan to garden together this summer.
She's getting seed and planning the garden; I get to do the
planting. Right now I'm half sick with cold or flu. I spent the
last two days on the bed studying speed reading.

Their first year of trailering was a resounding success. They
were at their best together when they were on the road. With
the house in Pettibone still rented, they continued to live in the
trailer, and family events were calling. Irv and I had moved from
St. Paul to south Minneapolis and I was pregnant again. Very
pregnant. Bonnie and Oscar had moved from Morton Grove to
a grand colonial house with an acre of yard in Winnetka. Giulio
was graduating and he and Claudia's wedding was planned for
September. It was not only the first and only formal wedding in
our family, it was an ITALIAN wedding.

Claude and Sue were in Chicago for Giulio's graduation and called to check on my status. "She's sitting here fat as a toad," my reporter husband reported. With my history of short labors, I was scheduled to go in on June 18 to have labor induced lest I deliver in the car on the way to the hospital. My parents headed back to Minneapolis with their little red canned-ham wagon to spend over a week of the hottest weather we'd seen in Minneapolis, riding herd on the three kids we already had.

JUNE 27 Rose and Irv went out to a farewell party for a departing staff member and got in about 4:00 A.M., so I got a chance to get acquainted with the night life of Cara Jane. She's a "good" baby, only cries when she's hungry. We went out to Lake Nokomis with McDonald's hamburgers, malts and fries for supper. It was a busy, hot day. Washed, ironed and made Rose's shift. We left mid-morning and stopped at the Lew Roberts resort at Howard Lake to look for a cabin for Bonnie and Oscar to rent. We're planning for all the families to gather there early in August. I hope everyone can come.

We got to Wally's' about eight and settled in, playing half a dozen or so games of Scrabble with Lue over the weekend. I shopped for a dress and shoes for the wedding and came up empty. I'm thinking of navy and white. I made tacos for supper; the three older kids are crazy about them. We left early Tuesday so Dad could get his blood checkup.

JULY 17 I have been painting the trailer and sewing for Claudia. I made six blouses and tops, two pairs of pants, and one shift. I have Arlene's bridesmaid's dress ready to fit. Last night I cut out and partially sewed a beige corduroy car coat to wear with slacks this winter. The trailer is all painted except the front end and that has primer on it. I hope to finish early next week. I found a navy rayon and acetate for the wedding and some navy heels.

On September 5 we all gathered for Claudia and Giulio's wedding. It was a big Catholic wedding in a cavernous church in downtown Chicago. Claudia wore white, a gorgeous thing with multiple layers of embroidery. Arlene was a bridesmaid. Dad finally got to walk a daughter down the aisle. He cried. We all cried.

Irv had a new Panasonic camera and got some pointers from the photographers on the Minneapolis *Tribune* and he was having a ball. I looked up in the middle of the recitation of the vows to see Irv prowling near the altar trying to get a good shot. He got wonderful candid pictures, much better than their hired professional photographer.

Then we were off to the Chateau Royale for a traditional Italian reception. There was food piled on platters beyond anything we'd imagined (and not a jello salad to be seen). There was wine. The band played the tarantella and the huckabuck and everyone danced. The evening was winding down and they had started singing old Italian songs when Claudia threw her bouquet and her garter and she and Giulio went off to find something for the rash that she was developing. Happily, she had just married a budding dermatologist.

A couple of days later Claudia and Giulio arrived in Pettibone. The next day was set aside for the bridal shower.

The Medina folks all came—Nellie, Frank, Ben, Brenda, Dennis, Cara and Jerry. That evening her old high school gang belched in with drinks: Mickey Rafferty, Dellwyn, Gerald Herman, Billy Dethloff, Mike Hingers and Merrill and Arlene with their kids. Claudia made sandwiches. Poor Giulio. He endured it bravely for a while and finally came in to talk with me. Kelly sat on my lap and looked at pictures.

The next morning was more of the same at church. The kids left about 3:30 and I pitched in and cleaned the house all over again, moving out the things we need for the winter. Arlene came in the next day or so and Monte let the front end of the trailer down on his shoe. Fortunately the shoe was too long and he only got a scratch — over his eye! Pete had to come running with a jack to extricate him. We left the next day.

The new renters moved into the Pettibone house and Claude and Sue spent the rest of the summer pulling the trailer from relative to relative, parking for a week or two and moving on. If they had ever worried about the uncertainty of this kind of nomadic life, those days were gone. Now they relished the independence and freedom it brought.

Our days at Wally's have been full and happy. How grateful we are for our nice family; our cup runneth over. Day after day the same, days filled with work and play; enough work to keep fit and feeling useful, the play mostly Scrabble and bridge with a heavy mix of knitting and other handwork. And then of course some reading, but never quite enough as the sewing and knitting use up my eyes. The older kids give us pleasure in their vitality and varied interests, particularly their development along musical lines and their unpretentious friendliness and the little ones in their innocent play.

It's been a busy time. We left for Pettibone at the end of the month for one last check before we leave for the season, stopping in Jamestown en route so Dad could have a physical. I bought a gay hat instead—red, green and gold bands, and had lots of compliments on it.

We stopped in Medina and the next morning we went to Pettibone for the annual church meeting and fellowship dinner. The next day was Election Day so we went up and voted for opposing candidates, thereby canceling each other out. Lyndon Johnson won.

Near Chicago they parked the trailer with a Shell station on the outskirts and packed a bag to spend a few days in the city with Claudia and Giulio and then to stay with Bonnie's kids while they vacationed in Columbia, South America. Sue wrote:

Dad left my suitcase and shoes standing beside the car at Giulio's. When we missed them two or three hours later they were indeed gone. So here I was with no nightie, robe, makeup, all my Christmas cards, stamps or stationery. But my angel was there on duty as usual and we lost nothing of much value except the case itself. Bonnie set me up with about ten dollars worth of cosmetics and promised a suitcase for Christmas.

The next day we boarded the city bus to tramp around the loop with 10,000 other nutty people. The weather was foul and sudden gusts of wind blew in several plate glass windows down there. Buses were running erratically because of Christmas shopping and we were babes where routes were concerned anyway. We waited in the biting cold for our bus and then got on one going only a few blocks. When we got our transfer and got off, Dad left his packages, the biggest and most valuable one included his leather case, so we were a bit crestfallen by that time and living out of paper bags. It was nice to get back to the trailer, relaxing and fixing supper.

We went back to Bonnie's the next day to help get ready for Thanksgiving. I made three apple pies. Their guests were a doctor from Columbia and his wife who couldn't speak any English and their two-year-old daughter. Also a Persian and his wife and their son about six – all so interesting to

talk to. The Persian was graying but young; he's studying
neurology – intelligent, sincere, interested. The wife was
younger, pretty, Americanized even to the slang, gracious
and lavish in her praise of the food. It was excellent.

Bonnie and Oscar are getting ready to leave for Columbia.
Sydney lost two pairs of shoes and they stayed lost in spite
of yelling and threats. Reid turned on the water in the basin
upstairs and it came running out the light fixture in the
hall. He got a spank for that and it didn't happen again. He
got into and lost one of Oscar's contact lens. Then the last
Sunday evening he stuck the hearth broom in the fireplace
and caught it on fire. He had a dandy little game going
when I discovered him. I guess he'll need restraints until
he's housebroken.

...We went to Claudia's on Wednesday and Bonnie called
while we were there saying they would be home that night,
so we went by way of O'Hare and picked them up on the
way home. They had a good visit in Columbia and even saw
bullfights. They spent part of the time in Bogotá and a few
days in Miami. Bonnie wanted to get home and we were all
glad except Oscar who hates the cold. We went out the next
day and got two nice pieces of luggage, our Christmas gift
from them as well as a thank you for babysitting.

Plans are going ahead for the European trip [with Claudia
and Giulio]. Reservations are to be made including the week
on the Queen Mary or possibly the Ile de France. In six
months I may know more about it.

We headed back to Wally's for Christmas. A window
worked loose in the trailer and whipped in the wind until it
broke just before we drove into Hudson, Wisconsin, so we
stopped there to have the glass replaced. It was cold and
raw when we stopped at dusk, and we slept in the street in
front of Rosie's. Irv is working days now. The next day was

Dad's birthday and Rose had a duckling and we baked dark bread and chocolate cake. Even had wine for toasting. Rose gave him a gift package of cheeses and a thermometer for the trailer. Rose spent the evening making a dollhouse room to go with Laurie's Penny Brite doll. Cute.

On the way back to Wally's we picked up a college boy from Madison going home to Valley City. He was so nearly frozen we were glad we'd felt moved to pick him up. He was a merit student but he said they only paid for tuition. We hated to leave him at the turnoff.

Lue was in the midst of Christmas baking and the house was bright with cards strung up across the kitchen wall and the tree set up in the living room. Ruby and Gaylord and kids arrived in holiday spirits. Christmas Eve and was as gay and good as ever. Five kids from middle-size to babies always add up to big fun.

On Christmas Day Lue's family, all of the Dalbols, were here for dinner. We roasted two turkeys and a seventeen-pound ham. Most of the women brought baked stuff, notably Ruby and Ladora. Bucky came from Hawaii and Harold from Livermore, California. The family went to Nels's the next day and Gordon's on Sunday and we went along. Ladora and I clicked along with our knitting. I made three stocking caps and a popcorn one for our girls.

It was January in Minnesota and they were pushing their luck trusting the winter to hold off until they had transported their little twelve-foot home to warmer climes.

We've been on the road two and a half hours as I write. It is cloudy and the air is frosty and visibility a quarter to one mile and slippery. The forecast is for snow and blizzard conditions so we are going to try to keep on for a while. A

big cattle truck was tipped over in a field and a large number
of cattle were wandering around. Two cars went off the road
and were stuck head first in the ditch. At 4:30 we found a
rest area unoccupied, and as the driving was getting a bit
hazardous with ice and fog, we stopped. It was a good quiet
night, but cold. The bananas froze in the trailer. We had
good traveling all day, through the rolling hills of Nebraska
and onto the flat Platte River. The snow disappeared about
Columbus and I haven't seen any since. We made over four
hundred miles today and aim to get into better weather as
soon as possible.

They traveled through the plains, the Texas and Oklahoma
panhandles as the hills got higher and the towns further apart and
mostly poor. They came through New Mexico and into Arizona,
stopping in Show Low for gas and groceries, and found both
higher than home.

We stopped at a nice rest stop with concrete table and
benches, boasting a palm frond covered canopy and two
palm trees. So here we spent the evening and night with
cliffs above and below and hairpin curves across the canyon
to show us what we are in for the next day. I fried the last of
our Minnesota fish and made slaw with the frozen Miracle
Whip and fried one cold potato. After supper I played myself
in one game of Scrabble, read in *The Unobstructed Universe*
and studied English grammar. A good night.

The next morning we continued with wonderful scenery,
pine covered hills and rocky buttes through the Salt River
Canyon and the Tonto National Forest. We reached Globe
about 10:30, got groceries and drove out to Roosevelt over
the Apache Trail (#88). It's a secondary blacktop road very
winding but not difficult and traffic was light. We stopped

at a rest park in Roosevelt which is little more than a trading post with a store, a café and a post office, none of them very impressive. The park had orange trees with fruit. The scenery was grand with mountains all around a lake formed by the dam further up. The weather is cool, but the sun is warm. We had lunch and napped. Both of us unexplainably sleepy. We were here to pick up our mail (there was very little) and we slept until nearly three.

CHAPTER 10

Blue Star Court

... more fun than I imagined

Roosevelt was an accident, albeit a happy one. They probably looked at a map of Arizona and thought Roosevelt was a good midway point to have their mail sent. It isn't. Driving the Apache Trail with a four-wheel drive requires a certain steeliness of nerves. They were driving it at the end of a travel day in a Chrysler pulling a trailer. But perhaps I underestimate the value of all those years driving the truck in North Dakota.

> When we emerged it was lovely out, warm and balmy, so we took the trailer over to the park (a dollar a day or fifteen for the month), and washed the dirt of the trip off the outside and washed windows. Then I took a walk down by the lake over rocks and through thorny brush. After supper I did some more English grammar. My days are happier and more satisfying if I do something to keep my mind functioning. I get an uneasy feeling that just looking for fun for me and thee will eventually backfire. Constant seeking for pleasure has never, so far as I've been able to detect, resulted in a happy full life for anyone.

We had an early lunch and explored the area camps and then drove to the nearby Tonto Monument, a cliff dwelling occupied five hundred years ago by Indians of unknown origin. It was a sunny nice day and the trip was rewarding, fun and instructive. We met several outgoing persons (men) who urged us to come to Apache Junction. We may do just that soon.

They drove down to check out Apache Junction. After inspecting several of the trailer parks that lined the main road, they settled on Blue Star Court and made a reservation to stay for two weeks.

Our spot was waiting for us at Blue Star Court. We pay ten dollars a week and have access to all the privileges and activities of the court. There was bingo the first night, a penny a card. Dad and I each won. We walked home with a Mrs. Riggs and saw her nice new trailer.

Saturday was the fifth anniversary of the court and they had a dance to celebrate with punch and cake from the management. It's the first time we've danced in many years except the two or three numbers at Claudia's wedding. It was more fun than I remembered it to be. We met the Gilberts and the Meyers.

It was a full week again. Monday we went dancing up the road at Sunset Court. Then on Wednesday we went out to the Rendezvous further on. There were live bands in both places and the last place had a good floor and dim lights. We've been doing our honkytonking with the Gilberts (Carl and Nora) and with the Stringfields (Brian and Ola).

On Tuesday we had pancake and sausage breakfast, the activity for the day. We drove out to Mesa and looked at used trailers and then to Goldwater's store in a shopping center. The store is rather elegant and expensive, but not the most so.

Thursday was ladies night at the Center Hall. I put on
my brown Dacron and cotton and went over and found
everybody dressed up elaborately. They played light games
and served a huge piece of cake for dessert. I decided that was
one party I could skip next time. I came home and started
my jersey dress as Dad was playing Yahtzee at the Holton's.

Saturday was chiliburger night. I had run over to the
Gilberts earlier to see if they wanted to go up the Apache
Trail with us Sunday for an outing. They did. Then he came
over in the evening with a new set of ideas. I was sitting in
the chair hemming my dress. They thought we should take a
drive south past the copper mines and on to Superior, south
and east in a loop back to Globe and back here.

So Sunday I got up before eight to fry the chicken and
make an apple crisp. We put on slacks and sweaters and
took off in Gilbert's car. Oh, it was a fun trip. Smog had
settled over the mountains near the copper mines and we
couldn't get a full picture of the magnitude of them. We
found a couple of trees and a flat bit of desert to set up the
Gilbert's little table and folding chairs and had our dinner.
Then we hunted rock specimens and came out of the cactus
with handfuls. Carl helped me find interesting ones since he's
an older hand at it. We also walked around the arboretum
and learned specimens of desert growth from all over the
world. Nora suggested we go dancing tomorrow night since
no one is interested in going to see slides at the hall.

Thursday I walked long in the desert behind the court and
hunted desert roses. I found a few and got sunburned.
I met Phyllis. She knows and likes poetry as I do. She is also
a psychic, she thinks. We heard it's thirty below in North
Dakota.

It was pot luck last night and such an array of good food —
and me off my feed! I borrowed a casserole from Nora and

made scalloped potatoes. Then I read in bed all evening. Dad played with the boys.

Friday I celebrated my birthday by playing bridge with the girls and dancing in the evening at Rendezvous. I got a card from Nellie and one from Marg. Dad gave me an eighty-cent mail holder. But the dance was recompense enough.

Sunday we went to church in Mesa, a beautiful little new church, the first stage of a big project. I was so impressed with the architecture inside. It was packed with seats clear to the end of the hall. They announced that they now had more people from North Dakota than from Minnesota.

We stopped on the way back to say goodbye to the Gilberts since they were leaving on the Mexican tour tomorrow and we were afraid we were too late to see them. Didn't want THAT to happen! So there were goodbye kisses and hugs. The warmth of these friends makes the heart sing!

The stay at Blue Star Court was over. By the time they got to San Diego and checked in with Marg, they were eying a bigger rig. But there were too many unanswered questions. Should they start to think about selling the house in Pettibone? Fall might bring big changes. Health? Family developments? Sue wrote, "Providence has the answers, not I."

Meanwhile, after a good visit with Margaret and her kids they were off with Marg and friends to "do" Death Valley. They saw the Charcoal Kilns and Furnace Creek, drove through Titus Canyon, "the most spectacular of our trips – a one way dirt road over pre-cipitous tight, tight curves, then into canyon proper where walls rose steeply on both sides" and reached Scottie's Castle before the end of the day. They toured the castle and listened to a taped meditation on an organ hookup while an older cowboy and his girlfriend made love in the back row.

The next day they all went to Las Vegas and Sue was uncharacteristically sniffy about the whole thing.

> Casinos all over the place and people frantically pulling on "one-armed bandits" to lose their nickels. Geneva lost about four dollars, Marg about three. I guess I ventured and lost about twenty cents and had not intended to gamble at all. Claude got one jackpot and came out a little ahead — five and a half dollars or thereabouts. We left about 5:30 and Joe drove up to ninety miles an hour — sheer madness. I was glad when that day was over as I'd been dreading it and wondering if I could neatly bow out, but it seemed I couldn't.
>
> **FEBRUARY 28** We arrived in Sacramento without a hitch. Last night we stopped below Carson City at a primitive camp with WPA toilets, tall pines and a rushing stream. Fellow travelers were building their wood fires near their campers. We dipped crystal clear water from the stream and I washed my head and took a bath. Had oatmeal with raisins and bacon and toast for supper and enjoyed it immensely. Morning took us onto excellent roads past Lake Tahoe where snow still clothed the hills and edged the road. Side roads were all still closed for the winter.
>
> We got settled and went straight to the Gores. Vern was home and Janie was arriving from school. Kris and Scott came soon after and then Keeny in her wig and driving the new Oldsmobile. Very nice. We spent the evening with them. Vern retired early as he had to leave at 2:00 A.M. to fly.
>
> The next day Keeny and I went pawing through the yardage and fabric store — one of the best things we do together. She has the most expensive Singer sewing machine made. These were happy days of good sewing, good food.

Now we are planning our return to Phoenix. Looks like a 1,000 mile journey, four days of continuous going. Oh well, it's generally fun.

MARCH 14   Got through Donner Pass in the afternoon and found it beautiful and no driving problem whatsoever. There was snow on the mountains but none on the road. We got well into Nevada and spent the night on the edge of a

The Gores Family: from the left Scott (trying to be taller than his mom), Keeny, Vern and Jane. Kristy is the little one.

town in front of a café. The desert is wild and barren in this area and towns are far apart. The next day we passed mass formations that appeared to be military pits of some sort and we guessed them to be atomic in nature. Hundreds of buildings there looked to be vacant. The desert is continuous but still not boring. We arrived at Las Vegas the next evening at dusk, driving through a stretch nearly solid contending for tourist dollars. Finally, close to dark and getting damp and cloudy and chilly, we came out at a place marked "recreation area" and found a high lookout onto Lake Mead. We decided to pitch camp.

I finished my blue knit braided belt and I like it. Read a little. I study Italian a little every day. I don't quite know how to approach it, but I am reading the dictionary, savoring and sounding out, hoping something will stick.

It was raining as we drove into Phoenix, coming in spits and small showers. I was elated at see 'old' friends again, like coming home. Gilbert's trailer is still here (happily), but they had gone to Vegas to see a sick brother. They are expected back Monday, I hear. Tomorrow we plan to go to church at eleven — Methodist this time.

MARCH 26 Mining Apache Tears turned out to be fun. We drove forty miles east and turned off on a gravel road and over a foot deep stream to reach the mines. Russell did the digging and we harvested a fine crop of tears. We went to dinner at Paul's, stopping at King's ranch to see the oldest living thing — a saguaro with 100 arms.

Carl and Nora came back on Monday too pooped to percolate. Said they'd seen us go by at Wikieup while I was sleeping.

Tuesday was bingo and this time we had a ball. Dad put an Apache tear on Edith Carson's board and told her now she'd win, and she won the next two games and two more later. He put one mine and I won three times.

I took a walk into the desert after I got back at nearly dark. These are the best parts of the day I always think. Carl and Nora came over to play bridge in the evening.

Monday the Hardy's wanted to go sight-seeing, so she made lunch for us all and we went up Beeline Road to Saguaro Lake where there were many tables and the weather was still and warm and overcast and the scenery superb. Multicolored cliffs lined the lakeshore and chipmunks scurried about. Then we came home and went dancing at Sunset. It was a happy day.

APRIL 1 We left this morning after a couple of days of goodbying. We went to Gilberts for goodbye drinks. It was one of the few times a drink seemed a good idea. It relaxed the tensions inherent in farewells. We left with goodbye kisses warm on my lips. I fell into bed and as soon as the soporific effects wore off I was wide awake as an owl and eating cornflakes at 3:00 A.M. to see if it would put me to sleep. Claude went over to take a shower to relax. We didn't even hear everyone leave at the crack of dawn – Thompsons, Gilberts, Hills, Lytels, Haltoms – just as well I guess. Art, Mary and Russell came to empty the coffee pot and render more goodbyes. Everyone says, "See you this fall." And well they might. It will be like homecoming. The desert was in full bloom as we left the area. Like a final benediction. Sweet sorrow.

They headed for Chicago where Bonnie was scheduled for surgery, a hysterectomy, and arrived just before Easter. Bonnie and Oscar had hired a maid, anticipating that she would need help during her recovery, and now, at the critical moment, the maid had quit and they were muddling through.

Bonnie decided to have her surgery even without benefit of a maid so we went in Thursday and spent the forenoon getting her hair done, buying a robe, nightie and slippers. Friday was the day for the surgery – good Friday.

The men took the kids to the museums on Saturday while I washed, ironed and cleaned for Easter. Leones came out with Giulio and Claudia bearing gallons of spaghetti, Easter eggs, crumbcake, Italian pastry, cheese cake and chocolate cake (the last two Claudia's creations and delicious). Bonnie got home for the big event, but was not feeling very pert. She gave me a lovely sweater for Mother's Day. Dad bought a new slide projector.

We planned the trip (to Europe), talked about finances and paid the fare. I'm still reading in the Italian book and also in *The Art of Thinking*. It's much the same as I have been reading, but sort of a refresher when good ideas get dimmed with everyday living.

I weighed in at 122 pounds this morning, undressed. I had my passport pictures taken yesterday. He took only one shot and I look terrible.

MAY 15   We got a new (to us) trailer, a twenty-four-foot Pathfinder. The next days were crowded with the business of getting things functioning and adding accessories. Wally was his usual helpful self – he can find the trouble with anything and get it percolating. He found a bathroom leak and fixed it. He also took the trailer to the terminal and he and Dad welded on bottle holders and made an ironing board to fit into the breadboard slot.

Back in Pettibone they settled into the new Pathfinder and prepared Claude to spend the rest of the summer on his own as Sue headed for the long anticipated trip to Europe. Harlan and

Sarah were still renting the house, so the Pathfinder perched in the backyard.

JUNE 1965　Got my passport, vaccinations and traveler's checks and I'm about ready to go. We plan to get tents and camp along the way (said to be for young in body and spirit only). Well I guess I'm as tough as they are. I wrote to Giulio saying I hoped I didn't feel too alone in my tent, asking "How do you holler 'help' in Swiss, French, German?" Then I realized I can't say it in Italian either for all the many happy hours I've spent pouring over it!

I dropped another four pounds in the last two months, down to 118. Feels good to have an acceptable shape again. Now wrinkles are the problem.

I've been playing the piano a great deal too – reckless sonatinas and more sentimental ones. It's not new for me to pour myself and my problems into finger work on the keyboard. I want to take some music along to Apache Junction this fall. I am looking forward to the winter and whatever it brings of joy or pain.

JUNE 23　Bible class at Jennie's last night and they had a nice party for me. They gave me a pair of white gloves and a bon voyage card and travel record book. Tomorrow we depart. I'm bombarded with unanswered questions: Is the trip wise? Worth it? The answer has generally been, "Yes!" with emphasis.

CHAPTER 11

Europe

. . . I have tried my wings and they work

Claudia, Giulio and Sue boarded the bus in Chicago for the first leg of a three month trip to Europe. In New York they settled into the H.M.S. Queen Mary for the three week voyage across the Atlantic. The trip was a major leap into the unknown for Sue, but she embraced it enthusiastically and prepared for it for months, sometimes with Claudia and Giulio, mostly on her own. She planned her wardrobe and sewed most of it. She studied travel guides and bought a book to learn some Italian in preparation for the visit to Giulio's Italian relatives. She got a new camera and practiced with it all spring. Her first passport and traveler's checks were safely tucked away.

> **JUNE 24, 1965** We said hello and goodbye to the Statute of Liberty, had lunch and settled in for a good nap. We needed it after our ten hour bus trip and the flurry of getting to the ship. Food is abundant and the waste is shameful. It's not particularly good, but adequate. The fruit is the best and the coffee is powerful. Tea is better. We are attended by steward Smith, who is always on the job keeping our cabins shipshape and handling our bags etc.

155

Every day she met and engaged new people – the young man who taught junior high in New York, the woman who confided that her son was a pianist of great genius, the French woman who recklessly challenged her in a game of Scrabble. She struck up a conversation with a young graduate student and "we discussed philosophy and existentialism, and the wisdom of searching for truth at any age." She and Claudia went to the concerts in the lounge. When the days were sunny she walked the deck, and when they weren't she read and practiced her Italian to the accompaniment of fog horns.

> There is quite an assortment of people on this ship from the highly colored Africans to the quiet colored Indians, from the bleach blondes to the snow white heads. There are several children and at least one infant. Yesterday I swam in the ship's pool and went down the slide, just to say I did, and got salt water up my nose.
>
> Giulio and I have been looking out at the Isle of Wight on the left and Portsmouth to the right, discussing our steward Smith. We agreed he deserved a generous tip. I said, "If I see him twenty times a day, he says, 'Hello, Mrs. Rawson.'" Giulio says, "He says, 'hello, suh,' to me and calls Claudia 'madam'." Then he left saying he guessed he would go and see what the madam was doing. Then we saw – and heard – them lower the anchor with a clang. An English accent announced that we would go in with the tide in the morning.

They disembarked in the city of South Hampton and boarded the train for London. Sue noted the narrow, winding roads with hedgerows, old, old houses with their tiny yards grown rank with flowers and the snow white laundry on the lines. In London's Waterloo Station Giulio called twelve hotels for "accommodations, as they say here" and finally found two double rooms.

It's the peak of the tourist season and I have a little greenhouse all to myself for $4.20. I washed up in the basin with water from a big plastic pitcher and emptied it into the pail that receives the waste. The railroad station had toilets with tanks overhead, flushed by pulling a chain. Pigeons flew around, alighting at our feet while everyone went dashing madly about. There were newsstands and fruit stands and others, all under a glass roof like a greenhouse. We looked for a restaurant to grab a quick lunch before taking the tour. One offered beans and sausages. Another had eggs and sausage with a good-looking flaky roll. The sausage was pretty tasteless. It's hard to win with English food, I guess.

They saw Hyde Park, Grosvenor Square with its statute of Franklin Roosevelt. They saw Regents Park, Saint Paul's Cathedral, the Tower Bridge, the Tower of London, Westminster Bridge and Lambeth Palace, Westminster Abbey, Parliament, Piccadilly Circus, St. James Church, and the Buckingham Palace grounds. "We'll do the Tower tomorrow, I guess. There are no towels or washcloths or soap in my room, nor a stove nor warm water – oh, well. I always brag I'm not self-indulgent, so now comes the reckoning, I slept well under two blankets. My shoes were still wet this morning."

The next morning they took the Tube to Westminster Abbey where guides herded and charmed them in turn with stories of the greats entombed there, especially the poets. Sue noted that the architecture of the Abbey itself was beautiful and awe-inspiring, inside and out.

The guide for The Tower of London described in detail the royals and scoundrels who lost their heads there and how exactly, pointing out suits of armor, swords and knives and instruments of torture. And then they were off to see the crown jewels. "At the toilets a woman stood with her hand out and demanded a penny and for that we got the whole bit with soap, hot water and a dryer."

We went to see the stage musical *Camelot* that night and the costuming was especially nice, and Claudia and I liked it, but Giulio went home in the middle — said he was tired. We had taken the bus and wondered if we'd find our way back, and we did. A nice-appearing man on the bus asked about a station and I asked him if he was English. (I was quite sure he wasn't.) He was from Canada and we talked about where from and how long we'd been here, and stuff like that.

Claudia sort of squared me away about talking to strange men, but I presume I will continue talking to anyone I take a notion to until I'm dead because of it or in spite of it. The new acquaintances I've made in my journeys have brightened my life a lot and I know I would have been the poorer for it if I'd always stayed aloof and refused to cultivate strangers. If this man turned out to be a bad character I would lose faith in my own judgment or character; but he was only a friendly traveler as I was.

JULY 14 Off to France. We had a nice train trip through more English countryside. I think I could easily grow to love it. Now it's 11:15 in the lounge on the boat bound for Boulogne. We had coffee and the last of the delicious English Cadbury bar with filberts. I'm on my knees on the sofa watching the ships in the channel and the waves breaking into festoons of drops and foams away from the boat. We just passed the White Cliffs of Dover and I took a picture through murky glass and murky sky. At least I have it for the record.

They landed in Boulogne and took a train through the French countryside to Paris. They stopped for a bite at a brasserie where a couple of Americans gave them travel lessons: Prices are high, cheating is wide-spread. They learned some of it first hand when a porter from the train rammed into them, annoyed that they were carrying their own bags. They rode the metro to their hotel and Sue noted that there was no toilet or bath in their room, just a basin and a foot bath (probably a bidet). Giulio asked for some towels and the maid said she'd bring them when he had a bath, only to discover later that there were no baths on the first two floors. Another lesson and a good laugh.

> We walked around, getting the feel of the place. This area is described in the guidebooks as "colorful." There is a street under our window swarming with unsavory looking characters of every size and color. The young people walk with their arms around each other; the French are quite handsome generally. The streets are lined with sidewalk booths where they sell junky souvenirs and sidewalk cafes with small tables under the awnings where the food is served at generally outrageous prices. The coffee is very strong and served in tiny cups. Tonight a Frenchman sitting across the table picked up my bill, which was much smaller than his, and left his for me. Gallantry is a lost art with the Frenchmen too, it appears.

The visit to The Louvre was enlightening and too short. Claudia and Giulio went to pick up the car and the tents. They came back with the Volkswagen, but no tents, no mail, no stamps. No matter, the weather continued to be rainy. They learned a few more lessons: French bread never comes bagged or with butter. One restaurant charged a cover charge and another charged for napkins. They decided from now on they would buy food from stands and eat along the road. They headed for Germany.

> We saw many food stands with luscious looking fruit and stopped at two stores and managed in our inimitable French to come away with a naked loaf of French bread, a round

of cheese of unknown name or quality, three bananas, three macaroons, a bottle of orange and a coke. A pat of butter salvaged from the hotel completed our dinner. We continued through lovely countryside and came into Strasbourg at five o'clock. We finally ran into good fortune as even innocents abroad can do occasionally, and found hotel rooms for $2.80. (Theirs was a little bit more.) A little Scotsman showed us to our rooms and we questioned the price, incredulous that the rooms cost so little, but it seems they do. And for good reasons. Our keys are huge, like our old skeleton keys, linoleum floors, feather quilts and turn button switches. But the beds are good and tables have tablecloths. We spread our feast and 'lay to' and it disappeared like the gingerbread man. We declared it good and what's more, wise. Giulio is doing a great job of navigating; his judgment is usually sound (at least it agrees generally with mine, which I think is pretty sound as well).

JULY 19   I went out and got $2.40 of food – fruit butter, French bread, ham and preserves for all day and more. I feel better when I can take care of some of these things by myself, so it was achievement of more than gastronomical import. We stopped in the autobahn rest area for lunch, perfect weather and food and we're all happy again...

Autobahn is like our freeways with many rest stops, tables and trashcans and lush grass. We can see women working in the fields (as in early North Dakota days) with their long black dresses and black babushkas, pitching hay and probably turning it to dry. We got into Stuttgart about three. It is a burgeoning city, running up and down beautifully clothed hills, big leafy trees everywhere, making the quaint, top-knotted old buildings look especially colorful. People here seem happy and friendly.

Giulio and Claudia are looking for a camera. Giulio manages things somehow without any knowledge of the language. I guess I know more German than either of them and I wasn't aware of knowing any. We exchanged money at a residential bank; it seems there's always someone who speaks English to bail us out in tight spots. The banker spoke English and he was a charmer. Most banks have signs in the window saying, "English spoken." All the stores seem well stocked — I hear they are the envy of East Germany. My room in Stuttgart was about $2.25, extra if you eat breakfast. Maybe I'll get some coffee since I haven't had any since Saturday morning and it's now Tuesday — a long drought. My room here is small with a single bed and a contour sheet and a light, fluffy quilt enclosed in a sheet sack, white as snow. There's a feather pillow, big and square, an immense wash basin, but no stool, no bath anywhere in sight, no closet. The door is six to eight inches thick. An eight-inch square beam across the corner of the room looks about ready to topple.

In Augsburg, Giulio took a wrong turn into an unmarked, one-way street where an Opel was making a left turn and hit the front fender. Crunch! No one was hurt, but soon a crowd gathered and everyone had an opinion. Giulio was fined $1.25 and repairs to the Volkswagen would be $25. We decided to 'do Denmark' while the repairs were made in Frankfurt.

That evening we came into Dinglebuhl just at dusk. This is the quaintest place of all and famous for its medieval architecture. It looks like a place out of a storybook. You almost expect these buildings to be made of gingerbread. Our hotel is the Golden Rose. The stairs are wide with ornate wood grills enameled black and three times as wide as usual or as necessary. Plumbing is old style except for the basins, which are big enough for baths (and we'll need them since baths aren't easy to come by). The pillows are twice the size of ours and the featherbeds enclosed in gleaming white covers, no bedspread – a good idea that makes for an altogether clean, fresh bed. Double doors again. My window looks out on a cobblestone street where very ordinary looking people go by, talking gaily. You wonder how such modern folks fit into such a fairyland. We noted that the babies all have lovely clothes and carriages. People are well dressed and coifed.

We had dinner at the dining room downstairs. Two carved wooden figures decorate the light fixtures, ceilings of carved beams and wood paneling on all the walls. Our dinner was served on huge silver platters and the waiter dished the guest's plates from them. Claudia and Giulio had Hungarian stew with dumplings about the size of our screw-shaped pasta. Mine was a smoked pork chop with a spud and sauerkraut. The waiter spoke English and brought coffee on a silver tray with sugar cubes and a tiny silver pitcher of cream for each. A group of probably sixty little children went by, playing or carrying band instruments and dressed up in colonial style uniforms and wigs. The streets were hung with flags commemorating some historic event.

JULY 23   We're on our way to Denmark: It's still raining torrents at times. I bought Betty Friedan's *The Feminine Mystique* at a book stand and then left my billfold along with the ticket and money at a booth where I stopped to buy airmail stamps and cards. The clerk retrieved it in time and I was vastly relieved. A good lesson. I remembered too late that I should have tipped her. We boarded the train at midnight and it was packed. A herd of young French boys with their leader got on earlier so it was nearly full before it

even got to us. We sat in the aisle and on little square seats
that folded into the wall and rested as best we could. We
perched there by the door with passengers coming and going
through, letting in the cold air until we were stiff with the
cold. Still the night went quickly.

Sue took the seven-hour tour of castles with moats and ancient
tapestries that told her all she needed to know about Denmark.
She watched the acrobats in Tivoli Gardens and made friends
with fellow travelers from London and Bangkok. Evenings she
read and wrote and reminisced about the time in Arizona. The
rain continued.

My little Danish porter always stands at the elevator with
my key when I come in as if I'm anticipated. My bed is laid
back and the spread put up. It rained again today but the
clouds seem to be parting overhead and may, just may,
give us a break and some sunshine. It's a strange July to
one who has never in her fifty-nine Julys seen one that was
without heat and only a few with very much rain. Still the
hours in my room have been pleasant. I finished the last of
Iris Murdoch's book, *The Bell*, showered and fixed up a bit.
I have been reminiscing sweetly at times and hopelessly. I
guess I should have been one of the characters in *The Bell*, all
of them seem without much hope. Still the uncertainty of
the future imbues it with anticipation, a sort of wait-and-see
promise, and so I go happily on in my fool's paradise. So it's
goodbye to Denmark.

Claudia discovered that she had left her three hundred
dollar ring back in the hotel in Copenhagen. We seem to
manage to leave something behind, and to have it be an
important thing. Giulio was for getting off and catching the
next train back. Claudia would have to go with him since

their passport picture was together. I would have had to go on to Frankfurt alone and try to make contact with them later. Had it happened earlier in the trip I would have been severely handicapped, but now I have tried my wings and they work quite well, I find. Then they remembered it was insured. Giulio called and they had found it so we were happy once more.

The train trip was fine this time, not crowded, and our reservations insured us good seats. Reading occupied us all. I am reading *The Feminine Mystique*, an informed and intelligent appraisal of the woman's "dilemma." The rain spits on. A Danish boy, seventeen, joined us and has been telling Giulio about teen life in Denmark. They can sleep together with parental permission; they learn all about birth control at thirteen or fourteen in school, and generally get pregnant only when they're drunk. Booze is available to all. Theirs is a socialized system in the country where older people are taken care of, but it results in heavy taxes and consequently high prices. There is no sales tax or income tax, none who are very poor or very rich, and it's easy to see why. This along with my book has given me new insights and new attitudes about sex and I wonder where it might lead.

I've nearly finished *Feminine Mystique*. It's always gratifying to find someone of stature who says what you've believed and defended for years, always wondering if maybe you're rationalizing what you want to believe and only rebelling. It appears to be what forward looking women have felt all along. How many husbands have lives important enough to spend two lives maintaining?

Back in Frankfurt they picked up the Volkswagen and continued on to Nuremburg and Dachau.

AUGUST 2   I met a Brazilian on the elevator and he said, "I've just returned from Dachau and I'm sick, sick." I asked what there was left to see after all this time and he said, "Everything." Our book says it's not pleasant, but one should see it firsthand and then resolve that it shall never happen again.

We did the Nuremburg Gardens in the morning and in the afternoon I took the train to Dachau. A bus took us to the internment camp, and we watched combines harvesting wheat across the road. I wondered how, with so much of God's beautiful bounty here, men could be so inhuman and monstrous. The first buildings were compounds entwined with barb wire. As we entered we saw huge square pillars, each bearing the name of a country. Later a guide told us they were put there by the countries as memorials to their dead here. Newspaper stories and lists of the inmates lined the walls of this big building, the original concentration camp, all in German. I felt quite defeated and got out my German book, hoping somehow to piece together the story.

A young man stepped up and in broken English asked what it was I was trying to find out, and so I told him. He said he was French but he knew some German and English and would try to help me. I asked if he would walk through with me and explain it and he readily agreed.

He made the infamous story come alive as we walked through the loosely arranged rooms, walls covered with greatly enlarged pictures. Towards the end there were pictures of mass graves filled with emaciated bodies, one with SS officers standing over hundreds of bodies. The boy explained that they shot benzene into their veins so they were unable to run or even to move, but they appeared far too weak to do it anyway. Long lists of Russians and Poles who died in great numbers; I believe 67,000 of one or the other, and less of other nationalities. Then on to the horrors of the massive Jewish elimination, a picture of a mother pulling three children along by the hands, hurrying towards the gas chambers; one of piles of shoes like big grain bins salvaged for further use, and on and on. My erstwhile friend explained, reaching for unfamiliar words as I tried to grasp his meaning, and mostly I did. He was most patient and I was most grateful. I was reminded again of how infallibly help comes according to my needs, never measured by my desserts.

The boy was a second year university student at a Catholic college in Lily, bright, handsome, and full of promise. Why he chose to help and befriend me, I'll never know. I hope I convinced him of my gratitude. We reached the big rounded stone memorial – it's like a watch tower with one side broken out. He said it was a symbol of the prison, the broken side connoting liberation. Metal symbols jutting out in front and on top were thought by some to symbolize the barbed wire.

At this point the boy had to leave and so we shook hands and he directed me past the crematory, behind which were beautiful, cultivated grounds with memorials over the many mass graves, some holding many thousands of unknown dead, each one no doubt dear to someone. I took pictures. We returned by bus to the station and the train stopped almost across the street from our hotel. The room begins to seem like home.

They continued on through Bavaria and into the Alps, stopping for tours of cathedrals with relics and palaces with crown jewels. She remarked on the beauty of the country and kindness of the people, on the accommodations and the food. She made peace with the strong European coffee and switched to tea. She began to miss the simple pleasure of communicating in her own language. But she always found interesting people to talk with. Usually she stayed in the same hotel with Claudia and Giulio, but often enough she stayed in separate accommodations where she gained confidence fending for herself in unfamiliar territory. Claudia was pregnant, but the announcement didn't appear in this journal.

AUGUST 9   We are in Zurich. Switzerland is not yet as mountainous as we supposed, like a continuation of Austria and Germany, as of course it is. We went to the museum of modern art, and found it quite different from the others with many impressionists that we didn't know about and then rooms of Matisse, Renoir, Donat, Picasso, Degas, Van Gogh and Cézanne. Interesting, but I still prefer the old Masters. We walked down to the lake and then watched hundreds of well-dressed people just walking around with their dressed up children and their dogs. The swans and ducks came up to beg for food. I bought an orange for fifteen cents to keep me happy tonight.

AUGUST 10   I took my bun and a peach and a map and started out to find the Zerba show. I sat by a fountain and ate my lunch after milling around in the swarming shoppers for a half hour. I enjoyed the Zerba show from the last row. A Swiss lady sat next to me and spoke enough English to make a conversation. I always have questions I want to ask about the country or the city. I started home about eleven and I got lost. These streets are the worst I've ever seen for irregularity and I'm not notably famous for finding my way.

We found Lucerne teaming with people and the hotel rooms swallowed up before our arrival, so we decided that the town had little appeal anyway and were willing to move on. We stopped at the American Express. These have come to be like an oasis to us. Claudia's ring arrived and we had a letter from the Lenit kids. We always need money exchanged and there is something cheering about seeing the lines of happy faces reading airmail letters from home. Here you can always hear English as people exchange opinions on European costs, cuisine, and climate. Today I met a very Oriental girl speaking perfect English. I guessed she was from San Francisco and she was! At dinner tonight I got a chance to try out my halting Italian with *"voglio l'aqua calda, per piacere."* (I would like some hot water, please.) She understood at once and brought me *heis wasser (hot water — in German)*. Oops.

We checked out the trip to the Jungfrau and even went to the train to buy tickets but decided they were too much. Giulio had his heart set on it so I was sorry on his account. Anyway, we left and drove through the most breathtaking mountain beauty I ever hope to see through two or three mountain passes winding up and up, and then down and down, with sharp hairpin curves. We cut back to Interlaken and on to Airolo where we stopped for the night.

At the border they exchanged their last francs for lira and picked up a red aide (emergency sign) to be used in case of an accident, free passes to museums and brochures of things to do in Italy. They had dinner at Como together and then sat on the bench by the lake and watched the lighted mountainsides and water reflecting the hazy mountains above. It was raining again. In Verona they stopped at the Santa Maria de Grazie church to see the original *Last Supper* by Da Vinci, disappointed to find the painting was faded and flaking and the church itself dirty, gloomy and in need of repair. The car was broken into in the night, but they had taken all their valuables with them to the rooms, so it was a minor inconvenience and another lesson.

In Venice they explored St. Mark's Square with its crowds of people and pigeons and souvenir booths. Over the next few days Sue ventured forth into the confusing labyrinth of Venice streets, sometimes getting lost. She watched the gondoliers poling their fares up and down the canals, playing accordions and singing "Funiculì, Funiculà."

> The people wave at me from their seats in the boat and it would be fun, but I presume going alone would only emphasize the loneliness in a setting made for love.
>
> "Presently my heart grew stronger, hesitating then no longer," and I ventured forth again, carefully checking landmarks, mostly to buy pastries and lobsters in the food shops, I confess, since the fruit stands and junk foods are discouragingly alike. I was better this time which gives me a hint. In lieu of a map, venture forth a little at a time and then retrace my steps. If I reach out a little further each time, by the time we leave I'll no doubt be ready to try the Vapareto, alone.
>
> **AUGUST 16**   I started out on the devious route to Friars Church — no main streets here, only alleys and bigger and smaller alleys — and I slipped through a street corner with about four feet clearance to come out on the church piazza. The church was pretty clean for a pleasant relief. Some are downright depressing with their filthy windows, their dust and cobwebs. Many of the famous paintings and sculptures are here — *Assumption of the Virgin*, and Bellini's *Madonna and Child*. It's all there. But their churches have unfavorable light for viewing the large paintings and they are dulled with candle smoke.
>
> And so I returned with no trouble, having checked my course well en route (if one ever can with these maize-like alleys). It was late and balmy with a hazy sky, too nice to

go in, and besides we were leaving in the morning and it's farewell to Venice forever (a horrible word), and so I sat on the steps leading into the water, carefully avoiding the bottom one covered with moss and slime and slippery as ice. I studied my Italian book and watched the boats coming and going. Presently an Italian fellow came and sat by me. We had quite a conversation since his English was no better than my Italian, but we still we managed to communicate and I got to practice putting my small Italian vocabulary into halting sentences.

I left then and freshened up a bit for supper and the kids came to the door just as I was going out. I decided to quit resisting the Romans (the last one excepted) and ordered wine with my dinner. The gondolas are going by again and some of these boys have good voices. It will make quite a memory.

AUGUST 17   My *LIFE* magazine says Europe is having the worst spring and summer weather in a hundred years. Actually, if we could have been warned, it would have been fine with me. I'd have gotten a good raincoat, ready to grab every minute. Also I would have made a warm suit instead of the summer ones that I brought. We have not suffered, probably not as much as if it had been hot. Speaking of weather, it rained again this evening, quite hard. The water was running down the street in rivulets in Boulogne.

Now we are in Florence – *Firenze*. We have a really palatial hotel this time that must have been built before electricity and plumbing since they are all outside. My bedroom window is a tall one and the bottom is above my reach. Our rooms are reasonable – Giulio is a real sleuth when it comes to bargains.

We toured the National Museum at the Bargello and the Gallery of the Academy where we saw the original *David*, along with several unfinished Michelangelo's. It was not known why they weren't completed. *David* alone is a great art experience, huge and perfect. I went alone to the tower to see some Cellinis, but there weren't many good ones. The guard smiled and asked if I were English and I said, "No, Americana," and he smiled again and said, "Ah, bella Americanas."

We took a bus to the Michelangelo Square and walked around in the sun awhile and viewed the city from above — hazy and congested in the valley, the buildings climbing the hills until lost in the haze. The cathedral loomed large, even from above, and from the street it's massive. The exterior is covered with geometric designs, sometimes in stripes and rectangles. Inside it's clean with marble floors and high, vaulted ceiling with stained glass high above. Very impressive.

The buildings are enormous; some are ancient fortresses dating from the fourteen hundreds. For blocks there isn't a blade of grass anywhere. People lead their dogs everywhere and let them stop to poop on the sidewalk, so you must watch your step as you do in the barnyard. The shopkeepers and street cleaners are out with their crude brooms, sweeping the streets and sidewalks, so the litter is not old. The pigeons are thick in the squares and so bold that you can hardly avoid stepping on them at times. People feed them and they climb all over you. The cats are tame but they're generally skinny. I saw a beautiful Siamese in a doorway yesterday.

We walked past miles of shops with lovely things, and I bought a few things for the kids. They expect you to bargain and in the end Claudia got some beautiful soft leather gloves.

Florence is a wonderful experience in art, and if one saw no more on the entire trip, but fully experienced Florence, it would be enough.

CHAPTER 12

Pietracamela

...*our grazie milles and buon giornos*

*L*ate that afternoon they reached the home of the Italian Leones in Pietracamela, and Giulio's mother was already there to welcome them and act as interpreter. The atmosphere fairly crackled with ebullience and good cheer from all sides, none more so than Giulio. The Italian Leones settled their American guests into their rooms and then drove four miles of switchbacks to the hotel in the hill for dinner.

> The food was marvelous and we had mixed feelings of delight, gratitude, humility and embarrassment to accept so much good food and good will with no possibility of returning the courtesy. This is a fantastic place; my description will not do it justice. The village is small and set on top of a hill and the stone buildings continue the line of the stone cliffs and sit at arbitrary angles with each other and with the world. We left the small main street of the town, a square piazza of cobblestone fronting the few shops, and entered an alley, climbing the rise of the hill. The alley is cobblestone, sometimes with easy, wide steps, sometimes narrowing. The stone houses huddle together as if in fear of impending

172

attack, and I dare say that was a distinct possibility in its early years. The houses seem to sprout out of the alley on a whim. People lean out the upper windows as we advance, smiling and calling out greetings. Other steps and smaller alleys opened out into scenes of spectacular mountain scenery. Almost every alley features a pair of mules with packs. The buildings all seem irregular, most are in sad repair.

At last we came to the home of Mrs. Leone's sister. It is nicely finished inside with marble floors. All the rooms are off the square to be sure. They have exercised great ingenuity in making do. An old fireplace encloses a work table with a marble top; a sink is made entirely of ceramic tile with a flexible tube hanging down for rinsing and a small basin portioned off one end for dishwashing. The sweet old *nonna*, in her gathered, long black skirt and black blouse and black headscarf, does all the family wash in the sink and they come out snowy white. She also insisted on doing ours. She sits and smiles quietly.

Saturday evening they had a gathering of family and friends who come any time of the day, but especially in the evening. I watched TV awhile on the big set. There are musical instruments to play, a guitar, one resembling a banjo, and another bug-shaped stringed instrument. Presently everyone joined in the singing (except me and Claudia who didn't know the songs). Young and old alike joined in, from twenty-one-year-old Flora Parogna to eighty-year-old Nonna Bonaduce, who sang enthusiastically with her toothless smile. Eventually everyone got a little glass of wine. I found it strong and rather bitter and I was glad the servings were small. (At the lodge we have the sweet white wine I find delicious and could easily get addicted.) Italian coffee is espresso, served in tiny, toy-sized cups, demitasses, and it's very strong. In my desperate attempts to get a good cup of coffee, I found that if I got three parts hot water to one of espresso, it was quite acceptable and I've become quite adept at badgering the waiters for "bring *carafe de aqua calda*" and "bring *tassa cafe*."

Monday we went to Teramo — four of us in the back seat of a Volkswagen. The mountain roads wound around endless switchbacks as we descended into the city. Mrs. Leone bought four watches, a gold bracelet for Claudia and nearly twenty dollars worth of jewelry. Pierina bought Claudia a sweater set and another for Giulio. I bought the dinner for the six of us, but little else. By then it was siesta time.

The next day at breakfast Pierina came in with an armful of sweaters. A trucker had arrived and set up a tent to display his knitwear and she had brought up a few for us to see and try on. We went down the cobblestone alley to the piazza where he had set up the tent with a marquee so he could unload in the rain. Our group must have come away with twenty sweaters. I got six myself, lovely twin set Italian sweaters for $7.50. Men's jacket sweaters were $6.50 or less. I got some for Dad and Wally and now I'll need two new skirts. They should be great for Arizona.

Francesco is learning a few words, like "sit down," and "goodbye," They stumble over our words as we do theirs. They generally understand my bumbling attempts to communicate.

In the evening twenty people gathered to see home movies. I could see a pile of rolls, all weddings and receptions, and I was prepared for the long show. Then fate intervened and a bulb burned out and the show was dramatically over. Then TV was turned on and an old Clark Gable picture came on, dubbed into Italian. Claudia, Giulio and I left as soon as we decently could. Mrs. Leone is a great help to me, interpreting and telling me words when I ask. She says, "Oh, you smart, I'm always a jackass."

And still it rains. Rained all day. They had a drought until the day we arrived; the rain seems to follow us.

AUGUST 25 We walked to the cemetery to take pictures of the graves to take back to family in Chicago. The whole back of the cemetery is a mausoleum with the drawer-like graves backing into the rocky hill like dresser drawers. The older graves are overgrown with dead grass and flowering weeds, but mostly they're just gray hard pan and stones. Most of the graves had glass-covered pictures of the occupants. The sun came out and it was a pleasant walk. The ubiquitous Aligi appeared en route to walk with us. He's quite a kid. Flora also joined us. I asked last night if she had English in school and she said no, she had French, Greek and Latin, but not English. Since she goes to a Catholic university, I presume Greek and Latin are required.

We returned to the house and changed clothes to go out to dinner at Babbo's cousin's house. It is even nicer than this one with marble floors, lovely furniture and marble steps that circle the second floor. She sat us at the table and we visited a half hour or so. Then a seven-year-old girl set a soup plate full of spaghetti on each plate. It was homemade and delicious, and since it was somewhat past our lunch time, we cleaned this up. The soup plates were removed and replaced with a fresh plate with slices of delicious roast veal and cold, cold green beans. This also went down fairly well, being low in calories. But wait! These plates were removed and replaced with a whole, roasted breast of chicken and two browned potatoes. At this we all began to groan and shake our heads and rub our tummies, but we made the grand effort. At last these were removed, partly eaten, and two bowls of fruit arrived — one of large peaches and another of white and red grapes. It's strange, even when you are full to bursting the fruit always appears as a welcome addition. Maybe because it is the last course or maybe it speeds up digestion.

Meals are never hurried. Two or three extras dropped in to talk animatedly in Italian and seldom did Claudia and I even know the subject. I reminded myself that most of our own table talk could be skipped entirely with no great deprivation. And so our fruit plates were taken away and a tiny saucer brought in, each with a tulip cup of gelato (a chocolate chip ice cream) and lastly the sixth course: espresso. Mercifully the cups are small. I asked for a *mesa forte*, half strength, and then Mrs. Leone explained that I wanted it weak, and they understood and nodded agreement. When it came it was not noticeably weaker, only sweeter. Thick and black with two heaping teaspoons of sugar to a tiny cup. At four we said our *grazie milles* and *buon giornos*, Mama Leone stayed on to finish the conversation and the dishes.

At home I removed all confining garments and crawled into bed, it being past siesta time. The hills were bathed in sunshine and I wanted to walk among the rocks, but not so much as I wanted to sleep. Pierina and Annina were cleaning the little fish when we returned and now it's nearly seven and I smell them frying. All I'd like is a piece of fruit and a cup of tea, or a pot of good old U.S. coffee. The scales downtown, if they don't lie, place my weight at 123.

Mrs. Leone and I took a walk in the morning sunshine down past the church to the public washing place where cold water ran in a steady stream through a shallow tank. Sheets were drying and bleaching in the tree branches. Workmen had cleared a rocky path and we crossed the creek and walked among the thick trees and brush. Raspberries, roseberries and hazel nuts were thick but not ready to pick, and so we returned with the clouds gathering for our daily shower.

We dressed for another big dinner at the lodge and it turned cold as we boarded the bus for the mountain. They had a long table spread in the upper room. First course was scallopini, a noodle dish with meat and cheese and peas cooked in custard cups. It was delicious and I ate it all. Claudia and Giulio were less enthusiastic. And then there was veal and chard, and finally the native cake, yellow with chocolate filling and flavored with some strong liquor, then fruit and tea and coffee. And more singing and conversation.

SATURDAY I walked down the rocky path this morning to sit on a grassy hill that dropped abruptly to the valley below, a perfect day. Then I walked the long, long path over the bridge. This is a perfect nature walk, rocky, up and down, wet in places, even tiny streams and always the shrubs, the trees, the creek bubbling over the rocks below and, always looming near and far the rocky hills and mountains. I must have walked for miles and I didn't find the end of the path. On the way back I took a picture of two women carrying their laundry on their heads.

SUNDAY The morning was filled with packing and cleaning and sorting out and disposing of. I gave Aligi my air mattresses. He was pleased as a boy with a new whistle. I gave Francesco an Apache tear for good luck, Aligi all the U.S. coins I had. I left twenty-five cents for Toni. The family just came from church and we took pictures on the balcony, a handsome family. Old Annina had spruced up and put on a Sunday dress and did her hair for the event. Then we went to the lodge for dinner. Pierina says she is going to bake a cake so we can be happy for a little while tonight before we cry tomorrow. I went to sleep practicing for tomorrow my "you are very kind" and "I am very grateful," "a thousand thanks" and the famous Italian *"arrivederci"* and *"arrivederla"* (farewell).

In Rome they saw the iconic landmarks and heard the ancient stories of the gladiators and the Christian martyrs and walked the cobblestones that chariots once clattered over. They saw the Appian Way and the Catacombs. They threw coins into the Trevi Fountain and they visited Saint Paul's cathedral and saw the bronze statue of Saint Peter, worn down by the kisses of the faithful kissing his feet. They visited the Vatican Museum and the Sistine Chapel and the Basilica of Saint Mary with its gold ceilings, the gold brought back from America by Columbus. In between it rained.

> The rain beat into the openings of my raincoat and my feet were soaked as we hurried to the bus stop. The people who had set up their fruit and vegetable stands on the square had been closing shop for the day, and the streets were covered with rubbish and garbage and rain all mingled together. It's getting serious and the sewer water mains have been washing out, leaving large areas of the city without water, at least for drinking. Plenty to drown in, I'd guess.

They stopped to watch an American film crew shooting a movie with Peter Sellers, and Sue was somewhat amused to find herself the target of the infamous Italiano.

> A man stood by me and inquired in Italian what picture they were making, and was that a 'grand' name. He sized me up and down as I watched him out of the corner of my eye. It seemed he was always closer than necessary because of the pressure of the crowd, and finally he was trying to hold my hand. And that wasn't all. I told him he was an Italiano and to *"sab bueno,"* to be good. And so we left. He appeared to

be the typical, respectable family man, well dressed and reserved.

After Rome came Naples and a train trip to Pompeii.

Pompeii was the most amazing thing we saw on our entire trip. The whole city is excavated and appears to be of the highest civilization even though it was destroyed in the year 79 A.D. It reminds me of the prophecies of the end of the world. There were lovely marble counters, far more elegant than those in any of our homes, with holes for water jars and marble and terrazzo tile floors. The houses were built around center courtyards with pools, pillars, wall pictures inside and out, fireplaces and ovens. In one basement there were glass cases containing bodies of people who were cut down in their tracks. Some huddled together as if in terror (and who wouldn't?), like Lot's wife, a pillar of salt. The shapes are almost fully preserved and some teeth exposed, white as pearls. Roads like the Appian Way lead between rows of houses still showing the ruts worn down by cart wheels. Many hundreds of earthen jars stand near nice dishes and cookware.

SEPTEMBER 5 It's the kids' first anniversary and what a place to celebrate it! The Isle of Capri. We arrived after an hour and a half boat trip and took a walk along with a couple hundred others. It's very nice. The Mediterranean was navy blue, changing to slate gray with my dark glasses on. The island is mostly just rock falling shear into the sea. The town lies in a cradle between two high points built up on multiple levels with the tourist in mind with shops from shabby souvenirs to elegant ones with expensive clothing and footwear. Americans were everywhere. Giulio approached a woman to ask some directions in Italian and she answered,

"No capicio." She was American, and we all laughed. The children are always adorable with their masses of curls and they are much loved apparently, and seem happier than ours.

By the time we got on the boat to come home darkness was settling down in the mountains and the lights of Naples appeared. A little rain shower shooed us into the lower deck, the crowd leaning out of an open window to watch the fireworks on shore.

I visited with a family also going home on the *Michelangelo* on the seventh. I appreciate these human contacts though I often insist that I am a loner. I guess I need both alternately, though I often feel more alone with people than without.

The kids were going out to celebrate in the evening, so I went out to find some pastry and fruit for supper and breakfast. I carefully checked the corner building so I'd get back safely, having been warned about Naples. Cops were everywhere. I turned a corner into a rather dimly lit street and headed for a fruit stand at the end of the block when my masher of the day fell into step with me. He inquired was I Deutch or English. I'm not in the habit of being rude and I didn't want to start. Since he was clean and well dressed and mannerly, I talked to him; he helped me select and buy some peaches and walked back to the hotel with me. He asked if I'd like to walk around and see the city. I would have liked to very much since we haven't really seen it and he was a native. But I didn't.

SEPTEMBER 6   Our last day here. The kids were having breakfast in bed, they said, and I had my peach and glass of tea and felt it was a feast. Giulio went out and got some money for the trip home. I have about forty-four dollars in lire left to pay for the hotel and food for the rest of the day. The kids got all dressed up and went out for a last night dinner. I declined and found a place that offered a perfect supper of chicken with bread and salad. A cat came in and gratefully ate scraps that I fed her. Poor thing had a crippled ear. The kids stopped by, in good spirits after their evening out. Claudia is getting crowded out of her dress and sighed with relief as I opened the bra back. We're all eager and excited to be embarking tomorrow.

SEPTEMBER 7   Today we said goodbye to Italy and to Europe – no doubt my last trip abroad. It was a great experience and the harvest will no doubt be in the memories.

They boarded the *Michelangelo* with a minimum of bedlam. Sue settled into her accommodations with three other women and their eleven pieces of luggage and set about trying to put together a foursome for bridge. Before they could pass the Straits of Gibralter and officially out of the Mediterranean Sea, there was one more celebration of Italy when a scattering of Italian merchants in rowboats came hawking their last souvenir offerings – rugs and pillows with the likeness of the Virgin Mary or Jesus or the expanded version with the Last Supper or bucks with locked antlers. Or a cigarette lighter. A skull cap. Baskets were passed up and, if they were lucky, returned with money. Shouts and gesticulations provided accompaniment. Then the whistle blew and the boats drew in their lines and straw baskets, waved and shouted the final goodbyes. Sue wrote: "I love those Italians."

SEPTEMBER 14   We're home. We got through debarkation without difficulty but were held up for three and a half hours in customs and missed the Chicago bus by ten minutes. We went to a terrible show to get off our feet while we waited for the next one. It left at 8:45 P.M. full to the last seat. Our frequent stops at Howard Johnson Restaurants were pleasant and the American hamburgers even better than I remembered.

CHAPTER 13

America

...and all the comforts of home

The trip to Europe only amplified the call of the open road and widened the horizons. A month later they took off in their new 1965 Dodge pulling the almost new (and bigger) Pathfinder travel trailer. It was definitely a step up from the little red trailer. Heading west, they swooped across North Dakota with just a perfunctory wave at the relatives and on to Arizona. Mostly Sue rhapsodized about the scenery and their good fortune. Sometimes she grumped. She was planning for Christmas, but her eyes were on Blue Star Court. She began to write "Claude" more often, instead of "Dad."

NOVEMBER 1965 We stopped in Billings for groceries and then drove on to reach Greycliff and tucked into a truck stop. We even have lights! I made spuds in their skins, meatballs, cottage cheese, apple celery salad for supper — not very camper-ish food. We feel like pampered darlings. Read a little *Cloud of Unknowing* and *Unobstructed Universe* and then finished Becky's mittens except for final touches. We are trying to freeze up ice for the next lap of the journey which should take us to Pocatello tomorrow.

We took the scenic route south of Bozeman with a creek flowing below the road all the way. It's the scenery you dream of. We came all the way into Pocatello before we found a stopping place, following our usual pattern of "don't stop until it's dark and we're exhausted and hungry so the evening won't be so long." (They're never long enough for me.) So we find ourselves in cities bumbling around looking for stations with extra space. Our angels must be on the job drawing overtime since we always manage to set down someplace before we get killed or arrested. This time we pulled behind a service station near the railroad tracks. Three trains went through while we were awake and paying attention.

I called Lue tonight from a gambling joint. Wally still hadn't got his deer as of Tuesday evening. Rick was accepted into the school chorus. I'm making doll caps and sweaters and mittens for Laurie and Polly's dolls.

NOVEMBER 17 We got to Apache Junction tonight about five and walked around and greeted old friends. Many old-timers are here already. Nora and Carl won't get here until December 1, Virginia said.

DECEMBER 22 Dad's birthday. The month has sped by and we've been as happy as seems possible and grateful for our great good fortune in being here. The weeks have been full with Dad playing golf and cards and I knitting or crocheting a little, writing Christmas letters, walking in the desert (O Joy!), playing bridge, bingo, sing-alongs, slides, potlucks. Dances have started here and there are some new folks. There's been quite a bit of rain which keeps us trailer bound, but makes the desert green.

Browns went with us to Saguaro Lake. We took a fried chicken and some 'pickup' lunch. We all went to church first, so we were starved by 2:30 and ate like vultures. Then Ed and I climbed the mountain. Claude and Zana declined, but Ed was game. It was quite a climb and quite a revelation. Ed had to get on top of some rocks and pull me up. I even had to pluck a cactus from my side. We stopped on the way home to get ice cream which turned out to be our supper and then played a couple of rubbers of bridge. They have been here (to our trailer) or we to theirs once a week (at least) since.

We dance at Sunset every Monday and have a good time every time. Dad has two "dancing widows" he helps keep happy.

The rains were interrupted for a day, so I took a long walk in the desert. One large arroyo was washed clean and smooth and a couple of palo verdes nodded to each other from the banks. I walked an hour or so and then sat on the bank to read awhile before starting back. I was gone all afternoon. We're getting ready to go to Margaret's (in San Diego) tomorrow. I've wrapped eleven gifts to take along.

JANUARY 8, 1966   We had Christmas Eve at Tom and Joan's — turkey and ham with all the fixin's and margaritas. I got a hair dryer from Roses, electric scissors from Claudia and Giulio. Bonnie sent some shares of stock and Keeny and Vern sent See's candy. Tom always gives me a box of stationery and envelopes (from his print shop). Good ol' Tom. Marg came along home with us to take in the New Year's Eve dance at Sunset. She left Sunday. We took her to Phoenix to catch the bus.

Carl and Nora were over for drinks and bridge on Friday. Friday was quite a day!

JANUARY 12   Monday we danced at Sunset with the usual good time. Rosenlofs, Moorheads, Jarvis, Carls, Arts and

Olsons, Riggs and Hills – such a bunch from here. Nice, nice time! Makes us feel young and desirable again.

Saturday we went to a new market, Skaggs Fruit Farm, for a heaping half bushel of navel oranges for $1.50. Mmmm good – but not as good as my desert interlude. The ocotillos are bright and green now. Dad keeps warning of snakes, but I wouldn't let a mere snake take that away from me.

FEBRUARY 15, 1966   We got the good word of Allison's birth on Tuesday while I was at bridge. So we used Wednesday to get ready and make last goodbyes and rendezvous. We reached Fort Worth at three the next day. Claudia and baby are fine. She weighed eight pounds ten ounces. The baby is darling in her little nighties. She had colic the last night we were there. We started home on Saturday.

We took the scenic route through Tucson and Florence. Recent rains have made the desert green and inviting. Old Superstition is wearing a crown of snow again and looks great. Unbelievable how glad I am to get "home" to our own bed, food, freedom and friends. The trailer is clean and nice to come home to.

Monday we went to a Valentine Party in the evening. I won a heart candy box of chocolates playing musical chairs. We played Proverbs and carried beans on straws and had lots of fun. Then we were on to Sunset for the usual good time dancing. I had supper with Carl (others got partners with valentine numbers). I don't sleep well after these – too much reminiscing or too much stimulation and coffee, I guess. But today I'm bushed. I wrote two letters and walked in the desert and did one lesson in Italian. Now on to *Lezione #10*.

FEBRUARY 22   Delicious reunion with loved friends – what I've been anticipating since the day we left. I keep thinking these wonderful times can't last. Unfortunately they can't, so we grasp each one hungrily against that day.

Got another disturbing letter from Keeny. Vern left for Vietnam in February. Heidi, their cat, also left and also her best girlfriend.

APRIL 2   We left Thursday. Every day was an unhappy one with 'departure blues' this last week. It was a good thing I didn't know my last walk in the desert was my last. We had martinis with Carl and Nora until six. Then that big goodbye that wasn't 'goodbye' but *'vaya con dios.'*

I was practicing piano in the hall when Julie came in for a last lesson and sing-along with "How Great Thou Art," "I Don't Want to Play in Your Yard," "Won't You Come Over to My House" – she's insatiable. Before I could get away the folks arrived for the sing-along and since there was nobody else to play I stayed to play for them. While I was there a dozen or so stopped by for farewells. We dropped around the next morning for final kisses from the whole flock. I told Gill Moorhead and Lee Riggs they were no better than anyone else and they got theirs too. Carl came around for a bonus one later. All this fond affection makes me regret leaving and guarantees the pleasure of my return.

On the road again, they planned a stay in Fort Worth to see Claudia and Giulio and Baby Allison, but first they stopped in Tucson and Tombstone and made a side trip to the Mexican border to buy bargain booze. That was a first.

Allison has changed and is fat and happy. She talks such cute little baby words and smiles. They (Leones) are moving on Monday and I suppose we'll help them. We had days of mornings in the trailer and evenings with the Leones sewing

baby dresses of pastel and print challis. I'm due for a trip
to the fabric shop. We had our Easter service over coffee in
the trailer since we didn't find a church. Claude and Giulio
have been fishing with mild luck. The kids moved. Their new
address is 328 Tinker.

Back in Minnesota, Wallys bought a lot on Leaf Lake, a smallish,
meandering lake among the hundreds around Detroit Lakes. They
spent weekends clearing brush and putting in a dock; they planted
a little green used travel trailer to serve as kitchen, bunkhouse
and home base. Lue's brother, Gordon, bought the lot next door.
(Gordon married Arlene Leoppke, my erstwhile best friend and
college roommate.)

Claude and Sue checked into Pettibone and found out the
teacher that had been renting the house would not be doing that
again. Once again they thought about selling the house. But who
might buy it? Pete and Bev Kaczmarski stepped up. They were part
of Wally's old high school cohort, now settled in as the adults in
the community with three kids of their own. Pete took over the old
R&K garage his dad ran with Uncle Willard, and Bev was already
an established teacher in the Pettibone School. It would be a busy,
hectic summer, dismantling over twenty years of family history and
detritus. But first they headed to Minnesota to check out The Lake.

We left Moorhead and headed for the lake. We ran into bad
wind all the way with gray skies, but it was better at the lake.
The kids have a terrific time. They got fish and two turtles
and garter snakes and numerous frogs and toads and put
them all in an old bathtub to make an aquarium. Mitzi was
in the midst of the fun yapping and running and grabbing
discarded socks and shoes to carry off. The men built a dock
and the kids waded along shore in the shallows. Lue and I
took a walk in the woods around the lake watching out for

poison ivy. The little goldfinches and orioles are back and
the chipmunks and squirrels keep us enchanted.

My parents sent out the word to the family: The house is sold.
If you want to come for one last visit, one last chance to retrieve
the vestiges of your childhood, now is the time. Family by family
we responded. We heard the call in Minneapolis, loaded up the
Volkswagen hatchback and headed west. Our kids (Laurie 7, P.J. 6,
Polly 4 and Cara 2) were full of anticipation. As you might imagine,
we didn't travel much. When we saw the PETTIBONE sign and
turned off the interstate at Tappen, Laurie looked around, crestfallen. "They didn't finish it yet!" she observed. It was a chaotic
few days in which Mom managed to gather together many of my
old classmates and friends, some of their mothers and their mul-
titudes of offspring. I remember she and Dad nattering at each
other (and who could blame them?) until one suggested that they
load the trailer and follow us back to Wally's place at the lake. All
the nattering stopped and they worked together like a well-oiled
machine, so relieved they were to be set free and on the road again.

JUNE 23   Our last night in Pettibone, a tender nostalgic
night in several ways. Rose, Irv and the kids came for three
days. It was a busy hectic time going through old pictures
and year books and all the stuff in the basement. The last
day we had a get-together: Mary Joan and her four kids
and Margaret; Carol and her two kids with Ella and two of
Kenny's kids, Marla and one of hers, Ardelle and her three —
nineteen kids in all. Arlene and Merrill and kids came that
evening. They made a visit or two to Zana's to buy paintings
and to Esther's for coffee and walks around town to see the
changes, for better or for worse. Florence and Marla dropped
in. So it's been quite a week. Then we all left for Moorhead.
Rose and family left Sunday morning taking Terry with them.

The deal for selling the house is going forward. Bev
and the kids came in the evening. She thinks the house is
"perfect," she said.

They parked the Pathfinder at the lake and oversaw the comings
and goings of the family. With Gordon and Arlene on the lot next
door this included Lue's family, the Dalbols. She had five brothers
and three sisters, so there were lots of them.

The Arizona friends, the Gilberts, stopped on their travels. "Carl
and Nora came mid-morning and left about 3:30. It's so good to see
them – like a breath of Blue Star alive and smiling," Sue wrote. But
first they went east, not west. The trip through Europe only whet-
ted her appetite to see more of the older historic sites of her own
country in Boston, Philadelphia and Washington. If Claude had
any reluctance, it wasn't recorded here. My guess is he would just
as soon have skipped the museums, but he loved hauling that rig.

The Thursday before Labor Day we left for Minneapolis
and arrived at Rose's late afternoon. We all went to the
State Fair Friday and Irv took us out to Chinese Monday
evening. They have a new black Wurlitzer piano. Rose and
I played duets. The kids are having lessons. P.J. eats it up;
Laurie fights it. We parked the trailer behind a little shopping
center on Nicollet for no charge and an invitation to come
back. I wonder if these kind people know how much they are
appreciated.

We headed south on I-35 and then over to Blooming
Prairie to visit the Meyers and on to the Mississippi, pulling
into a lovely county park just out of LaCrosse. The scenery is
lovely with lush green trees and hills all the way. The leaves
are beginning to turn red and gold but not yet at their peak.
We arrived in Winnetka right after lunch. Bonnie and I went
out and bought two pieces of fabric for skating outfits for

her. We made two skating costumes with lined top and trunks, a jumper for Amy (also lined) and two pillow covers. Plus two skirts taken in and hemmed.

They made their way along the edges of the Great Lakes, sometimes unhitching the Pathfinder and exploring by car.

Stopped for lunch on the rock wall in Cleveland and took pictures . . . got a basket of tomatoes for thirty-five cents and a deteriorating cantaloupe for fifteen cents. It was delicious . . . the area before Buffalo was a series of grape vineyards along the sandy shores of Lake Erie . . . It is lovely along the edge of the lake as the road curved and sloped . . . drove through Lewiston and Youngstown — old villages with ancient buildings mingled with the new. All

*Claude and Sue leave the lake for the first long trip
in the Pathfinder trailer.*

in lovely green surroundings. We stopped in a park out of Lewiston to eat our lunch on the shore of Lake Huron. A perfect day.

We drove through horrible downtown traffic to see the Niagara Falls, crossing to the Canadian side into a main street that reminded me of European traffic. It was bound up tight while a wedding procession went by with crepe paper streamers flying and horns blaring. A harassed officer was trying to steer traffic around two cars that had run together. As we waited on the railroad tracks, a train came through and we backed up to save our hides. Somehow everyone got his due and we got back to the observation tower. All was quite new and incomplete. Then the fast ride 522 feet up to the observation level in a glass cage elevator and our first glimpse of the magnificent falls – both Horseshoe on the Canadian side and the less spectacular American ones. We had early supper in the 'lounge' and sat next to a window where we watched nature's great show for an hour. Then we went down and stood above the falls and watched until dark when the lights were trained on the falls. Then back to the trailer for oatmeal and toast and apples. Very nice day.

SEPTEMBER 20   We got to Walden Pond about noon. Claude set up camp with all the fixin's: WES (Water-Electric-Sewer), the works. It was like money from home. I walked down to the Pond which was officially closed for the winter. It is a charming little lake. A small sign said the site of Thoreau's hut was down the shore a piece. I saved that for later. We had lunch and went into Concord. It is obviously an old town with many old buildings in good repair and few new ones. The streets converge on the center of town like a wheel and that is bedlam. We saw Emerson's room with his

own books and furnishings, a Thoreau room reconstructed
the proportions of his hut and his own equipment and
Paul Revere's lantern – the real one. Then we drove to the
old cemetery containing the graves of Emerson, Thoreau,
Hawthorne and Louisa May Alcott. Rain is forecast for
tomorrow and it's getting a bit chilly. And we may be
running out of bottle gas. But it's fun to be in and have all
the comforts of home.

SEPTEMBER 21   We left camp and zoomed into Boston with
the rest of the zoomers with no regard for life or limb. The
spot where all the early history was made was hard to find in
the part of town where urban renewal is in full swing. The old
and the new mix together in a hodge-podge of narrow littered
streets with decaying buildings in some sections – reminiscent
of Europe. The streets run at crazy angles, inherited I
suppose from their beginnings way back in the seventeenth
century. We barely started the Freedom Trail when Claude
got sickish – the chill dank air and uphill pull, I suppose. We
had clams and chips at a lunch counter and then continued
to the cemetery where Paul Revere, Ben Franklin's parents
and the victims of the Boston Massacre are buried. It was
long and hard to follow, with detours, unmarked streets and
vague directions, but people were good to help.
    I saw only two pairs of slacks all day including mine.
About half the women wore hats. Boston is living up to its
reputation for sensible shoes, suits and tweeds, and stolid
straight-laced faces. Traffic was horrific. Had oyster stew for
supper. Crocheted on Allison's cap and played cribbage with
Claude. I weigh 123 today.

SEPTEMBER 22   We went in search of bottle gas. Folks here
don't seem to know what we're talking about. The day was

warm and pleasant and overcast. We drove past produce markets dotting the roadsides with apples, peaches, melons, grapes, squash and pumpkins. Got a gallon of cider for a dollar. I found two yarn shops and bought some white sayelle and orlon for baby caps to continue my Christmas creations.

We walked down to Walden Pond to eat our lunch. Brisk little chipmunks darted up to grab the crumbs of dark bread we dropped for them. A gray squirrel struggled by, cheeks bulging with acorns. Then we walked around the lake to find the site of Thoreau's hut (it was discovered in 1945 after being lost to view for 100 years.) Now I must re-read Walden again to see what else of Thoreau we have in common. Tomorrow we leave for Plymouth.

They checked out Plymouth Rock (a disappointment), the Mayflower (shockingly small) and the first pilgrim settlement (spare, but cozy). Tomorrow, Cape Cod.

On the way to Philadelphia they went through Rhode Island ("...the many immense ancient houses set us to wondering did people really need all that room?") and New Jersey ("...appears to be a nice place to live, but I guess there are too many people for us"), finally settling into the Valley Forge Trailer Park. They unhitched the Pathfinder and drove into Philadelphia where they inspected all the usual suspects: Independence Hall, Ben Franklin's grave, the Quaker meeting house ("...bleak with simple cheap benches with well-worn pads"), and the wax museum ("...impressed with the Washington Crossing the Delaware and the Marines Planting the Flag on Mt. Suribachi").

Leaving the Valley Forge Trailer Park through heavy traffic and continuous commercial development, she was reminded of the threat of population explosion.

They drove through Lancaster with its "solid rows of boxy ancient houses with scarcely a crack in between, dormer windows

or balconies leaning out over the street" to Gettysburg National
Military Park where they watched the cyclorama of the battle of
Gettysburg.

> We went up a circular ramp into a round room with battle
> scene on the wall all around us. Lights directed us to certain
> spots as details were explained. Fifty-one THOUSAND men
> were killed here in three days! It must have been ghastly. We
> drove around the battlefield to see the many monuments
> and memorials as well as Devil's Hole, a rocky hilly area
> where heavy fighting took place. So sad. And it's such a
> beautiful spot. We came home starving. I stretched the
> leftover hash with some fresh potatoes cut fine and it was
> delicious. The peaches we got in New York are ripening now
> and disappearing fast.

Outside Washington they parked and spent a day or so planning.
Sue scanned the brochures and picked out one of the bus tours
and then decided to focus on the Smithsonian Institute and the
National Gallery. "That should do it," she wrote.

> **OCTOBER 1** A quiet day at home. It rained all night and
> nearly all day so we agreed to sit it out. I read, played
> scrabble, crocheted, played cribbage and two-handed whist
> and made an apple crisp. Trailers came and went all day.
> Claude went out with his bathrobe hanging under his coat
> to chat with neighbors. One family has a small trailer and
> five kids. The weatherman predicts wind and cold tomorrow.
>   We picked up our mail at Greenbelt and stopped to have
> coffee and read letters right in the parking lot — two from
> Claudia, one from Bonnie, one from Arlene, one from Lue
> and a couple of others — a good haul. Then we went on
> toward Mount Vernon stopping at a picnic table to have our

sandwiches, apples and coffee on the shore of the Potomac. A nice fall day with full sunshine and the trees turning gold and red and discharging a flurry of leaves with every gust of wind. Mount Vernon exceeded our fondest expectations.

We walked through the landscaped gardens with their thick boxwood hedges and flower beds, through two or three museums featuring Martha Washington's clothes and jewelry plus George's long silk hose, white pants, embroidered vests. In the kitchen of the main house dummy ducks, pigs, turkeys roasted in the fireplace, rolls fresh from the oven (a bit dusty to be sure) 'cooled' on a sideboard amid a great array of black cast iron pots and polished copper kettles. In the smoke house, hams, bacon and sausage hung curing. The barns and carriage houses housed two carriages; the insignia on the bridles matched those on the carriage. A bucket on a chain hung in the covered well.

In the master bedroom of the main house we saw the king size bed in which George died. His remains and Martha's lay below the slope towards the Potomac. It's a lovely, lovely setting. I never knew it was on the banks of the Potomac.

The next day on the grand tour they saw Arlington Cemetery and the (temporary) eternal flame at John Kennedy's gravesite. They visited the Lincoln Memorial, the Washington Monument and the Jefferson Memorial on the Mall by the reflective pool. They toured parts of the White House, Supreme Court and the Capitol Building where they heard Senator Wayne Morris speaking in favor of a new appropriation. Senator William Fulbright spoke earlier against the bill.

In the Archives they saw the originals of the Constitution and the Declaration of Independence and were overwhelmed with pride. From the viewing area at the Bureau of Engraving and Printing they looked down on machines and people printing money, stacking one dollar bills into stacks of $230,000 each and $20 bills in stacks of $4,600,000. Sue wrote: "I never expect to see so much money again in my whole life."

After a day of extreme touring and fighting traffic, they were happy to get 'home.'

> I made a cabbage apple pineapple salad and dark toast with smoked beef and cheese. We always feel like pampered darlings to get home and sit down to our own choice of food.
>
> I took clothes to the laundromat and a woman came into the telephone booth there to call. It could have been me. "I'm about wore out!" she said. "My feet are killing me" and "Oh, I don't know how long we'll stay, a day or two more. We don't try to keep strict schedules. We're retired, you know." And she, like me, had got into her housecoat, but she'd gone a step further and had her slippers and curler cap on.

The next day they took the bus to the Mall and walked several blocks to get to the Smithsonian. Once there they went off in separate directions to explore their own interests. Sue saw the women's styles from the nineteenth century on, the First Ladies' dresses, and fabulous jewelry. She explored the Museum of Natural History and the mineral and gem gallery with the Hope Diamond necklace. At the National Gallery of Art she was amazed at the sheer number of greats displayed there – Renoir, Corot, Gauguin, Rubens, and on and on. Presumably Claude saw guy stuff.

They made one final pilgrimage to the Washington Monument and took the elevator to the top. Through the apertures they could view all they had toured in a great tableau laid at their feet. And they were impressed. The wind had come up and was blowing a gale, so they took a cab to the bus depot, had coffee and then boarded the bus for home, relieved not to have to drive.

In Richmond they toured the Governor's Palace and ate chicken stew served in pewter bowls at a local tavern. In Yorktown they visited the house where Cornwallis surrendered to Washington. In the reproduced, restored Jamestown colony they marveled at hardships the early settlers endured and the smallness of the ships that brought them here, and the skill of the live actors that portrayed it all.

> We drove around the historical tour of the island in which Jamestown stood. Tame deer came out to have their pictures taken. A beaver scurried over the wall. Gray squirrels were busy burying acorns. The magnolia trees are sprouting red shoots or berries — probably a prelude to blooming. The air is a reminder that we are getting farther south.
>
> We heard on the news that Hurricane Inez has been tearing up the Mexican provinces and has been badgering and threatening Texas of late. We got into North Carolina tonight. It looks much poorer here. We passed up some good trailer parks and then finally checked into this pretty bad place, very rough with many shabby trailers. It's a little creepy. We came by two accidents close together — always a sobering sight.

In Charleston they visited friends who showed them the sites, provided the first familiar faces they'd seen in weeks and sent them on to Jekyll Island.

> Daisy left us sliced ham and two pieces of pie for our journey. They were really wonderful. The trip to Georgia was nice, the weather fair and the roads good. Jekyll Island is a big tourist attraction featuring the "the Marshes of Glynn" made famous by Sidney Lanier. This is one of our mail

pickup sites but we got only five or six bank and business
letters, no others. The island has a lovely beach, golf course,
good motels and eating places. The enormous houses here
(called "cottages") were owned by millionaires, but are now
in assorted stages of decay. One owned by Will Rockefeller
is used as a museum. Dust lies thick on everything pointing
up starkly the transience of wealth. I have often thought that
beyond a certain point, wealth becomes superfluous.

When this trip was only a dream we saw the film, *Along
#1*, and decided to do it. So today we are following it down
to Key West. On one side we see sand dunes heaped up and
covered with palmettos and scrub oak along the beaches
for many miles, and across the highway on the other side
tall pines and other trees I can't identify hang gloomily with
Spanish moss. None look very well-nourished or groomed.

We turned off at Titusville to take a tour of Cape
Kennedy. The sultry humid weather lulled me into napping.
But encouraged by the enthusiasm of our guide, I was at
last aroused to the awesomeness of the whole thing. They
explained how huge carriers weighing millions of tons
carry the missiles to the launching pad and showed us the
huge building – the largest in the world – where they are
assembled. It's some satisfaction to know we've seen it.

The rain was coming down in earnest as we proceeded
down #1. We pulled into a trailer court and let it rain while
our chicken cooked. We had it with dumplings and a big
salad.

Our court man warned us that the water in the main
tap was contaminated and to draw drinking water from
another. So come morning we debated which was which. I
filled the coffee pot and tea kettle before we left to keep
us in water until we sat down again. Our coffee was pretty
bad, so I tossed that out. The water in the pot was salty and

contained one visible six-legged creature, and this morning a little frog jumped out of the toilet. It is sultry and humid.

OCTOBER 15   We drove into Miami Beach just to see the huge luxury hotels all new and flourishing. Driving south, we went through the edge of all the tourism buildup, a great expanse of dredging and filling and building. Florida is almost ocean and the ocean around the keys is almost land, and in between lay swamps as wasted as the Arizona mountains. What is the Bible prophecy – "The mountains shall be brought low and the valleys raised up"? We kept going on #1 towards the Keys and the swamps got wetter. Only scrub trees, reeds and palmetto now. A dark snake with a painted back like the old rulers we had in arithmetic crawled sluggishly across the road. I think we may have run him over.

We put the trailer in a court eighty miles east of Key West at Islamorada, about half way down the keys. The man came out and parked us and gave us a piece of sewer hose. Then he brought us a coconut. He noticed we had a flat tire so he got the station agent to come and change and fix it. Hence our first use of AAA.

They drove the long, long bridges to see the southern-most point of the U.S. ("not very pre-possessing," Sue wrote) and drove the eighty miles back to the trailer for biscuits and chicken "and rice pudding for dessert since it's Sunday." They set out through more heat and humidity than they were used to and drove through Sarasota, up to St. Petersburg and on to the Florida panhandle.

That night we got to a court just short of Mobile. It had rained so the yard was sodden. Claude set the trailer up while I went in to pay for parking. The woman was large and

dark. She said she was part Indian and I said I thought that
was something to be proud of. At which she brought up the
fuss people were making about the Negroes in Cicero and
Berwyn (recently in the news). Someone had said they didn't
want any damned niggers living next to them. She'd said,
"Why? They are people and were put here and they need to
live, too." She said she worked with them and they were
cooperative and when she needed anything at work they
gave it to her or did what she asked. She seemed to have
no hint of racism. This in Alabama! As I left for the trailer
I thought, "She would make a fine neighbor. I wish I could
know her better."

They followed the coastline with its beaches of white sand and
hummocks with coarse beach grass and watched the locals fixing
up their properties for the approaching winter tourist season –
"children's storybook playgrounds, amusement parks, eating places
with fetching facades." Consulting the trusty *Woodall's* Directory,
they found a camp and set off to explore New Orleans. They
walked the narrow streets of the fabled French Quarter, looked
half-heartedly in gift shops and had French coffee and beignets –
"a cross between raised doughnuts and cake, deep fried in squares
and dusted generously with powdered sugar. Very good."

So it's Westward Ho! The next day we entered Texas. You
can tell the difference immediately. Everything is grander.
The Welcome Station was all shiny grandeur with cute little
belles wanting to know could they 'hep' us. They could and
did. We got to Fort Worth about four. The car has been
getting somewhat balky – wouldn't reverse at times. Claude
began to suspect it needed a big overhaul. But it kept going
until this morning when it gave out. The mechanic we talked
to said it would be major, so we are scheduled to go into

town Monday for fixing. We are fearful the warranty won't
apply as there is a trailer involved.

We found the kids (Claudia and Giulio) fine and went out
to supper with them. They came to get us today. We hung
around, washed clothes and hair and I made a cap for Cara
for Christmas. We gave Claudia and Giulio their Christmas
picture and Allison her pink popcorn cap.

OCTOBER 29   It's been a busy week of Christmas shopping.
I have a box almost ready for Rose and one for Wallys, and
had the kids over for Claudia's birthday. We babysat several
times. Allison is quite the charmer. The car was finished on
Wednesday.

NOVEMBER 1   We pulled out today after driving by Leones
to say goodbye to Claudia and Allison. I'll miss them but it
was good to be on our way again. We're both getting itchy.
It turned windy and chilly, down to eleven degrees in the
panhandle we heard. We got to the Texaco station where we
stayed last year and unhitched, and then went to Guadalupe
for booze for cocktails for Apache Junction. We picked up a
barbeque supper that was less than so-so and came home.
I made popcorn and we played cribbage and two-handed
whist. I won, but Dad was not his best tonight.

CHAPTER 14

Arizona

...in love we live

NOVEMBER 4 We arrived at Blue Star Court about 2:30 and it was like homecoming. I got busses from Stringfields, Chance and Al Kohler. Al found me when I went to the hall to practice and he nearly toppled me from my piano bench. It was fun getting back to that too. I love that old piano with its easy action and lovely deep voice. Lovely, lovely night, cool and dark and still bugless. It stirs deep longings I can't seem to dispel. Claude played cards all evening with the boys.

NOVEMBER 16 Never time for everything unless you want to keep pushing which I don't. Still, life shapes up quite fully. We danced twice at Sunset and met new people. They urged us to come back. I've gone to the desert every day to walk. Some days the temperatures got up in the eighties so I sought shade in the arroyos under the palo verde. I spied a discarded mattress bleached through many months in the blazing sun and spread my plastic case over it had my little pillow along. On this I studied my Italian at length and am making notable progress. I surprise myself at how I amass the words and go forth each day with enthusiasm. I exercise each morning and play piano much more than I exercise. These eat up large pieces of time and energy but also make my days.

More murders have been reported in Mesa and Phoenix and I have been pressed to stay out of the desert. It seems I am worried about. So I promised to say within "safe" areas – whatever they are. I am too close to trailers to be comfortable conversing with myself in Italian. I'll have to work something out. I could cry! Under every eye, subject to every opinion!

Monday's dance was lovely – never more so I guess. Our own bunch was there – Stringfields, Moreheads, Gilberts, Rosenlofs, Williams and us. And many others we knew casually.

I made two crocheted sweaters and caps for Rose's girls' dolls and I'm knitting a set for Keeny's Kristy.

Gilberts arrived Thursday when I'd about given them up. We went to Trail Riders Saturday evening for a very nice time, and we have plans for next Thursday evening to dance at the Holiday Inn. Planned a Sunday outing with Carsons.

NOVEMBER 25   ...two good letters today, one from Lou Morrow and one from Helen (Vogel). Funny how the letters we appreciate most are those that express appreciation of us. Helen is so devoted and has such an exaggerated opinion of my "insight" and intelligence. I only wish I could fit that image to the real me. I guess I did have quite a lot of potential if some great soul could have molded and led me. So much time and energy is wasted in our floundering, and other lives consume so much of us.

DECEMBER 18   It's almost a month since I wrote, a month filled with writing Christmas cards and letters and playing with the natives — happy times. Nearly every day filled with friends. Carl and Nora left Friday for Las Vegas to visit his brother and then home to Long Beach for Christmas. We plan to go to Marg's Wednesday and may go up to Long Beach for a day if things work out.

The journals don't give a very clear idea of Claude's life in Arizona. In a Christmas letter written in 1966, Sue wrote this:

Claude is back at his golf and goes around several times a day; I swear he has more energy than I do when he finds something that interests him. When he has done that he goes to the hall and plays smear with the fellows for pennies. He spent a whole day uptown one day, looking at trailer houses. I wonder how many of those salesmen he had convinced he was all but signing on the dotted line. He came home dragging his tail, but we went dancing in the evening. He wasn't quite the gay young rake that night, though.

Sue was in love with life, with nature, with the freedom of the open road. And with Carl Gilbert. It's unclear exactly what the relationship was — a crush? A temptation? A flirtation? An affair?! I doubt it ever reached such a conflagration. Let's call it Sue's Dalliance. They met the Gilberts almost the first day they arrived in Blue Star in 1964. Both couples — Claude and Sue, Carl and Nora — were among those that went from court to court in Arizona to dance, and on short forays in the desert to explore their new world, mine Apache tears, drive the Apache Trail. Carl was the object of all the romantic longings she felt in Europe. As couples, they partied, visited each other's summer homes, traveled together on short trips. As couples. There were whispered endearments and prolonged embraces saying "welcome back" and "Vaya con Dios" at the end of the season. We kids knew about it. She told Claude, "I love him." Claude's only response, as recorded here at least, was hurt silence. Whatever Nora knew or thought remains a mystery. And then, as happens, it was over. I have left the hints exactly as they appeared in her written journals, no more and no less than she recorded them. By January 1967, the hopelessness of the situation was wearing on Sue.

> I'm trying to get back in the groove again after roaring through the holidays. This living on the epidermis of everything gets me in a semi-depressed state and I am more than glad to get back to normalcy. We had Christmas in San Diego and Marg came back with us.

> **JANUARY 15, 1967**   Life goes on, mostly pleasant but a few depressions when I remind myself, "This too shall pass." I still walk in the desert and practice my Italian. I have to keep drawing myself back to concentrate, but it works and pays off in learning. C scolded me for walking in the desert and threatened to start smoking again — we made a deal.
>   . . . Friday we met at Gilberts for martinis, ten of us. What a bunch of nuts! Fun evening.

> **JANUARY 23**   Another week of our waning lives — what a thought! And how quickly they fly. And how often I wonder how best to use them. I go to the hall for exercises though my body protests vigorously. Then there is the piano workout and I ask again: could I be better employed? Is our first duty to improving ourselves and our gifts, if such they be? But no answers come. Even when I was vigorously delving into religious literature I didn't have a clear cut sense of going in the right direction.

JANUARY 31   Carl and Nora left today for Mardi Gras
though Carl said yesterday he'd rather not go. He brought
over their extra oranges and tangerines. After "so long kisses"
(goodbyes are verboten) and safe journey felicitations, we
picked up Fay and went to the dance. It was nice, with
reservations. It's a good week to get caught up with guests
and to keep busy.

Friday I got ready for my birthday and party. I baked buns,
beans and cake and all turned out good, I thought. I had
everything ready when the five arrived – Art, Mary, Bryan,
Nora and Carl. I had seven paper placemats on the table
with napkins and little rhymes with their names clipped on.
While they had their appetizers I asked them to read their
verses. It went over well and they all took them along.

Here is Carl's:

> Here sits Carl, that frisky knave
> Tell the barkeep what you crave –
> Mountain Dew or Witches brew
> Or will you guzzle what we have?

Mary's:

> Mary, Mary quite the canary,
> Why do you sing so queenly?
> Do you sing for the sinner,
> Or sing for your dinner,
> Or sing you for a martini?

Bryan's:

> Twinkle twinkle little star,
> Bryan's place is where he are –
> In between two lasses yummy,
> Sit ye down and fill your tummy.

Nora's:

> Gentle Nora, so petite
> And charming, too, we think;
> Sit ye down and rest your feet
> And sip your little drink.

Claude's:

> Here sits Claude the host and master;
> Hope his drinks are no disaster,
> Take your seats and hold your hat,
> You'll soon find out what he has on tap.

We played Yahtzee and had cake and coffee later. I thought it a lovely party with good friends to help make it memorable.

Cards have been dribbling in from everyone. Rose says she is sending something in keeping with my new southwest swinging image. It was a picture of an Indian Maiden with a rhinestone in her navel saying Happy Birthday. She knows just what delights me. Also Claudia. We seem to communicate if infrequently and often wordlessly. And of course, our dear Lue – so faithful and understanding. Every day it proves more true: "In love we live. We die to life in proportion to how we fail in loving."

I had some 'making up' to do and it was done in such a thorough way! Ah, me.

Thursday was potluck with my big baking of dark bread. It's still accepted with great enthusiasm so I keep baking it in gratitude for its gracious acceptance.

Ah, yes, the dark bread. Sue developed the recipe for her iconic dark bread back in the 1930s or '40s and it was a staple of my growing up years – a combination of whole wheat and white flour made slightly sweet with molasses. For daily use it was hearty and healthy toasted with chokecherry jelly, fresh from the oven it was heavenly, with sour cream and brown sugar it was ambrosia. (That is, sour cream as it was in the old separator days of North Dakota, thick and glossy and tangy and probably a hundred and fifty percent butterfat.) Sue began taking a loaf of her dark bread for the potluck dinners at Blue Star and soon she was taking a full batch of four loaves it was so popular. Often she gave a loaf to a friend as a special gift; sometimes she sold it if there was a special request.

Occasionally I made it myself. Here is the recipe as she first recited it to me:

Mom's Dark Bread

Take your biggest mixing bowl, put in four cups of warm water and add half a cup of molasses, half a cup of brown sugar (packed), about a quarter cup of oil and four teaspoons of salt. Stir all this together until the sugary parts are dissolved. Then add a good tablespoon of yeast (one envelope) and stir it in. Let this sit in a warm place and go make the beds while you wait for the yeast to start working, maybe twenty minutes to half an hour. It should be all bubbly and frothy when it's ready.

Stir in four cups of whole wheat flour and then start adding white flour (flour made especially for bread is best), stirring it in as you go. Eventually, when you can't stir it in any more you have to turn it out onto a bread board to knead it. You'll probably use about eight cups of white bread flour in all. Let it rest on the bread board while you clean out the mixing bowl and grease it. Then you start the kneading process, rolling and pressing and adding handfuls of flour until the dough is soft and elastic and no longer sticky — probably about ten minutes or so. Put it back in the mixing bowl and cover it with a dishtowel and set it in a nice warm spot with no drafts and let it rise. After an hour or so when it's doubled in size, punch it down and let it rise again. The next time it doubles in size, punch it down and dump it out on the bread board or counter and divide it into four loaves. Grease your bread pans lightly, shape the loaves and put them in, cover the pans and let them rise once more. Start the oven set to 350 degrees. When the loaves have doubled in size, bake them for thirty minutes or so. You can test one to see if it's done by thumping the bottom of the loaf. It should sound hollow. Careful, though, it's hot.

The spring wore on with the usual dances and outings. The journal entries were further apart; they lost the sense of enthusiasm: …finished my red dress, looks nice…went to a new Methodist Church…groceries…

FEBRUARY 5 Spring has come to the desert and doves are nesting in the cholla. One had her nest all lined with cotton batting, but when I reached in to see if there were warm eggs, the cactus spines grabbed me like watchdog. Smart birds! I found a little oasis out there, spread my coat and looked at the sky through the palo verde and cholla. So lovely it's hard to concentrate on Italian.

MARCH 18 Saturday we had a party — hard times, St. Patrick's, pie social and dance all rolled into one. Several of the men dressed for a "fashion show" — Forbes, Riggs,

Nelson, Olson, Gilbert, Roselle and Rawson. They brought down the house. Carl went over and planted a big red kiss print on Walter Wickum's bald head. Then they auctioned the pies. Mine was the first and Joel Nelson got it. He still had on his frilly blouse and jumper, hat and gloves. The pie was pineapple lemon and a goodie. I made a hard times dress of an old sheet with a red collar pinned with a big safety pin, red belt and pockets, fringed at the hemline.

Tuesday we had a trying picnic at Lake Canyon that was almost a fiasco, with six couples. I'm getting panned, it seems, for being anti-social, which only makes me more so.

I wore Clara's green two-piece knit for the St. Patrick's dance. I only missed one dance, but there were strained relations.

*A couple of times during the season there would be
a dress up costume party at Blue Star.*

MARCH 19   Palm Sunday, just home from church. The choir sang "Open the Gates" with "I Know That My Redeemer Liveth" at the end. So beautiful. I shed tears through most of the service. Guess I'm a crazy mixed up "kid" as His Honor says. I used to think that as one matured his problems were wisely solved one by one until none remained. But now it seems it never changes. We only exchange one conundrum for another, and each seems overwhelming in its turn.

MARCH 26   Easter Sunday. We went to sunrise services with Gilberts and Stringfields at the Methodist church. It was chilly and most came in summer coats. The service started with people standing in the courtyard as the sun rose over the Superstition Mountains like a ball of fire.

Our time for parting draws nigh and it seems as if we cling a bit more to our minutes together and I feel the ties of friendship more keenly. There were sixteen or eighteen of us at the dance in the hall tonight.

Stringfields left...A pall settles over the Court as friends leave two by two. It's a quiet thing like October days, a token of separation...It rained – the first rain of 1967. Rain and tears fell together.

...Carl and Nora left today.

APRIL 3   Our last day in Blue Star. It's like pulling a tooth. Let's have it over with. There were chores and last visits among friends. I took a box of leftover sandwiches to desert birds and animals and took pictures of the blooming palo verdes out there. Then one last dance at Sunset with goodbye kisses and hugs.

They headed back once more to their alternative summer life. Mom told me once, "In Arizona we're Claude and Sue, up north

we're Grandma and Grandpa." The grandchildren were the consolation prize. They stopped at Claudia and Giulio's in Texas.

> The kids got away for a few days while we babysat Allison
> all week. Her most notable accomplishment was blowing
> her nose enthusiastically. Yesterday morning she sat in a big
> chair, took off her shoe and then her sock, which she put
> to her nose and blew hard. She looked very puzzled at my
> uncontrollable laughter.

Back in Moorhead they arrived in time for spring programs of
Wally and Lue's kids.

> Wednesday was the kids' orchestra concert. Patty played
> (violin) with the seventh grade group. There must have been
> a dozen violins, cellos and piano. Then the junior high came
> in with more instruments and finally the senior high with
> brass and more strings. Just awe-inspiring! Ricky played the
> piano for the second group. Friday I showed the Arizona
> pictures to Terry's grade and they seemed pleased.
>   Claudia's baby was born May 13th — Jill Erin, seven
> pounds, nine ounces.

It was a cold, rainy spring. Sue was looking for new areas of the
country to explore and this time it was to be a summer trip west
through Montana and into Canada. They planned stops at the
Fort Peck Dam and Many Glaciers in Montana and into Canada.
The weather was alternately rainy and hot.

> **JUNE 10**   We're all hooked up and ready to sail come
> morning. We have had a nice seven weeks here (at Wallys'
> in Moorhead), much as usual with busy days seasoned with
> some fun like bridge, scrabble and concerts. We saw one

movie: *A Man for All Seasons*. We're ready to leave for the
Gypsy Trail.

...we went to Banff. It was all it was reputed to be. We
took all the drives for which there were roads and some
of the nature walks. The first day we drove out to see
Hoodoos – weird shaped rocks in Tunnel Mountain Valley.
There is a fabulous lodge there with the Bow Falls nearby.

...we stopped at an Indian rodeo. I had the camera
aimed through the fence taking a few shots. I decided to
shoot just one more and caught a cowboy just as his horse
pitched him off. They carried him off on a stretcher with
what looked like a broken arm.

...We took a snowmobile ride over the glacier. Claude
couldn't take the rough ride – his angina acted up. For me
the ride was great. Columbia Ice Field, Athabasca Glacier, I
think. Later we stopped at Sunwapta Falls.

We got to Jasper about 6:30 and sat in the tent area
without a hookup until the next day. It rained, so we ate,
rested and played cards. Then I sewed on my wild screen
print blouse. I think I'll like wearing it. We plan a trip to the
east entrance tomorrow.

...picked up our mail at Lake Louise before going on to
Kicking Horse Park. Lue wrote about Rick's accident with a
loss of four teeth – what a misfortune. Also a letter from Carl.
Unhappiness over Keeny's letter kept us from full enjoyment.

On the way we stopped at Emerald Lake, a lovely spot with
blue-green water. It was a balmy perfect day. I walked a ways
down the hiking trail. Further down the highway we stopped
to see the natural bridge with water charging through weird
rock formations. Bears came every night to tip the garbage
cans for goodies to carry into the woods and chomp down.

Wednesday we took the drive six or eight miles to
Takakkaw Falls dropping 1,284 feet from the upper valley. We

stopped to eat our lunch at a wayside and then back to the trailer to find the bread I'd mixed pushing its hat off. I put it in tins while Claude hitched up and we drove to the Hoodoo Camp and took the nature trail through the Beaver swamp. When we got back to the trailer the bread was ready to bake.

Gilberts had been to the court twice to find us, so we set out to find them. We had drinks and then went out to eat. It's so good to see them again. Friday I packed a picnic for all and we drove out to Finn Creek. We made a fire as it was cloudy and chilly and sat and played cribbage until nearly three. Then we went back to the motel for drinks and home for tacos and pinochle. We had a nice evening together, but I think the prospect of parting again sobered us a bit. I had a lovely letter from Helen to cheer the barren hours that followed.

The trailer was hot so we put our Formica board on the water can outside and spread a rug and cushion and it worked fine. I found a radio station with good two-piano selection on the radio and read from my Ayn Rand and studied Italian. And so I called it a good day in spite of the heat. It's eleven o'clock and the trailer is just getting tolerable.

We drove another hour and the heat went up to 102. We asked at a camp if we could sit under their weeping willow and cool off. She said, "of course" very graciously, so I fixed a thermos of iced tea and we took our cribbage board and pillows and picked our way down the hill. A foot- wide stream ran by and we set our glasses in the cold water and they kept cool while we played two games of cribbage. Then on our hot way again.

They made for the Pacific and ran into traffic, exploring the coast they ran into forest fires and road construction. They headed back to the U.S.

AUGUST 21   We gave up seeing Vancouver. The Canadian customs dispatched us without incident, but in our pleasure in getting back to our own U.S. we inadvertently ran through U.S. Customs, at which important oversight they took out after us with siren screaming. Didn't we know, they demanded, they could impound our car and trailer over such an indiscretion? I said, "Oh, come now, you wouldn't do that to us would you?" and he returned, "It isn't me, it's the LAW!" They took six potatoes and two oranges to appease the insult. We took a side road through Kirkland to escape the sprawl that is Seattle, vowing to duck into the first trailer court that presented itself. We found a wonderful one and stayed two nights.

AUGUST 30   Saturday we took a picnic and went to Mount Rainier Park and Monday we took off for a two-day trip around Olympic National Park. We took a branch road up Hurricane Ridge where we looked out on the wilderness, a mass of snow-frosted mountains, some with glaciers. We saw a doe and two fawns on the road returning, so tame we got good pictures. Douglas fir loomed three hundred feet in the air. Later we stopped to pick wild blackberries and later still to run barefoot down the wet beach as the tide came in. Returned home about five, tired and glad to be back. But it was a lovely trip.

SEPTEMBER 17   We left Green Meadows court on Monday and spent the next night in Yreka, then to Sacramento. Claude called Keeny and she said we could come if we wanted to — a cold and dishearteningly formal invitation. But we did go out the next day. Nice house. Nice kids, Nice Vern. Good food, but no food for optimism. The preacher on the radio just said "Pray to God to make your tears make you a rainbow." I should someday have a nice one.

So we soon left and headed for Yosemite. We spent several days seeing the sights – Yosemite Falls, Glacier Point, Sentinel Dome and the Fire Waterfall Drop, Washburn Point Lookout and up Big Trees Drive, Hermosa and back home. One loop took us 135 miles.

Dalbols [Lue's family] came out the next day at noon. Bucky, Sharon and Paul, Harold, Edna and Tori. We did have a great time. We ate on the picnic table and then came in and played whist until 4:30. Then we took a picnic and went to Indian Caves, Mirror Lake and back to Yosemite Falls, returning with wood to make a camp fire and eat on our own tables. We sang around the fire until nine and then inside for more whist until midnight. Bucky's family slept inside while the others stayed in sleeping bags in the yard. A big black bear came in the night and raided the garbage, and we were all glad he'd found enough in the garbage to satisfy his appetite.

SEPTEMBER 28   Sunday we all had bacon and eggs in the trailer and then packed up and all (leaving the trailer behind) headed for Tioga Pass for a look see – three cars full. We stopped for lunch at Porcupine Camp. The sun came out of the clouds and we built a good bonfire, warmed the beans, buns and dogs and had a big fruit salad besides the dregs of yesterday's salads. Deer came up with two fawns and there were blue jays scavenging. A clear creek ran nearby. We played more whist – Harold and I won the final game for the record. Then we said goodbyes. Tomorrow we learn if we can negotiate Tioga Pass.

I put all our perishable food in our gasket box and set it on top of the car as it was near freezing. But quicker than scat a big bear came up and pulled his whole body up on top of the car and rummaged in our food supply. I shooed him off, flashlight in hand, at which he lumbered off with our Danish bacon. I put the rest in the car and soon he was back climbing up on the trunk. More shooing. Then Claude went out and turned on the car lights and here he stood with his feet up on the radiator looking him in eye. I guess that did it as he disappeared for the night.

Next day Tioga Pass came up quickly and we crawled along about ten miles an hour, but we kept intact and the drive was less frightening than we expected. We reached Rosamond before closing time and got a nice packet of mail.

Claudia and Giulio were in L.A. looking for an apartment. We went over next day to see the babies. Clemmy was feeding Jilly, so I got to see her. Sweet and adorable, of course. Allison woke up in an hour. Claudia and Giulio came out to our campground the next evening. They were busy apartment hunting and baby tending so we didn't see much of them. They move into their new place on Monday.

After a week in Long Beach visiting Gilberts, we spent a couple of days with Claudias. Giulio got a nice wage increase to about $916 a month, he said. They went out and bought a desk and a dinette set since we were there to babysit. We stayed over to celebrate Claudia's birthday and then went over to Gilberts to say bon voyage.

OCTOBER 31 We made the trip in one swoop. We arrived in Blue Star about five and the gang was having hamburgers in the hall and we were received with hugs and kisses. So wonderful! Gilberts arrived a week later — past due. Then they took off two days later for Flagstaff and returned for two more days before returning to Long Beach for their Golden Wedding Anniversary. In the meantime I'd been shopping. I got them a Guy Lombardo record containing "Lara's Song" from *Dr. Zhivago*, "He," and "What Now My

Love." Nora had expressed a liking for Lara's song. Now
it breaks them both up and especially Carl. I also picked
up the sheet music for it, mostly to learn the words. So
now "You Don't Know Me" and "Vaya Con Dios" have
a substitute.

They spent another Christmas in San Diego. Sue formed a real
affection for Marg's kids and their families. Tom always provided
her with stationery from his print shop and a box of See's chocolates. It seemed that Gene was called upon to fix their watches
every year.

Back at Blue Star things were not going smoothly.

> ... Gilberts returned again the fifth of January – on time this
> time. We've been spending lots of time together, dancing,
> eating – and quarreling!
> ... early March Marg came with Jackson and we danced
> ten times in fifteen days. Orville and Bill [Marg's ex and son]
> blew in and nearly sabotaged Marg's vacation. We were
> having our own family jar so everyone was upset for a couple
> of awful weeks.
> We left Blue Star on April 19. That morning we packed
> up, hooked up the trailer and said some goodbyes. Gilberts
> left and didn't come back for so much as a bon voyage. I left
> two little dishes, half a loaf of bread and Clara's letter on
> their step. Maybe it was better this way.

That was about the end of the Carl Gilbert saga. After that they
were just part of the crowd. Elsewhere, you may remember, 1968
was piling up horrendous events. Sue recorded the assassinations
of Martin Luther King and Robert Kennedy, noting that the lurid
TV coverage was getting almost commonplace. They were back in
Moorhead in time for the spring concerts, recitals and graduations.

CHAPTER 15

Accommodations

...Now here I am where I wanted to be

In July, 1968, my family arranged to spend a couple of weeks at Lake Le Homme Dieu not far from Wally's lake place. The folks moved their house on wheels to be our neighbors for a while and gave us a little taste of their life.

JUNE 30   We set up in the trailer court on Lake Carlos *[near Alexandria, MN]* on Friday. Rose and Irv arrived at their rental cottage on Lake La Homme Dieu so we went over and got them launched. We were there for pancakes on Saturday and they came here for dinner Sunday. Irv took the bus back to Minneapolis on Sunday and Rose stayed on for the week. We all went to the Runestone Museum in Alex and saw the stone claiming that the Norsemen had been through this area over 600 years ago, way before the Pilgrims.

JULY 4   ...took chicken and potato salad and went to have a picnic with Rose and the kids. Lots of folks around today with assorted trailers and campers. The state park filled up.

JULY 12   We all went back to Wally's lake lot today. Claude and I packed up and left as always with pleasure and ready

The Letofsky kids at Lake Le Homme Dieu, 1968.
Clockwise from the left: Polly, P.J., Laurie and Cara.

for adventure. I'm always ready. Claude took Laurie and
Polly with the trailer and we finished packing the Volkswagen
and tidying the cottage and then left with the rest of the
food and the rest of the kids. Bonnie is due in Monday by
plane with two or more kids.

AUGUST 31   We had a final weekend together at the lake. Wallys left Monday and we gathered up loose ends and went the next day. I got a blue blanket for Lue and Wally for three books of gold bond stamps and left it for their Christmas. . . . stopped in Jamestown for doctor's checkups and picked up warm sleepers for Arlene's kids so we can leave their Christmas box on the way.

The trip back took them once more through the Black Hills and Yellowstone Park. By now they were like old friends, but Sue never tired of their beauty and the restorative powers it held for her. This time, instead of going west, they went through the Rocky Mountain National Park in Colorado on the way to visit Duane (my cousin Butch) and Cookie who were stationed in Denver, Colorado.

Our next lap was through some of the most beautiful country I'd ever seen and I got some good shots. It was a hard pull with the trailer over the 14,000 foot divide and we made frequent stops for pictures and look-sees and to feed the chipmunks. They are so dear!

Nature has a way of soothing away fierce resentments. As beautiful as the drive was, I was glad when it was over. The last part went through Estes Park — too beautiful to describe. We got into a court about three, tired and sullen. But then we both slept and woke up somewhat refreshed and walked all around Bear Lake. The backward trip was all downhill, winding and descending through the golden apricot trees and snow frosted mountains.

We called Butch. The next day we went to their place on Aspen Terrace and drove out to Cherry Creek Recreation Park. Then back to Butch's for steak supper. I did so enjoy the kids both big and small.

OCTOBER 5   We entered Utah and the desert surroundings appeared as we headed south toward Bryce Canyon. At The Arches Monument we unhitched the trailer and drove and walked the arches. It was nearly dark the next day when we got to Bryce and set up in a campground. We spent most of Monday touring Bryce. The scenery is very striking and spectacular, but the park is small and not much variety. I walked to Inspiration Point and down another trail, but it proved to be one mile down, one across and one UP! And I do mean up. But it was very rewarding, filling the eyes and the heart. If I'd taken more time it would have been less strenuous, but Claude was waiting. I should learn to follow my own counsel. I met and visited with several couples. It's always interesting to chat with fellow travelers and we have yet to find a dull one.

Next day we toured Zion. Towering rocks erupt from the valley floor. I thought it might be another Bryce which was also lovely but so different. We viewed Bryce from the rim looking down into a vast expanse of orange colored pinnacles and weird formations, but we viewed Zion from the valley floor nearly falling over backwards as our eyes moved up the face of the solid rock cliffs. We took the mile and a half trail to see Weeping Mountain where the water ran off in sheets and the mountain was dewy wet – so lovely. I thank God every day for the privilege of travel, for health, for a zest for life, for not losing the sense of awe at the wonder of it all.

Evenings find us sated with travel and a bit dull of spirit and weary from it all, but next morning we do our appointed chores and are ready for the new adventure. We take off like little kids to the vacant lot to play ball. Claude seems to like to drive and I have my knitting which adapts itself neatly to the routine. I am training myself to knit without looking whenever possible. It works better than I dared hope, and it saves my eyes and lets me enjoy the views. Wearying of that, I take a turn at my Italian. If anything, I grow more interested not less. I've been through the little book several times and I'm reviewing the big one.

Wednesday we drove the fifty-six miles to Jacob Lake, the launching pad for the north rim of the Grand Canyon. After settling into the National Park campground, we packed lunch and started out for the north rim expecting one look and return. But after going the appointed forty-four miles, a spur led off to Angel Point round and round, up and up through evergreen forest punctuated with flaming golden aspens. We stopped at half a dozen lookouts, some quite awesome, and walked the course to a jutting point over Angel's Window. I drove most of it, stopping to take pictures wherever I chose. I was particularly charmed by the perfect little fir trees sitting proudly beside their elders, like well-behaved children.

When we came back to the trailer, a happy-faced little man approached and asked if he could park beside us. He was a widower pulling a little trailer and seeing the world. He said he was wholly on wheels now. He had such a wholesome outgoing disposition I'm sure he is not lonely very often. We had martinis and I fried the chicken wings and stewed them in wine. I thought them delicious. Whether it was the martini or the wings, I'll never know.

The return to Blue Star was more subdued. The journals began losing steam and became less enthusiastic and more cryptic, many tinged with sadness:

Bob and Dotty stopped and decided we weren't home, so we missed the Trailer Village dance. Just as well. . . . cleaned trailer for Sunday's party...nice turnout for the dance in the evening, bad night...warmth of friends and family here and away very uplifting. Just withdrawn sullenness at home.

Claude took a nap and golfed. I hit for the desert – it has a healing quality. Who said, "If thou art worn and hard beset with sorrows that thou wouldst forget, go to the woods and hills; no tears dim the sweet look that nature wears"? [It's from Longfellow's "Sunrise on the Hills."] Italiano didn't take that day, so I dredged up Hound of Heaven. Some lines I had to probe for, but it had the same old appeal once it surfaced.

FEBRUARY 22   Arlene's Grant Stewart was born, weighing in at seven pounds thirteen ounces. She had to stay over a few days because of blocked roads.

FEBRUARY 27   Much saddened by Helen's [Vogel] death – my dear, dear Helen – always staunchly defensive of me. She felt, she always said, that I brought her much in ideas, insight, and inspiration. I know she did for me. She was one of the greatest people I've ever known and so long as I live I shall no doubt be most grateful for her gentle understanding of my plight through the years, especially during the Dexter episode. Looking back I see how ridiculous were the accusations hurled at me, but perhaps all things do work together for good. Now I have a better perspective and am better able to ignore and surmount intrusions into my life and thought. As the song goes, "I gotta be me." Helen was not only willing to let me but rejoiced that I was. So when such an outstanding personality passes beyond the veil I wonder again: Does all this wisdom and accumulation of abundant living cease to exist? Is she in some fairer sphere watching above us? Can her influence still be wielded on my behalf?

...returning to the trailer I found the knitting bag with a number of autographed books Helen had given me and some of mine to her, and I recalled again our most precious friendship. Truly, those must have been the best days of my life, and at the time I thought them hardly endurable. And I wouldn't have endured them except for her understanding and encouragement – "and the greatest of these is love."

Back in Minnesota Claude and Sue spent more and more time camped at Wally's place on Leaf Lake while their family came and went as their time allowed.

AUGUST 12   Lue went into town *[Moorhead]* early for various appointments leaving only Tootsie *[the dog]* and Wally. She returned around seven with Raul (a Mexican boy), Patty (who'd been relieved of her job), Terry from the orthodontist, and Tony from his swim test. The kids swim like fishes, and it's a relief. Becky played in the tree house with Robin all afternoon. Laura and I played scrabble. I fried a heap of sun fish and had fried spuds, slaw and fresh buns, ice cream with hot chocolate sauce. MMMmmmm.

This was to be the year of Eastern Canada – Montreal, Prince Edward Island, Nova Scotia and Newfoundland. Sue was running out of travel routes in North America. Claude was running out of patience. The diaries were beginning to repeat themselves. They left at the end of August, stopping at the usual places. They got to our place in South Minneapolis the week of the Minnesota State Fair – again. They parked behind the Dairy Queen on Nicollet again and, as a special treat, Polly and Cara got to sleep in the trailer one night. Then it was on to Bonnie and Oscar's in Winnetka outside of Chicago. They visited the Ford Museum in Detroit and crossed into Canada through the Windsor Tunnel. After a flurry of going through customs, getting tied up in traffic and briefly lost, they pointed the Dodge toward Montreal.

SEPTEMBER 6   We continued on to Montreal and settled into a court across the river. We planned to go to the World's Fair the next day, but it was cold and cloudy and Claude couldn't take the weather. I tramped around until four on my own and then got on the metro going the wrong way – it took me into Montreal. The men at the terminal there got me squared around and I went back to "Man and His World" *[World Expo]* and continued on to the next terminus. Now here I am where I wanted to be.

SEPTEMBER 9   We reached a little town just beyond Montmarti in the rain. Today I spent writing letters and resting, crocheting and napping. Our landlord is a good Joe who comes to see if we are all right and urges us to be sure to let him know if we need anything at all (unlike the guy at the magazine stand at the metro who flung our twenty dollar bill at us after refusing to give us exchange).

The wind went down and it was a beautiful day. We went to find our friend chopping wood and on the way discovered a bunch of chokecherries, large and ripe to bursting. So we picked a pail full plus a couple of tin cans we scrounged from a dump. He showed us his woods, going on in his broken English with a French accent and dropping his H's and putting them in front of the vowels. He is a sweet one! He stops in several times a day to ask if he can help. As we were getting ready to leave he arrived with two loaves of homemade French bread, a quart of cream and a pound of butter not yet proven.

So we took our leave. The road led up the coast of the St. Lawrence with its rocks and islands, in and out, up and down through many little French villages and out into higher mountains covered with pine with the river between. We are gorging ourselves on white bread toast and chokecherry jelly, peaches and real cream.

SEPTEMBER 12   We took a very rough road that shook up the trailer rather badly. I kept going in to put stuff away. We finally got to a trailer park in the country near Tormentine, New Brunswick, where we will get the ferry to Prince Edward Island. We left the trailer and took the car across. We had fried clams for lunch and then explored all afternoon. We saw the famous house of Anne of Green Gables. The area is dotted with small farms and fishing villages.

They headed for Truro and near the gateway to Nova Scotia, they found a beautifully landscaped, sunken rock garden and a Scotsman playing his pipes. They parked the trailer in a lovely terraced court in Antigonish and set out on the Cabot Trail. They stopped in Sydney where they booked passage on *The Leif Erickson* to take them to Newfoundland. In Port aux Basques they went out to explore on foot when a car stopped and asked if they needed a ride anywhere. The driver was Reverend Best, a local pastor, who proceeded to give them a personal tour of the town, with commentary on its history and geography. It's built on solid rock with winding streets and narrow roads, up and down hills, mostly unpaved. Retracing their steps they hooked up the trailer and turned south along the coast of Maine, back in the U.S.A.

By this time Vern had been reassigned, and Keeny and Vern were at Otis AFB in Massachusetts. This time the welcome was warm. They celebrated Scott's seventeenth birthday with tacos and angel food cake. Sue admired "Keeny's excellent knitting that makes mine seem primitive. She does all things well." And then they went off to the Yarn Barn and got thirteen skeins of imported yarn for fifty cents a ball, enough for crocheted vests for every granddaughter with some left over. Janie wore hers to school and reported that her friends all "wished her Grandma would make vests for them."

> So they all got early Christmas presents. Not the best way to give Christmas gifts but it's sure nice to have it done. We have left some at each place we went through.
>
> Vern got in late from his flight. It's hard to imagine a nicer guy – always amiable and generous. He urged us to come back soon. He and Claude fixed the water heater and refrigerator. Keeny made swordfish for dinner—delicate and flavorful and rich.

They drove through White Plains, through New Jersey's upscale neighborhoods of exurbanite New Yorkers and through their run-down cities and bad traffic. They drove through Amish country and ate soft pretzels and shoo-fly pie. They drove through the Shenandoah Valley on a clear day, and Sue took pictures with a guy from Canada while Claude rested. They went out of their way to see the Natural Bridge near Lexington, one of the seven natural wonders of the world, and were impressed. They broke a hook off the trailer hitch outside the Smokey Mountain National Park and enjoyed perfect weather and fall colors while it was being fixed. They survived the traffic and tourist shops of Gatlinburg, Tennessee, and stopped at a campground where they stayed six years ago in their first little red trailer.

Outside of Oklahoma City they picked up a young Indian boy, drenched and cold from hitchhiking in the rain, took him into the trailer for lunch and dried his sweater. Sue was about to give him a dollar, but he darted from the car at the freeway exit before she could offer it. She found New Mexico to be barren and monotonous, but nevertheless fascinating, and they entered Arizona near Springerville. They came down again through the Salt River Canyon and arrived at Blue Star early, about October 15.

OCTOBER 25 A nice letter from Keeny made our day.

The diaries dwindled, recording only the most mundane events in short and cryptic entries. And then they stopped altogether for almost a decade.

CHAPTER 16

Settling

...I often think I am singularly blessed

The families were on the move. Oscar, sick of Chicago winters, persuaded Bonnie to finally make the move to Florida even though it meant starting over building his surgery practice. They moved to Plantation, a suburb of Fort Lauderdale in 1970. Vern was transferred to Homestead AFB south of Miami, so they were nearby. Wally was transferred from Moorhead, Minnesota to Mandan, North Dakota, and so they moved from the lakes to the western plains. Giulio finished his armed service and residency and they moved back to the Chicago area, settling in Palatine in 1971 where he eventually opened his dermatology clinic.

We Letofskys stayed put in Minneapolis where events moved in on us. In the sixties our neighborhood was a microcosm of what was happening in the country. My two best friends, Becky and Cyndy, and I shared coffee and recipes, hauled kids, and went camping together. Our husbands – a cop, an Urban League executive and a newspaper reporter (and now comedy writer, too) – sort of covered the social and political landscape of the time. But things change. By the mid-seventies Becky had returned to teaching, Cyndy had earned her RN, and I had gone back to graduate school and was working for an educational publisher. All of us were divorced.

Claude and Sue were still traveling, spending summers at Leaf Lake and winters at Blue Star and in between they pulled the trailer from kid to kid, friend to relative. But the grand theme tours of the sixties were pretty much over. In the fall of 1972, as they were navigating the short stretch between Bonnie's in Fort Lauderdale and Keeny and Vern's south of Miami, a driver cut in front of Claude. He braked, moved to the shoulder, but in the move back into the traffic lane a tire on the Pathfinder caught, flipping the trailer and then the car. Amazingly, neither of them was hurt. Vern came to collect them and salvage what they could of the trailer's contents. Over the days that followed he helped them navigate the chaos that such an accident brings – the insurance, replacing the car, calming their nerves with good food and bridge.

Their daughter Janie remembers: "I came home from school that day and the garage door was open and it looked like it was hit by a tornado, debris everywhere. Grandma and Grandpa were very quiet and subdued – in shock maybe. Grandma talked about a premonition she had the night before when she woke out of her sleep to a voice telling her to be careful on the highway."

Then, hauling their rescued belongings in a U-Haul hitched to a new car, they made a beeline for Blue Star. Undaunted (well, maybe a little daunted) they replaced the Pathfinder with the Kenskill.

In Blue Star their activities stayed the same, only now they were different. They still went to dances at the hall in Blue Star and to the courts nearby. Sometimes Claude and his buddy Shorty went to the Elks Club dances and Sue stayed home (She couldn't stand the smoke). They still went on picnics in the desert, to Saguaro Lake and the Apache Trail, but now those trips were to entertain visitors. The desert around Blue Star where Sue once escaped to practice Italian and watch the sky and pine away in solitude was being transformed into yet more trailer courts for snowbirds from the north. She still baked dark bread for the potlucks, only now she was baking twelve loaves at a time. She played bridge, bingo and pinochle, carefully recording the scores and winnings. She started a bingo pot and at Easter the winnings were added to her Easter offering.

She still went to the hall to play the piano and provided the accompaniment for sing-alongs. Somewhere along the way she discovered Bill Streu, a fellow musician who played the saxophone. Or at least he had played it thirty years ago and dug it out on his retirement. Bill was delighted to find someone to play music with and his wife, Jean, was delighted to have him entertained. It took a while to find the right mix. Bill pretty much played popular music and so she played along, relearning the old favorites like "Galway Bay" and "Peg o' My Heart."

Gradually she introduced him to classical music, combing the music stores for arrangements that could be adapted for piano and sax. Then she eased him into the more religious classical – "Ave Maria" and "The Holy City." He balked at hymns, however, and she balked back and declared him to be "out of line" when he downright refused in a snit to "play all that hymnal stuff." Before too long they were providing the entertainment for gatherings in the hall and booking Christmas concerts in the nearby courts.

They had to practice in the hall – the only place with a piano – and since the hall was the center of activity for the court, this was not always easy. Other groups were pretty good about sharing and it was not unusual for Sue and Bill to provide musical background for the ladies' quilting group in one corner, the guys' game of smear in the kitchen, and the committee decorating for the next event. Sue longed for a piano of her own that she could play whenever she wanted to. Claude vetoed it.

At Christmas Sue wrote long, chatty letters to dozens of relatives and friends she had accumulated along the way – first hand written, later typed on the old portable Smith Corona I had in college. Every year the list grew longer. She scorned the practice of sending form letters. "I try to read the mind and soul of the one addressed and see if I can judge what they are interested in hearing."

Sue crocheted a couple of afghans, developing her own patterns, and was pleased with the results. She set out on a mission to make an afghan for everyone in the family. She consulted us, one by one, on our preferred color and pattern. Then she turned to making them for the grandkids (by then there were about 25) and smaller baby afghans of the softest downiest pastels for the new babies. She sleuthed out yarn sales, puzzled over new stitches, experimented with new color combinations and learned to crochet without looking, while she watched TV and when they were on the road.

By the mid-seventies Marg had retired and remarried and was living in a trailer court nearby. Laura and Willard moved into that same court. Unlike Claude and Sue who were still traveling back and forth with the seasons, Margs and Willards stayed through the blistering Phoenix summers. Laura returned from shopping one day and found Willard on the floor outside the bathroom, dead.

When Claude and Sue left Blue Star in the spring they dawdled along the way, parking in welcoming spots, but mostly the destination was the lot on Leaf Lake. Wallys no longer lived close enough to be there regularly, but it was still a magnet for holiday weekends. Gordon and Arlene's cabin was just a few paces away and there was room for campers and tents in what amounted to a family compound.

Then it happened again. On the Interstate near Valley City, North Dakota, the trailer was caught in the wake of a passing semi, flipped over and took the car with it. Again, they escaped major injury. Sue had a scrape on her leg. Claude was seventy-five. Reluctantly they got the message: it was time to stop dragging their home behind them on that long drive twice a year. They bought two permanent mobile homes – one in Blue Star and one on Leaf

Lake that replaced the little green "toaster"camper that had been the anchor for Wallys.

Their summers at Leaf Lake took on a rhythm all their own. They would arrive in late May, brush the spiders off the windows, empty the mouse traps, mow the grass, prime the pump and prepare for the weekend. During the week it was quiet enough, time for leisurely games of Yahtzee with their morning coffee, walks to the mailbox when Sue relearned the poetry she'd memorized in earlier years. The weekends were busier when the younger generations came to camp and party and get away from the humdrum of the work week.

The bookend holidays, Memorial Day weekend ushering in season and Labor Day weekend wrapping it up in the Fall, defined the summer along with the really, really big 4th of July in the middle. Year by year these events grew as the families grew. They came with their campers and tents and coolers and grills; they came with their toddlers and teenagers and their teenagers' friends. They came with their boats and canoes and water skis and fishing poles. It was where the cousins really got to know each other paddling in inner tubes and hunting frogs and inventing games in the tree house.

And they came with their food. Somehow, without a great deal of coordination or fuss, grills would be lighted and communal meals would materialize on the picnic tables outside. Sue usually contributed a double batch of dark bread, an enormous pot of baked beans, and her special chocolate Texas sheet cake. "Twenty-one for dinner," Sue recorded once in the mid-seventies. Then it grew. Forty-five one year and the top, in one gigantic reunion, they fed seventy-five.

A long weekend might feature one supper of Sue's tacos. She made her own tortillas, a Betty Crocker cum North Dakota adaptation, and multiple electric fry pans were set up with long extension cords to fry the tortillas to be filled with not-too-spicy hamburger, lettuce, tomato, cheddar cheese and tomato sauce with the faintest whisper of chili powder. A Mexican might not recognize them as tacos, but we loved them.

Not everyone was into action. The guys usually had a project or two – pouring concrete for a patio or repairing the dock – the women had sewing and craft projects to share. The Scrabble board was always in mid-game. They could almost always round up four for a revolving marathon game of bridge at the round table under the tree, and when things quieted down at dusk and the mosquitoes descended, a group would gather on Gordon's screen porch for the ever-expandable, age-adaptable game of Shanghai, or at the fire pit for s'mores.

By Sunday evening or Monday they would begin to gather their soggy, sandy towels, their empty Tupperware containers, their tired, cranky, mosquito-bitten kids and head back to their real lives.

Bonnie and Oscar vacationed several times at the Fair Oaks resort nearby where there was golf, sit down dinners and less chaos. Keeny and Vern came through once in a while in their RV. Arlene came occasionally, sometimes with Merrill and the kids, mostly alone (it's not easy for farmers to get away in the summer). I couldn't get there often, but once in while we loaded up and headed west for a little lake rehab and extended family fix.

In the summer of 1977 Claudia and Giulio rented a cabin on Pelican Lake, an easy drive from the compound at Leaf Lake. Claudia drove up with the three girls, Allison, Jill and Paula, and Giulio flew into Fargo with "The Guys," their surprise bonus born in 1975 – the twins Nathan and Matthew. By the end of the summer Claudia had arranged to buy a cabin of their own.

That summer Claude and Sue celebrated their 50th wedding anniversary at the local Cormorant Inn. We all came and celebrated with food and wine and toasts. Someone suggested I write up a clever re-cap of their fifty years together, and I tried, but I couldn't do it. All I could see were hard times and conflict – not funny. Among the articles and journals Mom left me is a magazine

The family at Claude and Sue's 50ᵗʰ Anniversary. Standing from the left: Keeny, Rosemary, Wally, Claudia and Bonnie. Sue and Claude seated.

clipping that features a very elderly, very dour couple sitting lump-ily under a sparkly "Happy Anniversary" banner. The caption is, "But they'll always have Paris." It tickles me every time I see it, and it must have done the same for her. There's something to be said for surviving the storms and vicissitudes of fifty years of marriage, but I wasn't ready to say it then and I'm not sure she was.

Sue discovered Elderhostel, the program of mini-courses of travel and education for the adventurous retired. She attended her first Elderhostel in 1976. She came to Minneapolis on the bus and I drove her down to the beautiful campus of St. Olaf College in

Northfield. She was excited to be on a college campus again; I was jealous. This one featured classes in music, religion and poetry – just her cup of tea. Claude wasn't interested; he was content to putter around the place.

I spent most of the seventies on the edge of chaos and poverty as a single mom trying to steer my four kids through their teenage years without calamity. Fortunately they were better at it than I was. Irv helped, of course, but he had moved to California. I was trying to make it as a freelance writer, writing almost anything anyone would pay me for – company newsletters, multi-media scripts, brochure copy, speeches, magazine articles. For eight years I was a local "stringer" for *People* Magazine back when it featured real profiles of interesting people. One of my contracts was with the Ebenezer Society, a large non-profit organization in Minneapolis that specialized in care for the elderly. I wrote their fund-raising appeal letters, the employee newsletter and the quarterly magazine.

One spring day as I was waiting in line at the photo shop to pick up pictures for the next issue, I noticed the guy ahead of me in line. He was holding a blank check and I could see the name on the top – John Rawson. Hmmmmm. Rawson. The line was slow and I struck up a conversation. "I see your name is Rawson. My name is Rawson, too...there aren't that many of us..." "Where do your people come from...South Dakota? Mine are from North Dakota..." "...coincidence..." We picked up our photos (his were also for a company publication), shook hands, called each other cousin, and I went home to work on my deadline. Mid-afternoon the phone rang. "Is this the Rosemary Rawson who was picking up pictures at Brown Photo this morning? ...You know, I have a book of Rawson genealogy I think you might be interested in. Could we have lunch?"

We lunched in the safety of the tea room in Donaldson's Department Store in Southdale. He was a widower with young adult kids, three boys and a girl – the mirror of my three girls and a boy. His girl and my boy, within two months of each other in age, were both pursuing careers in music. He liked camping and canoeing in the Boundary Waters. I loved camping, but hadn't ventured beyond the state parks. He had OPERA TICKETS! He invited me to dinner and the opera the following week and I accepted. We met each other's kids and introduced them to each other. We were engaged by fall and married a year later. Our kids were giddy with relief that their aging parents had found somebody.

He did show me the book on Rawson genealogy, and with a little sleuthing and consultation with my parents, we discovered that our last common ancestor was born in 1653 in Massachusetts Bay Colony. William Rawson married Anne Glover and they had nineteen children. Seven of them survived to adulthood. William junior began the line that led to John. His brother Nathaniel, seven years younger, began the line that led to me. I didn't even have to consider whether or not to change my name. It seemed like destiny.

Here is Sue's account of the wedding:

> **JUNE 27** We arrived in Minneapolis at their new home on Girard Avenue for the rehearsal gathering. John gave Rosemary a string of pearls that his dad had given his mother. All John's kids were there except Chuck who had to work. His stepmother Ruth and her daughter Sue (who is very young and pretty) were there with Sue's hubby Dave. Gobs of food and snacks with wine and soft drinks. We stayed there overnight. John has moved in (into the new house) and Rosie is still at her old house with the kids. It's our 53rd Anniversary.

> **JUNE 28** The day of the wedding dawned beautiful and sunny but not hot. The wedding was in the Fireside Room of the Mayflower Congregational Church, simple and nice. Rosie wore a dusty rose silk wraparound dress with embroidered yolk — beautiful. They wrote their own vows. P.J.

played a Beethoven sonata and Kathy a Chopin nocturne. John Jr. and his wife Dianne played and sang "You Are My Miracle." It ended with a lighting of the candles, the kids from each family taking turns until eight candles were lit and Rose and John lit that last one, symbolizing the joining of the two families. After a flurry of picture taking we all went out to the Olympic Country Club where we had a most delicious brunch of melon, blueberry muffins and eggs Benedict. Friends started arriving at the reception at one o'clock. More great stacks of food appeared, and of course, the wedding cake. I saw Winnie and Becky, her old neighbors. It was a great celebration with many of family gathered together.

I was astonished that the whole family drove across the country to attend my second wedding. Only Claudia and Giulio's family were unable to come. Claudia's twins, The Guys, were already booked to be ring bearers at a Leone wedding in St. Louis.

1980 was the spring of granddaughters for Wally and Lue. In the space of three months Patty had Christina (Stina), Becky had Sarah and Ricks had Rachel.

Claudia and Giulio had settled nicely into life at their cabin by then. That included a garden that came to play a major role in lake life, especially Sue's. Typically Claude and Sue would arrive from Arizona in late May and one of the first priorities would be to plant the garden. Usually the garden was rototilled and ready to plant by Claudia's neighbor, Felix. By the time Claudia arrived with her brood the radishes were peeking out in a neat row beside a ruffle of new lettuce.

JULY 3 Getting ready for the Big Gather. (4th of July) The day dawned cool and windy. I used up the day making chokecherry jelly from last summer's juice and went to Claudia's to pick spinach. The peas and beans are full of

blooms and little zucchini are on all the plants and should
be ready to pick in a couple of days. Made sheet cake and
beans, ironed and cleaned. Wallys came in (from Mandan)
just as we were finishing supper.

JULY 15   Went to Claudia's to pick veg and got seventeen
quarts of beans, three or four of peas, plus beets and the
last of the spinach. Found I had two wood ticks attached
when I got home.

JULY 21   Claudia says the beans and peas are READY.
Good day for picking. Picked two gallons of beans, shelled
two quarts of peas, plus onions and half a bushel of
zucchini. Also some cucumbers and carrots. I had a nap in
the bunkhouse and when I woke up Claudia was making
spaghetti and salad for supper. We played Scrabble and
Shanghai and got home late laden with bags of vegetables.

By the end of July the copious harvest from Claudia's little
garden was supplying fresh vegetables to friends and family and
complete strangers who happened by. Little Nathan complained,
"I hope we're not having those little green balls again."

The arrival of August signaled it was time to be on the lookout
for chokecherries. Keeny's Jane remembers Sue in chokecherry
season:

"When Grandma picked chokecherries, she was on a mission —
she'd be up on the ladder with her white plastic bucket strung with
a string around her neck, both hands reaching and stripping like
a windmill. She out-lasted and out-picked all of us."

Sue wrote:

We all picked until nearly dark and got about twenty
quarts I would guess. Most of the next day was given over

*The Leones at the lake. Clockwise from the left: Giulio, Paula, Jill,
Claudia with Nathan, Allison with Matthew (or the other way around).*

to extracting the juice. It made a terrible mess. Every large kettle was conscripted plus all utensils, pans and dippers and strainers. Tins were full, drainers filled . . . stove was a disaster. Claude picked over and washed most of them which helped enormously. By three o'clock I had cleaned up and fixed my hair and was more than ready for a nap.

AUGUST 8   Got a letter from Carl saying that Nora can no longer eat or talk and she is skin and bones. I lay awake last night thinking and praying for them. I can see him sitting there crying. Poor guy.

AUGUST 11   Cool and hazy today after fog in the morning. Giulio's plane was two hours late getting in. Claudia and kids came for hot dish, green beans with bacon, cottage cheese, fresh bread with chokecherry jelly. Shanghai and cookies for dessert. I wrote to Carl. Keeny called from Fargo. Vern's mom is very bad.

AUGUST 14   Went to Claudia's and got her loaded and started out with five kids and two cats. Keeny and Vern went into Fargo again. Nice day, sunny but not hot. Lovely puffy clouds in a clean clear sky.

AUGUST 15   I called Claudia to see if they got home okay. She said it was a wonderful trip home and it had been a wonderful summer. I feel the same. We sustain each other in many ways and our lives are enriched by the other. That's as it should be for everyone, though I often think I am singularly blessed.

SEPTEMBER 1   Went to Claudia's and picked about ten pounds of tomatoes and found two enormous zucchini;

pulled up the plants. Claude cleaned the freezer in the shed and scoured the oven racks and the bread pans – that was a real help. The men pulled in the dock and the boats and buttoned them down for winter and before dark they were all gone.

SEPTEMBER 9   I got a note from Carl. Nora died August 26, buried on the 30th. . . . Nellie *[Claude's sister]* fell again and the decision was made to move her to the nursing home. It's sad to see old friends deteriorating and I thank God again our health is as good as it is. Claude went in for a blood test.

Back in Arizona they settled again into the life of Blue Star. In November Sue fell on the concrete patio and broke her arm. They went as planned to Florida and spent Claude's birthday and Christmas with Bonnies and Keenys. While they were there, Oscar arranged to have the cast removed from her arm. "I couldn't believe how wasted my arm was. It's very sensitive, but the splint acts like a security blanket. I took a bath in hot water and was happy to learn I was able to squeeze the sponge."

In January, 1981, Wally's Becky had a baby boy. They named him David. He was premature, a six-month baby and very small and frail. In February Sue recorded, "Baby David is still doing okay." But in May she wrote, "Wallys are pulling themselves together after burying baby David. Such a sad homecoming, but everyone is coping beautifully." He was wearing a monitor because his breathing was irregular, but they woke one morning to find him still and gone. He was the only baby we ever lost and Wally never forgot to list him among his grandchildren.

That fall Sue went for the second time to the ALCW (American Lutheran Church Women) retreat at Garrison Camp in western North Dakota. The first time she reported enthusiastically about the sessions and the fellowship. This year she was invited to be one of the speakers to present a "lay sermonette." She worked on it off and on through the summer, recalling the difficult days of the early fifties and her spiritual and intellectual awakening with Dexter Marsh.

> This is the Big Day. The church was packed for my sermonette. I got many kind remarks and I was quite astounded at the response. It was an altogether beautiful two days. I hope the inspiration lingers for at least a year or until I can go again.

Sermonette — ALCW Garrison Retreat, Summer 1981

As John the Baptist came preaching a gospel of repentance, so a young student minister came out of the east teaching a gospel of love. I well recall those June days as he came and sat on the front porch with me, a young man full of the spirit and fervor of his youthful conversion.

It had been a rather difficult winter for me. I was keeping high school students, rooming and boarding them since it was in the days before bussing. Also I was teaching private piano lessons, sewing, washing, ironing, doing whatever I had opportunity to do to earn a few extra dollars to help our older children with college expenses. Days were full and demanding. I would awaken at night still exhausted from the day's demands and would be overwhelmed with the thoughts of the treadmill nature of my life. That is not to say that I wasn't also going to church, teaching Sunday school and playing for services.

So this fresh approach to the gospel of love entered my soul and life and gave it a new meaning. Though the poignant, breathtaking first flushes of conversion ebbed and surged again, life was never the same after that. I looked at the golden stubble fields with a new vision since now all things were of God in a special way. The sunsets were almost painful in their beauty. And that winter the lights on the new fallen snow sparkled with a new brilliance.

I pondered deeply of the "eternal verities": If God is love, then all love must be of God. And if that be true, then can sin be only the failure to love in our lives?

The First Commandment tells us we must love; thou SHALT, it says, love the Lord your God with all your heart, with all your soul, with all your mind and with all your strength. "With all your heart" suggests that we love with all the power of our emotions. We are to offer him the first place in our emotional lives. "With all our souls" demands that our spiritual strength is to be all His. He is to have our worship and praise daily, hourly, always. The First Commandment says moreover, "You must love the Lord your God with all your mind." This suggests to me that we must meditate upon the words of scripture — read, grow mentally by study, reading and thought, into the knowledge of God. Then, also, we must love God with all our strength. Does this not suggest to you that we must direct our physical energy into activities that will serve God and glorify Him?

And then Jesus put on the crowning touch with, "You must love your neighbor as yourself." Ah, here is something you can get your hands on, so to speak. Something palpable. How wonderful to be able to love God through loving each other. And what wonderful wealth of opportunities present themselves to us throughout a lifetime. And what a comfort to know that every loving thought, word and deed is from God Himself, since God is Love — and Love is God.

And so, reinforced with a new interest in knowing better how love works in a workaday world, I decided to put it to a test. For instance, how would it work in the business world? Well, I am no business woman, but I do know that when I have been treated in a kind, loving way in a place of business, it makes my day. And how gratefully we return to those merchants who treat us fairly. And how we appreciate the workman who gives his time and skill to serve us in our need without exacting the last possible dollar for it.

How then would love work in the political arena? Have we not all longed for someone who cares, someone who can be trusted, to represent us in government? Yes, someone who does love his fellow man more than his job.

Or take the world of crime — does love work here? Is it a practical way to deal with the criminal? Statistics prove that it is. They tell us in unmistakable terms that most crimes are committed by those who feel that they are unloved (and they probably are). If we love enough, could we, indeed, empty our jails?

Or take the mentally ill. One chaplain who served our church when we were temporarily without a minister and who had been serving as chaplain to the mentally ill in the state hospital for the insane, told us that not one person there felt that anyone loved him; could enough love also empty the mental hospitals? Would anyone who loved his neighbor set his house on fire or vandalize his place of business? Would anyone who loved all people everywhere want to drop a bomb on them?

It seemed to me that the only extent to which love had failed in any area was the extent to which it hadn't been tried.

The heart of the Christian aches to see and hear of the results of man's inhumanity to man, throughout the world. And he wonders how one person can love enough to make any impression on the vast sea of suffering. My conclusion is that every least loving act or thought diminishes by so much the sin and sorrow of the world. Multiplied by millions of loving hearts and caring people the impact should be substantial.

So let us never weary of well-doing, reminding ourselves constantly that faith, hope and love abide. But always, the greatest of these is love.

Shall we pray: Gracious Lord, thou living source of all love, spread thy love abroad in our hearts, that people seeing us may say with those in our Lord's day on earth, "Behold how they love one another." Amen.

CHAPTER 17

Claude

...a year of mistakes and broken dreams

Sue was getting more involved with her church – her churches – both Epiphany Lutheran in Arizona and St. Peter's in Minnesota. In Arizona she joined the Bible study group and the choir, sometimes providing the special piano music for the offertory at Sunday services. When she was asked to be a lector, reading the scripture for the service, she accepted. In Minnesota she provided the special music for the service whenever she was asked and when Pastor John asked if she'd like to go with him to the Sunnyside Nursing Home and do the music for his small church service there, she happily agreed. "I was a nice experience," she wrote. "It is a real joy to contribute to something like this and I get ever fonder of Pastor John."

She carried the practice back to Arizona and she and Bill played for a nursing home there. She lived her faith every day, but gently and quietly, more by example than proclamation. When the grandkids had questions they knew they could go to her – not so much for answers as a listening ear and an open heart.

She still made most of her own clothes and continued working toward her goal of blanketing the family with afghans.

It had always been difficult to pry money out of Claude for anything but the basics, and she carefully guarded the pittances she had of her own, her small social security check and whatever she got selling bread, now that she no longer had piano students. It allowed her to shop for music for her and Bill to learn and to give freely to the church and charities she believed in without begging and negotiating with Claude. But for the big stuff, he had to be consulted. So when their home needed a facelift, she would begin a long term strategy to get him to go along. Inevitably the aggravation would get the better of her. She wanted to replace the shabby kitchen linoleum and the carpeting in their Arizona mobile home and started scoping out the possibilities with predictable results. "Claude pulled a typical Claude Rawson on me and said I would have to pay the $1,000 for flooring and furniture if I wanted it that bad."

They had begun the practice of flying to Florida for Thanksgiving with Bonnie's and Keeny's families. The first time their tickets were paid by others. Come time to buy their own, Claude went out and bought one for himself, leaving her to pay for her own. She seethed – and then adapted. Again.

> Funny how our family income can only support one and I'm the one left standing without any apparent means of support. I often feel I am just working for room and board with no fringe benefits – but that is humanly speaking. The great gifts of God are still mine – beauty all around, great literature and dear friends. Last but not least a great, great family. I guess I'm rich after all. Still these nasty little deals do get to my very core and ruin an otherwise good night's sleep, which this one did. Lying on my back in the dark can be devastating, so I got up and played solitaire until I won.

Back in Minnesota, Keeny and Vern, who had been in and out with their RV for a couple of years, began to nose around the area for a cabin of their own. Claude and Sue kept an eye on the market when Keeny and Vern weren't around and checked out a couple of places that didn't pass the sniff test. They found a likely prospect on Lake Maud. That fall, as orange-red maple leaves swirled around them, Keeny and Vern went through it – Vern with his engineering nose and Keeny with her designer eye – and saw the possibilities. They bought it with their inheritance from Grammy Gores and, after a session or two with a camera and a tape measure, they headed back to Florida to make plans. By the end of the following summer the porch floor was sanded, walls painted, the kitchen counter was lowered, the curtains were up and a little sunfish sailboat was tied up by the dock. Now three of the families had places at lakes near the city of Detroit Lakes – Wally's at Leaf Lake where Claude and Sue summered, Claudia's on Pelican Lake and Keeny's on Lake Maud.

⁊

Claude turned eighty and his health was in decline. They had physicals every summer. Sue was fine. The doctor said Claude had a slow-growing prostate cancer and would need to have surgery in the spring. His blood was slightly low in iron and they struggled for a time to decide just what it was. They settled on aplastic anemia or something close. "Went dancing at Cherokee," she wrote in the fall of 1981, "but Claude was tired, so we didn't dance them all." He began getting blood transfusions every six months or so. His energy would begin to wane, like an old phonograph winding down, and with a blood transfusion he would be raring to go again. The blood transfusions got closer together. The process was a two-day affair, going first to get a "blood match" and back the next day for the transfusion. It took several hours each time.

... Claude went to the doctor; stopped by Mesa Lutheran Hospital to arrange for his blood transfusion on the sixteenth. It took eight hours in all.

APRIL, 1982   ... blood test showed his blood was down another three degrees. The doctor said it was about what they expected, and he would probably have to have blood transfusions every three months from now on.

JULY, 1982   ... Claude goes in for a transfusion and bone marrow test... an all-day affair. I shopped a lot and bought a little. He ran a temperature of 101 and worried us awhile but it was soon better.

Before long they had the routine down, even the routine of changing from the doctors in Arizona to the doctors in Minnesota. He had his prostate surgery and it was "unremarkable." "I have cancer," Claude would say, "but the doctors say something else will kill me before that does."

At the back of the journal for 1984 was a newspaper clipping, crisp and yellow with age, with the headline, "Death Book can help ease financial pain if spouse dies." It detailed what information would be needed in such a case. Clearly, they had had 'the talk.' Written on the page next to it was a listing of their accounts, some of it written in Claude's quavering little chicken scratches in pencil and transcribed in Sue's still firm cursive scrawl.

FEBRUARY 11, 1985

· In case of death, inform Social Security (addresses are in the phone book). You will need death certificates to send to each one:

Standard Oil (for pension)

Central American Life (certificate is in the safe at Wally's)

AT&T (bonds are in the safe at Wally's, $50,000)

- No need to inform the banks.
- Pay estimated taxes on April 15, June 15 and September 15.
- The key to the strong box is in the desk drawer in the shed or in the black case under the lavatory.
- Car insurance needs to be kept up.
- Mobile home insurance and the title to the car are in the strong box.
- Interstate Bank in Apache Junction has about $400.
- Robinson State Bank has $10,000 in CDs. They will send a notice every six months with a certificate to sign and return to tell them what to do with the interest.
- Claude's Social Security ($698) automatically goes to the bank in Robinson.
- First Federal has around $28,000 and maybe $8–900 in the access account; you can write checks for a minimum of $300.
- The will is at the attorney's office in Steele if needed.

In June of 1985 we all headed to the Diamond Jubilee in Pettibone. It was a chance to touch home base again, and the best chance we would ever have to see old friends who had left the area and scattered across the country just as we had.

Bert Neiswaag was in charge of directing people to the areas set aside for campers and he had reserved a whole plat for the Rawson clan. It seemed like every building and electric pole in town had three or four campers plugged into it. Keeny and Vern, John and I, Marg and Roy all came in our own RVs, Bonnie and Oscar had rented a big motor home; Claudia came with Jill by car and bunked in with someone. It was great fun.

Overnight the population of Pettibone swelled from maybe 110 to over 500. The planners brought in portable street venders who sold hamburgers and sandwiches. The second night was to be a barbecue. We went out the evening before to see where they dug a pit, built a good fire to roast an entire side of beef to a succulent fare-thee-well. The parade had over a hundred entries from all the little towns up and down the line – their fire engines, antique cars and tractors, Lions Clubs, 4-H Clubs. Best of all, old friends. That night we danced in the new hall – a vast improvement over the one of my childhood and in the same place. Saturday was a local talent show and a kiddy parade. We walked the town and I showed John the little house and the Thorstness house and the Schmitt house – where I'd grown up.

At the Pettibone Diamond Jubilee in 1985. Sue and Claude seated in front. Back from the left: Bonnie, Claudia, Wally, Keeny, Rosemary.

Arlene and Claudia at the Pettibone Diamond Jubilee, summer 1985

That winter we gathered again to celebrate Sue's eightieth birthday with chicken Kiev dinner at the Dobson Ranch, one of the many resorts in the Phoenix area. I realized later that she would have much preferred to have had a celebration in the hall at Blue Star with buns with ham and chicken and slaw and jello salad and maybe a big cake to serve 100. But Marg covered that with a reunion a few weeks later at her place in Meridian Court. We were all there except Keeny and Vern and this time there were cousins – Willard and Laura's son Duane (Butch) and Marg's son Tom from San Diego.

MARCH 11, 1986   Claude needs weekly blood tests now. He fell while I was washing dishes and hurt his leg. He had a rough night. He got me up at five o'clock to give him a urinal. I covered him up and turned up the furnace. I called the doctor who told me to take him to Mesa Lutheran emergency and ask for an orthopedic doctor and X-rays. I had to call an ambulance. He had surgery at five o'clock and was out of recovery at nine. Officially he broke his right femur, up near the hip. It was probably a spontaneous fracture, they said. I stayed all night and slept on a rollaway bed beside him, though rest was sporadic to say the least.

On Thursday she went home to concerned neighbors, potluck and pinochle where she won high. The kids called in one by one and two by two. I drove up from Tucson. (John and I retired to Tucson in 1984.)

The next week, on advice from the hospital social worker, she started looking into nursing homes and began tackling the medical industrial complex in the form of the mounting pile of medical forms and referrals that were accumulating on their desk. This had always been Claude's department. She ended up taking the whole pile to the hospital hoping that between the two of them they could figure it out.

With some physical therapy Claude did well enough that he was able to come home. He started learning the skills of getting out of the car and up the steps with a walker. Friends came to sit with him while Sue shopped and went to choir practice and Bible study. It was approaching the time to leave for Minnesota and Claude said they'd better plan to stay in Arizona this summer. Sue thought otherwise. He would be fine, she thought, once they got to the lake. The thought of spending a Phoenix summer in their shoebox mobile home steeled her resolve.

She was right. Wally flew in to drive back to Minnesota with her. They put Claude on a plane to Minneapolis and Lue picked him up and took him home to their new place near Anoka to wait. By the time they had been at the Leaf Lake place a couple of weeks, Claude was out mowing the lawn and getting ready for the Memorial Day weekend.

It was a good summer. But Claudia's family did not come. The kids were getting bigger and had activities that made it difficult

Claude and Sue, Fall 1986

to put together even a few weeks when everyone was free to get away. Claudia was back in school working toward her degree. (She had only an RN certification). Giulio was expanding his clinic and their new house on Turkey Court was in the planning stage. They decided it was time to sell the cabin. Giulio made arrangements for a truck to pick up the furniture.

August is almost half gone. It's hazy this morning but cool and fresh and MPR has delicious music on. Yesterday morning I watched our woodchuck munching grass over at Gordon's and the day before I saw red squirrel going round and around our big tree in front of the window. Finished Arlene's blouse.

Sue continued practicing poetry on the half-mile walk to the mailbox. She polished the "What is so rare as a day in June…" piece from the *Vision of Sir Launfal*, and *Hound of Heaven* that she'd first memorized while doing the ironing back in 1952. And she reviewed *The Leak in the Dike* from my childhood.

Bonnie came in October to drive back with Sue, and Claude went to stay with Wallys until they got there and could pick him up at the airport. They had crossed another marker.

In early December, returning from yet another doctor appointment, they stopped in a strip mall to get Claude's glasses adjusted. "Wait here," she told him, and went to get the car. But he followed her and as she turned to back the car out he put his hand on the fender to steady himself – and fell. He seemed to be all right and they went home. But later when Sue returned from a dental appointment she discovered that he had been unable to get up and had wet himself. She was going to take him to the hospital, but he wasn't able to stand on his feet, so they called an ambulance. He had a broken arm and a chipped shoulder.

Awoke at 6:30 after a good night's rest. I hope it isn't my last one. I feel refreshed but the full impact of yesterday's disaster is beginning to dawn on me. I cling to the assurance that God will provide. I'm going in soon to be with Claude for his transfusion. I have a sack packed with Christmas cards, knitting and a book. Claude's blood didn't arrive until around 7:00 due to difficulty in finding a cross match. He had a rough day. I wrote Christmas cards and knitted and read. I fed Claude and then went out for chicken nuggets and picked up a card for Claude. I talked to the doctor who told me he expected Claude to "deteriorate rapidly" due to his age and blood condition. I talked to a social worker. And went home alone (of course).

I called the hospital next morning. They said Claude would sleep most of the day. Wallys called; I called Keeny and Vern the next morning and they may come. Friends are stopping me to ask about Claude (and me as well). I called Pastor Botchen to ask if he would come out and give us communion and perform a laying on of hands and he said he would. Claude seems stable. Rosemary, Keeny and Wally all called in quick succession and they all said they'd come when I feel I need them.

I got a note from Ralph Gilbert that Carl died on November 27.

Claude had a good day, alert and rational and asking questions. I was encouraged. I'm getting worn out – or maybe jaded is a better word – but a good night's sleep helps. Rosemary came. She and John brought him a "five speed walking stick" like an old fashioned gear shift. It even has a reverse on it. Claude is eager to get home. They left and I stayed on until almost seven to feed Claude and see him bedded down.

DECEMBER 15   I met with Janet, the social worker. She's going to check on a room for Claude. She thought he might not get out until the end of the week. There is a question whether they could hospitalize him at all on Medicare, so we're not making many plans very far ahead – even two days. Janet said, "Do me a favor – go home and rest – put your feet up." Marg had me to supper – roast chicken and dressing, pumpkin pie. All good.

DECEMBER 16   I made jelly before I left as I want to give some for Christmas, and I got to the hospital about ten. Dr. Cavalcant ordered chest X-rays. A fever indicated some infection and he suspected low grade pneumonia. The pain in his arm and shoulder is diminishing and he didn't wince when the doctor elevated it. Janet is calling nursing homes to check on vacancies, but there will be no help from Medicare. Claude has no tubes or antibiotics now and he sits up to eat. I stopped at the nursing home to check it out. Still no word on how long he can stay in the hospital.

I went to coffee and doughnuts in the hall and left most of the doughnut, but being surrounded by loving friends was more delicious anyway. Friends in the Court offered rides, food, support — help of any kind.

Tomorrow is Claude's 84th Birthday. They had him up twice to walk and he got to the sink and back. I came home to mix bread and had a long session on the sofa with a glass of wine. Just like old times. Then I had a good nap. We were a fair crowd at the hospital. Marg and Roy came and Rosie and John. There was lots of joking around and Claude was in good spirits and joined in the fun, laughing as much as any of us. A great day for him. And great for us too, to see him begin to emerge again.

Trips to and from the hospital became routine. She enjoyed the natural scenery along the way with citrus groves and native desert and mountains in the distance. She sang favorite hymns providing her own background music. The car gave her trouble, sometimes refusing to start, only to have it work perfectly when the mechanic went to check it out. She fretted over what Medicare would pay and what it wouldn't. On Christmas Eve Claude was checked out of the hospital and into Casada Villa Care Center nearby. He was disappointed that he couldn't go home. She was exhausted and relieved. There was no Christmas Eve, only the blessed bed she crawled into as soon as she could get to it.

She got up early to do her hair and take Christmas treats to the Streus and then came home to read the paper and do the *New York Times* Crossword.

CHRISTMAS DAY   I took sweets, the Sunday paper, cards and some turkey sandwiches and went to see Claude. He was glad to see me. Wally called tonight and he is coming Saturday. Claudia sent $100 to do something nice for myself. How about a three-week vacation?

Claude is hanging in there and getting physical therapy. Hopefully he'll walk again soon. I played for the residents a while before I left.

Wally worked on the car while I took care of my large stockpile of "tired," napping and waking and napping again. Rosemary is coming on Thursday again. Claude was tired but lucid. (Heck, I was tired but lucid). Wally started going over the mound of medical papers.

NEW YEAR'S EVE   Claude weak and trembling and imagining that Thelma was there and Milt Larson *[old friends from Pettibone]*. Claude asked Wally how Mom was doing and said he worried a lot about her. He reached for my hand and held it as I squeezed his and patted it. They handed out hats and noise makers and served cheetos and crackers and punch – the saddest looking New Year's Eve party I ever saw. So goodbye to a year of mistakes and frustrations and broken dreams and ushering in another similar one. I hope we give a little better account of ourselves in this one. When we left I said to Wally, "He's failing, isn't he?" I called the doctor who confirmed my fears. He said he might go ahead with a transfusion next week "if his stability warrants it." So

we came home quiet and subdued. We haven't spread the
word yet except to Rosemary who is coming today directly
to Casada Villa. Wally called Lue, so she too knows our grim
situation. There was pie and coffee in the hall before the
New Year's Eve party and dance, but we came home before
the party began. I saw 1987 in with a kiss, a bath and bed.

She made the drive to Casada Villa every day, bringing food from
home and sometimes mail that wasn't too taxing. I drove up from
Tucson every weekend. Claude was confused more and more of the
time, but he perked up when they brought up finances. He agreed
that they should probably get a new car. His eyes widened when
I told him the Dow Jones had topped 2000. When I was about to
leave he puckered up for a goodbye kiss, which he'd never done
before. I kissed him and said, "You're a good Dad."

Sue took him by wheelchair to the hospital for a transfusion,
which seemed to make no difference whatsoever, except to con-
fuse him further. "Come on, Mom, let's get our clothes on and go
home," he pleaded. Keeny and Vern arrived in their RV.

Claude still exhausted. I sort of hated to leave him, he
seemed so frail. He had a spell of anxiety in the morning
when he thought he saw me in another room and demanded
that they take him in there to find me. He was confused all
day. He asked me how the "new marriage was working out"
and said he heard I was marrying "that joker" and didn't
even invite him to the wedding. Keeny and Vern think he is
over-medicated. Staff said he was mostly 'confused' but he
did talk sense occasionally.

Keeny found a sale of Hertz rental cars by the airport and there
was an '86 LTD. They consulted Claude in one of his more lucid
moments, and he decided they didn't need a car after all and then

wondered if he'd even get to ride in it. Vern talked with Wally and the next day they went to the bank and got $8,432 for the car, the warranty and four new tires. "I hope I have everything I need now, whatever that is." Sue wrote, "I scarcely know what I already have." Vern took care of everything, transferring title and insurance and went over the stack of papers involved. She was relieved and grateful for the help.

> The kids are getting ready to leave. I don't know if I'm ready
> for soloing on the books, but one has to make the leap or
> be dependent from now on, and I don't want that either. I
> cherish my independence and freedom.
>   I moved Claude's shirts out of the closet to make room for
> my blouses. If he does come home I can easily relocate them.

She began the long battle of medical bills and insurance and who owed what to whom. "I can't apply for Amoco [new Standard Oil Company] to pay for the twenty days of nursing care until we apply to Medicare and get their refusal. I don't know how to do this."

And every day she drove the twenty miles or so to Casada Villa and watched as he faded away, talking less, eating almost nothing, his confusion turning to simple dull wittedness. He would fall asleep between bites as she tried to feed him. In between she visited other more alert patients and sometimes played the piano in the lounge. At home she removed the bricks that Claude had arranged on the bathroom chest, an arrangement that always bugged her, and refinished the top with a new coat of varnish. "Now it looks neat and clean at last," she wrote.

> **FEBRUARY 3**   Claude is mostly sleeping or semi-awake. He
> seemed reluctant to let me go and I wondered if he'd make
> it through the night. I thought maybe I should stay, but
> my own fatigue called me home. I called at eleven as I was

going to bed and the nurse said he was 'fine.' Medical forms coursed through my head all night. I kept rousing to remind my unconscious to 'knock it off!'

FEBRUARY 4   The nurse called at 4:30 to let me know that Claude had 'slipped away' in the night – about 3:45 or so. I've been calling everybody. Ruth came and had coffee with me for an hour until Rosie got here about 7:30. We went to Bunkers to see Claude's remains. He looked surprisingly natural, as if he was about to speak.

She called me about 5:00 and said, "Your Dad passed away about 4:00 this morning." "How are you doing?" I asked. She told me Ruth was there and I promised I'd be there in two hours. I drove up through Oracle Junction and Florence in record time, trying to review his life and put some meaning to his death. I couldn't think of one meaningful conversation I'd had with him in fifty years, and it made me cry. Just outside of Florence I hit a coyote. Somehow it felt like the coyote was Dad's totem, wily and detached. It made me even sadder.

Bunker Family Funeral Home called to ask if she'd like to see him before the cremation. We looked at each other a moment and said, almost at the same time, "I think we should." She seemed smaller as we entered the place. He was on one of those high gurneys, still in his hospital gown, his still perfect little feet sticking out the bottom. They had (mercifully) put his teeth in for the occasion. I said he looked like he could have been simply sleeping, albeit precariously. Mom leaned over him and put a hand on his chest. "Claude?" she asked gently. Just in case.

Pastor Botchen came and talked quite a while and we tentatively planned the memorial service for Saturday. We picked up Wally at the airport that afternoon and he and Sue left on some of the urgent errands while I took on the list of people to call. Claudia arrived on Friday. Keeny and Vern had barely arrived home and understandably opted not to come back for the memorial service.

The service itself was simple, two bouquets, and a short sermon by Pastor Paulson. Probably about thirty people came. The ladies of Blue Star provided sandwiches and salad for lunch and the ladies of Epiphany Lutheran brought the cake. John and I left for Tucson and dropped Wally off at the airport.

> **FEBRUARY 8**   Claudia and I rested and finished off the sandwiches for supper and we spent the evening together visiting, reading, studying and eating whenever we felt the urge. We slept together. I set the alarm for five so she could catch the supershuttle to the airport at six. And so it is over and I'm alone again to make the best of it.

Whatever grieving she had to do over Claude she had already done. Some of it years ago. The rest of it on the long daily drive from Blue Star to the Casada Villa Care Center and back. I think they may have recaptured some intimacy in the last year of his decline and demise and she may have put her own health at risk in attending to his. But it was over. The next day she went grocery shopping for one and bought one rutabaga, one parsnip and Metamucil to "get her innards reorganized; they seem to still be under stress." Before the week was over, she was shopping for a piano. She dropped off the last of Claude's clothes at the Salvation Army and told them to come and get the sofa. Then she went to Sears and bought a Scandinavian style recliner with a footstool (at half price) and asked two husky men at Blue Star to move the TV from the living room to the little room.

More gradually she learned to negotiate the house maintenance, the bill paying and banking that she'd never done and never liked. But she liked the independence. "I'm adjusting to cooking for one and find it is not too difficult," she wrote.

Days are getting sculptured and full. Dressing-coffee-
exercises- journal-devotion-Tums. It will be easier when the
TV is moved and I have the radio or tapes. A quiet evening at
home will be attractive, I think.

   Went to pick up my lamp and stopped at Furr's
[cafeteria] for lunch. I keep my copy of *Guide to True Peace*
in my overcrowded purse and it gives me that – peace in a
crowded restaurant. What a happy loner I'm turning into.

   Went to Lenten services and Bible study – a real
significant one on death and heaven, dealing with seeming
contradictions. I heard dance music coming from the hall
when I got back, but it struck no nostalgic response in me.
I'm glad for that. I always knew a time like this would be
coming and I thought it would be good even back then.

Sue started riding with Kent and Ruth Martin to Bible Study
and they became good friends. "I never imagined that Ephesians
contained so much real meat of the Word." she noted. Arlene came
to visit for a week. Bonnie called and invited her to fly to Florida
and go with them to the Epcot extravaganza at Disney World. She
continued to confront bravely the medical morass of bills and
insurance that would go on for over a year.

When it came time to head back to Minnesota, I offered to
drive back with her in Brownie (the old brown LTD Ford) so she
would have a car at either end. It was a good trip and we went
their old preferred route, up through the Salt River Canyon, north
through Colorado and across Wyoming to the Spearfish Canyon
in the Black Hills. She recounted some of the stories of their
many trips along that route. Aside from the unfortunate speeding
ticket I got in Wyoming, it was a perfect trip. Wally and Lue had
the trailer set up and ready to go at the lake and we went on to
Wally's in Anoka for Mother's Day. My kids came and we began
a tradition that would go on for almost a decade, of marking the

switch from winter home to summer home with a joint Mother's Day gathering at Wally's. (John and I were looking for a summer place on a lake to escape the Tucson summers. We found it near Webster, Wisconsin.)

> Now it's time to get used to being at the lake alone – a feeling I must get used to. There are some advantages to be sure but a little scary otherwise. I have lots of plans. Wally and Lue are taking some vacation time to work on projects there and to ease the transition. The Scrabble board is in its permanent spot for the summer. Lue won the first one and almost had the second wrapped up when I went out on a triple word and got to count her seven tiles besides.

In early June Claudia and Giulio came to gather the last remnants of their cabin and say goodbye to their lake experience. Keeny and Vern arrived to open their cabin. Sue enjoyed the duck family that took up residence on the point of land that protruded into the lake. She enjoyed the walks to the mailbox relearning old poems and began making improvements on the trailer that it had needed for years. She signed up for the Women's Retreat at Fair Hills. "I've been wanting to go, but couldn't leave Claude. I'm so grateful for my contentment," she wrote.

She made plans for a memorial service for Claude in Pettibone, maybe after the 4th – like July 12, she suggested to herself in the journal. "I hope the plans fall together neatly. It's always a hassle when we run into conflicts of time."

CHAPTER 18

Loss and Recovery

...more sorrow than I have ever known

It was late when Giulio called Keeny and Vern with the news. They decided it was best to wait until morning before they told Sue. The next morning they made a pot of coffee and headed for Leaf Lake. Sue was surprised to see them so early. "You'd better sit down for this one," Keeny said. And, as gently as they could, they told her that Claudia was gone. She was killed instantly in a head-on crash with a semi-tractor – a Peterbilt maybe – driven by a young man who was just moving it to another lot. He wasn't even licensed to drive a truck that big.

Sue did not wail or faint. She simply did what was needful, got out her suitcase and asked Keeny to give her a perm before they left. And then she sank slowly into the deepest grief she'd ever known in her life. And it never quite went away. Never.

> **JUNE 24** This is the worst news I could have had. I can think of nobody close to me who will be mourned more or needed more. The family is devastated. Giulio keeps saying, "O, my sweet honey." The phone was going all day with notices and communications. Keeny and I went to Audubon for money and gas and then to Pamida for a Toni which she

gave me at her house. It was a difficult day. We tried naps
that didn't work. I came home about 10:30, though I had
taken a nightie and toothbrush along just in case I should
want to stay with them. Home began to look better as night
came on. Mercifully I had a good night's sleep. Arlene is
coming by noon and then we'll drive to Minneapolis and on
to Chicago with Tony.

In Tucson I was alone when I got the news and I did wail and
keen and sent the cat fleeing for cover under the bed. Nothing
close to this had ever happened to us. At O'Hare, Bonnie arrived
from Florida, John from the Twin Cities and I from Tucson all
within an hour of each other. Wally had already arrived and he
was dispatched to pick us up. We huddled together like emperor
penguins in a snowstorm; I found some comfort in knowing there
were people who felt as bad as I did.

At the new house on Turkey Court family was gathering. Giulio,
beset with grief and tearing up whenever he stopped to talk, was
tending to a thousand details. The kids stayed in their rooms,
sometimes with the comfort of a friend. Allison, now twenty-one,
kept a cool head and gathered The Guys and took them to the
mall to buy something appropriate to wear to the funeral. They
were twelve now, and outgrowing their clothes every couple of
months. I was assaulted at every turn with the personal minutia
of grief – that I was eating the leftover broccoli she had cooked
the day before, dental appointments for the kids were neatly listed
in her handwriting on the front of the refrigerator, her swimsuit
hung on the shower rail.

The family amassed. Giulio drew me aside to tell me he
recognized Claudia was what she was because of my
influence and he wanted me to stay close and help the
kids. He wants me to come back in September and maybe

stay for two months. We'll have to feel the pulse then
and try to decide if they can go it alone. I may find it a
healing experience – or maybe the opposite with her aura
permeating everything.

There must have been forty or fifty flower sprays at the
funeral home. They filled the room and ran along the walls
of the entry. She was much loved and deeply mourned.
Giulio stayed the whole five or six hours. I thought the casket
was just a prop (since she was to be cremated), but I found
out later her crushed, beautiful little body was in it and I felt
more waves of pain.

At the funeral home I was struck again when I saw her name
over the door of the room where she lay. When we found that she
was indeed inside the casket I went over just to stand by it, near
her. One of the boys, Matthew, I think, came up beside me and put
his boyish hand on the casket. I put my arm around his shoulder
and asked, "Are you going to be all right?" and he said, "I don't
think anything will ever be right again."

This *Parable of Immortality* was read at the funeral:

> *I am standing upon the seashore. A ship at my side spreads her
> white sails to the morning breeze and starts for the blue ocean.
> She is an object of beauty and strength. I stand and watch her
> until at length she hangs like a speck of white cloud just where
> the sea and sky come to mingle with each other.*
>
> *Then someone at my side says: "There, she is gone."*
> *"Gone where?"*
> *Gone from my sight. That is all. She is just as large in mast
> and hull and spar as she was when she left my side, and she is
> just as able to bear the load of living freight to her destined port.*
>
> *Her diminished size is in me, not in her. And just at the
> moment when someone at my side says: "There, she is gone!"*

There are other eyes watching her coming, and other voices ready
to take up the glad shout: "Here she comes!"
    And that is dying.

Afterwards the house overflowed with food and relatives. Neighbors offered their spare bedrooms. Lyla and Darold, Claudia's best friends from Pettibone and then at the lake were there, all the Leone relatives, all the Rawsons and Arlene. P.J. was going through with his band, and stopped. He played Scott Joplin's "Solace" on Claudia's grand piano as the crowd milled and mourned.

They drove home through a summer storm and the days that followed were full of rain and gloom. Only part of that was due to the weather. Sue sent this prayer by Peter Marshall to Giulio and the kids:

> *Father, I am only human. I need the touch of human companionship. Sorely I miss those I love who are with thee. I pray that thou wilt reveal to me unseen presences. Help me to know how close my loved ones are. For if they are with thee and thou art with me, I know they cannot be far away.*
>
> *Make real for me that contact of spirit with spirit that will reestablish the late fellowship for which my heart yearns. Give me faith shining through my tears. Plant peace and hope within my heart. Point me with joy to great reunion. But until then, enable me to live happily and worthily of those who are with thee. In the name of those who are with thee, in the name of Him who is the Lord of Life, I pray. Amen.*

The 4th of July weekend was subdued that year. Over the summer there were more phone calls between the siblings. For the first time in years, we paid attention to birthdays.

Played Yahtzee and had popcorn which rankled my tummy
and woke me up about 4:30 to think depressing thoughts.

I do thank God for the gift of sleep which he has given me nights so that I had the strength and courage to carry on through the days.

Marg and Roy (both in their mid-eighties) wanted to go to the memorial in Pettibone and I went along to do the driving. So I made my third trip in three months to the North Country.

On July 11, 1987, we gathered again in the little church in Pettibone with friends from forty and fifty years ago. I designed the program on my Macintosh computer with Claudia on one side and Dad on the other. June and Rudy Morlock provided the music while Nyra Jean provided the accompaniment. The service was conducted by the lady pastor who, it turned out, now lived in the house in Woodworth where Claudia was born when it was a maternity home. We dawdled for a time and then headed out, stopping to eat in Jamestown at the Wagon Train. There were twenty-one at the table — all relatives.

> **JULY 27** I got a letter from Rosemary telling of her grief; it struck a resounding note in me. I prayed as I've often done, "God, just send me a token, a dream to tell me she is all right; that she is happy. Take her in your arms and hold her." Towards morning after I had been awake and gone back to sleep, I dreamed that I went to Helen Vogel's to pick up some pictures that she was to have finished for me. There was a crowd of people there, but they were apart from me. I was looking through some torn open envelopes of pictures and I couldn't find mine. Then I started singing quietly. I know and love the song I sang, but I can't recall what it was. Then the whole crowd burst into song and sang it just beautifully. A man approached me and showed me some small gold tokens, and as he left he pressed two of them into my hand as if he didn't want to be noticed by the others. It was the cross and chain Claudia gave me. He bent over and

kissed me, and I thanked him and walked way. When I woke up "Because He Lives" was the song on my heart and lips.

Sue went to Giulio's in September as planned. She didn't quite fit into that upscale suburban lifestyle – meals were unpredictable, lifestyles unfathomable to her. There were good and painful talks with Giulio and sometimes with the kids one on one.

She flew into Phoenix, struggling with a season's worth of luggage, and back to Blue Star to face the closed trailer with no power, water, heat or groceries. With a little help from neighbors, she settled in. She was still new at this.

"Fell asleep watching *As the World Turns*," she wrote. "Everything terrible is happening there too." Her friend Ruth Drost lived in the mobile home directly behind Sue's. Their friendship started when their husbands were both alive and deepened after Ruth was widowed and Claude was failing. Ruth was the one she called when the call came that Claude had died. They began to share their suppers, first by invitation and later more casually: "I have chicken enough for two." "Good. I'll bring a salad and some ice cream." While never written in stone, it became the norm.

A year after Claude's death she was still dickering with insurance companies over his final illness. She still went to Casada Villa Care Center to play piano for the patients.

In April 1988 she finished one spiral notebook and began the next.

> This starts yet another page and book of my life. Who knows what adventures will be recorded or even if I finish it. There was more sorrow in the last one than I have ever known before. And still tears come. But I have been given strength and peace and even the will to carry on with activities of my life – my handwork, rugs, sewing – and even my music has become important again. God is still in His heaven.

Sue became accustomed to the new migration back and forth. She bought an enormous suitcase dubbed "Humongous" that was the center of those trips. It held her sewing and knitting projects, music, and on the way to Arizona a winter supply of chokecherry juice to be made into jelly, a staple of her breakfasts and for Christmas gifts. As far as I know – and I'm sure I would have heard – it never broke en route. On the way to Minnesota Humongous would hold a summer's supply of bulk yeast for baking dark bread. At the lake in Minnesota, Lue's sister Ruby's family bought the lot next to Gordon's cabin, thus extending the "compound." This was good news. That place, not Sue's, provided a new center of activity and more important, another bathroom.

Keeny and Vern became her anchor through the summer. Vern was always on call when the power went out, the pump quit or the car wouldn't start. Keeny had the serger sewing machine and was willing to do the finishing touches on the never ending, wardrobe-expanding sewing projects. They had a garden as lush as Claudia's and they took care of it themselves and shared the bounty.

They bought season tickets for the three of them to the Little Theatre Straw Hat Players at Moorhead State University. These outings typically included dinner at Chi Chi's, the Mexican restaurant run by Patty and her husband Steve. A liter of margaritas and a tray of Chi Chi's excellent appetizers proved the perfect lead-in to an evening of musical theatre. The first season they saw *Joseph and His Technicolor Dreamcoat, Man of La Mancha* and *H.M.S. Pinafore*.

In Arizona Sue became more involved with Epiphany Lutheran Church. She became a regular lector and won kudos for her careful and clear delivery of scripture. She joined the choir, singing in clear alto, later convincing them she was really a tenor now. When they started a bell choir, she joined that too, and found it a challenge. The music, weekly Bible study and occasionally sewing projects at the church plus weekly trips to play hymns and old favorites for nursing home patients at Casada Villa and later at nearby

Hearthstone became the heart of her days in Blue Star. On her eighty-third birthday she wrote:

> I feel great, certainly in the top twenty percent of the people my age, I should guess. I do the things I deem important to maintaining good health, and my blessings are so great there is no counting them. God has given me the great gift of warm, hugging friends and that's evident whenever I venture out to gatherings and in one-to-one encounters. The glory of it is, I find them wherever I am — in Blue Star, church here and in Minnesota, at the Anoka church among Wallys' friends and family and even in the response of the dear souls in the nursing home. I always come away feeling blessed with the encounter. And how I appreciate my little snowbird nest. Every time I return to it from a trip abroad a warm glow flows through me — my reclining chair provides perfect comfort for reading, listening to music from Public Radio, thinking — sleeping.

For a while she continued to play music with Bill Streu and his saxophone, but Bill was slowing down. He had heart problems and then it was clear he was losing his sight.

The journals record a dizzying parade of travel — to Florida for Thanksgiving with Bonnie's family, to San Diego for Christmas with Marg's family, to Chicago to touch base with Claudia's tribe. She came to know the shuttle drivers by name. She made plans for a bus tour of the east coast with Marg and Roy and Laura.

> I woke up at 3:00 A.M. and lay awake thinking of what I had to do. LOTS. But I didn't get panicked so it must be all right. I wonder how long I can keep up this hectic "before leaving" pace. I think I enjoy the challenge and sense of accomplishment in the doing. I'm getting my ticket today. Bill wants to play if I can work it in.

In the fall of 1988 Wally was having chest pains again. He'd had one heart attack and with determined diet and exercise he had recovered. Now they performed an angioplasty, hoping that would do the trick. As Christmas approached it was clear that it hadn't worked and the doctors recommended strongly that he have surgery – quintuple bypass – without delay. Three days before Christmas he was in surgery for ten hours.

Sue was in Minneapolis and so were his kids when he was wheeled out of surgery looking bloated and cold, hooked up to a frightening array of tubes and ominous machines. They were surprised to run into my cousin Joy in the family waiting room. Her husband was there in intensive care. He died the next day. But Wally was doing okay. It was a somber Christmas. By New Year's he was home and recovering. "He says he's doing okay," wrote Sue, "but coughing still tears him up and he's weak beyond belief. My baby boy!"

That summer the pastor at St. Peter's, knowing her interest in the annual retreat for Lutheran Women at Fair Hills Resort, told her about Holden Village, a Lutheran based wilderness retreat in northern Washington. They were hosting an intergenerational retreat around the theme of aging and death. Of course she was interested. A bus was to leave from Oak Grove Lutheran High School in Fargo and Two women she knew also signed up to go, but they both cancelled before the day came to leave. "I'm sure I'll make friends, I usually do," she wrote.

The trip was two days through the western states, a four-hour boat trip and an eleven mile bus ride over gravel roads to get to Holden Village. It was all she hoped for – deep woods, paneled cabins with rustic furniture. She was assigned two roommates, Tess and Gelina. She met Arden Barden (my mother must have had a difficult pregnancy, he explained) and signed up for his class on Aging with Grace and another on The Common Myths of Dying. It gave her a chance to talk about Claudia's death and her "Because He Lives!" dream. At the closing program she recited from memory "Billy Peebles Christmas" and "Chums." On the long bus ride home they extended the Holden experience.

> During sharing time Gelina told of her trip to Norway and Solveig and I led some harmony singing – "Harbor Lights" and "Vaya Con Dios," "When I Grow Too Old to Dream" and others. I got up at the last to say the Holden experience was "awesome" which made them laugh. Then I gave "Trees" which they liked. We went by the Pettibone turn off and the place where we rolled the trailer without even seeing them. We arrived before five. Brownie was waiting patiently for me and took off without much resistance. But not until we'd had hugs all around and sweet expressions of affection for each other. I got lots of orchids for my poetry and several said I'd added substantially to their enjoyment of the trip. Ida said she was going to memorize some poetry herself because of it.

Perhaps it was the retreat that prodded her. As the summer drew to a close she stopped one day to visit Delma and Felix, Claudia's neighbors at the cabin who prepared her garden each spring. There were hugs and tears. "…such precious, dear friends. How blessed are such expressions of true caring and how reticent we are to express them," she wrote. "I had resisted going over there sooner, knowing the memories would be too painful. The gardens, both of them, are ragged and neglected."

> **LABOR DAY**   One of the great days at the lake with perfect weather. The trailer traffic almost needed a cop. But there's lots of food and places for shelter. The dogs bark at everyone who comes in and at each other. In a bit of perfect timing, the kids picked up turtle eggs and then watched

them hatch. Keeny and Vern came over with pot roast and gravy and a gallon of apple cider.

TUESDAY Keeny and Vern stopped by in their RV, ready to take off. I resist the thought that they are really leaving, but on the other hand I have a multitude of things to do to get ready to leave myself. Today I play for the folks at Emmanuel, get my cholesterol test, tomorrow night I play two numbers for ELCW Meeting, Thursday wash and iron, Friday and Saturday to pack the car as I move out by degrees. Saturday evening is the turkey dinner. Sunday is church and the trip to Pine River (Elderhostel) and the first leg of my return to Apache Junction. I'm getting excited. I hope Brownie and I keep our heads with the demands made on us. The last days at home were festive...

In Florida for Thanksgiving that year Sydney, the musical protégé in Bonnie's family, got tickets for the two of them to a performance of *The Messiah*. She took along copies of the score so they could follow the performance.

We could listen for different sections as they alternated and overlapped and played together. Great experience. Handel drew from 1400 years of prophecy, all pointing to a Messiah, but it says he only used ten percent of the Biblical source material. Each selection had the Biblical source printed at top of the selection. Lots of it came from *Psalms* and *Epistles* along with the gospels.

All of my intuition and vision cries out for this kind of experience. When I anticipate LBI next month I get more excited and convinced I'm doing the right thing. Sydney bought me a tape of Christmas music and we played it on the way back.

After the successful stay at Holden Village, Arden Barden contacted Sue again in the fall and invited her to attend the January
Interim at Lutheran Bible Institute in Seattle. It was a month-long
intergenerational course for Lutheran pastors, would-be pastors
and others in that service and the theme was aging and dying.
They recruited Sue as a representative old person. They couldn't
have found a more willing participant.

> Debbie called from LBI and said tuition was $160 a class. I
> was astounded (sort of); all I really expect to do is listen
> carefully (and I may miss a passel of that), a sort of innocent
> bystander ready to receive some of the fallout. But on
> second thought I didn't really care what it cost. I'm just glad
> I could spend some of God's gifts to me on such things with
> some assurance they may contribute to my own growth. So
> on with the plans.

The registration reminded her of Valley City days. With Arden
Barden's help, she chose two classes with homework – Epistles
and Wisdom and the Bible and Aging – and three that could be
listened in on when convenient.

> In Arden's class he asked whether life is down hill after the
> middle years and I said that in the middle years we were so
> busy raising kids, making money and doing what had to
> be done that we had no time for things that would lead to
> mental and spiritual growth. These things were put on the
> back burner. Now, with age, we were eager to get to them. I
> told them that I did just that and it was a joyful experience.
> Arden quoted me in the second class. He said I was a good
> example for the younger students.
> We older girls led the worship service. I played "Eine
> Kleine Nachtmusik" for the prelude; Phyllis did the

introduction and opening prayer; I read from Browning. They sang "I Was There to Hear Your Borning Cry." Leone gave a short sermon and then Kathleen played a medley of hymns ending with "Beautiful Savior" when everyone joined in. I didn't get to give my Bach postlude.

On weekends Bob Cook, an old friend from Pettibone, recently widowed, wined her and dined her and took her to meet his kids. Was he COURTING?

She spent evenings studying and working on papers and socializing in the lounge with other students both young and old. She especially liked having the young people there. It was a welcome change from Elderhostels. The month ended with a cruise on the river with a fancy dinner and dancing. She came home bubbling with reports.

Back home in Blue Star Bill Streu complained that she "flitted around like a fledermaus." His eyesight was nearly gone and he came over to listen to tapes of the songs they had played together; it helped to have them to imitate. They played the songs he still knew from memory. He grew more crotchety. In April he came to tell her that he and Jean would be moving to a retirement home near their children in Texas.

Bill came by to say their place was sold and they would be gone in two or three weeks. He figured out he's known me one fifth of his life. So it's the end of another era. It's bound to end in some nostalgia and regret. For me the antidote is to return to the classics with new vigor. It's worse for Bill. I presume time is running out for both of us.

...the farewell party was hard on Jean. Bill got up and talked about their time here, how a few planned weeks ran into eighteen years and how great our years of playing together were. Jean stopped by afterward to say she

appreciated my offer to take them out to dinner at King's
Table but Bill wouldn't go as he couldn't see to choose
what to eat and ended up with what he didn't want, and
besides that he hated to dress up. Jean says he's spoiled and
selfish. I have noticed it myself. So I asked them to supper on
Monday. Guess I'll get a pot roast.

At eighty-four she had slowed down a little, but when Pastor
Botchen announced that a group from the church was planning a
tour of Europe and to Oberammergau to see the famous Passion
Play, Sue didn't hesitate to sign up. With some assistance from her
fellow travelers she managed to keep up. She slept on many of the
bus trips through the scenery she'd marveled at thirty years earlier.
Even at Oberammergau and the Passion Play – the whole reason
for the trip – she kept dropping off. What thrilled her most was
the Mozart museum where she saw his little violin and piano and
attended a concert of his familiar chamber music.

As they walked the walled city of Rothenberg she recalled the
European trip with Claudia and Giulio. "But this time it was quite
a challenge since it was up stairs and over cobblestones much of
the way. I attached myself to the Hamptons. I made a note to write
and thank them once more for taking of their own travel time to
make mine more secure and free from concern."

Their flight home followed the daylight west. Customs took two
hours, and then west across the country, with one last layover in
Las Vegas. Their luggage didn't arrive until the next day. "I went to
bed at 8:30 for the first time since babyhood," she wrote. Two days
later she had repacked Humongous, buttoned down the trailer
for the summer, and was on the plane to Minnesota. Before the
month was out she was considering a tour to Israel.

A couple of years earlier Sue got word that her cousin Justine
had died – Justine who was one of the cousins from the summers
on Green Lake in Minnesota when they were teenagers; Justine

who lived so precariously with crazy Aunt Tommy in Seattle when they stopped by back in their trailering days. Justine (who had a law degree) had died without a will and no near relatives. Then everything got quite complicated. Sue (and Marg, too) had signed a waiver relinquishing all claims to the estate and they understood it would go to her caretakers. Then came evidence that the caretakers were suspect and the estate was being challenged. This was the exactly the sort of affair Sue would shrink from. It became a running theme recorded in her diaries and went on for two years. She began to think of what she might do with any money she might get. She agonized and sought advice from Wally and Vern and eventually a lawyer in Detroit Lakes. Now it was finally settled and she was awarded almost $10,000 as her share. She opened a special account and supported a number of charities, causes and people with the inheritance from Justine's estate.

Back at Leaf Lake after a winter and spring of sometimes frenzied travel and stimulation, she savored the simple day-to-day chores of living.

> I'm running out of windows whose care has been eating up my days. I called it good. We seem to need physical work, maybe something in our rearing or a built in compulsion. When I see a shining window (free of spider webs) and filmy clean curtains it stirs a joy in my heart. Something is certainly missing in the lives of people who have no choice but to live in filth.

She continued to encounter what she deemed everyday miracles: finding exactly the shade of plum yarn she needed (that had been discontinued) in the remainder bin for half price; the car breaking down at the exact moment someone was there to take care of such a thing; a $100 bank error in her favor triggering a needed contribution to one of her charities or finding a lost key while searching for something else.

Summer days ran into each other, days lost to memory – a patchwork of mad parties (cards) that ran into the night leaving them sluggish the mornings after. There was the steady flow of traffic through her trailer, back and front—mostly to the bathroom. Teds left, Tonys came. Wally tore down the old shed and put new siding on the fish house. Together the guys put a new roof on Gordon's cottage. Rick came in the RV with his three kids for three weeks and before they left he tuned the piano and he and the kids cleaned the yard, marching four abreast, scratching up every cigarette butt and sunflower seed. They gathered bags of aluminum cans to go to the recycling center. Over at Keeny and Vern's there were extended visits from Janie's family (the McDaniels), and Scott's with their boys.

On her trips to the nursing home, Sue added poetry to the piano playing, reciting "Bless This House" and "The Speckled Hen" and "The Gingerbread Man." Soon she was putting together entire programs of music and readings for other groups. Always followed by conversations and hugs for the patients.

Sue formed a special bond with the grandchildren, following their progress and regress – their marriages and increasingly their divorces and remarriages and not-quite-marriages – all without judgment, only sadness for them when they were sad. There seemed to be at least one in each family that drifted into her beloved music. In Bonnie's family it was Sydney, in my family it was P.J. In Wally's family it was all of them.

> ...Sydney came, sunbathed on the dock and we played duets on the piano and had long talks about religion...she packed and repacked and finally left about two-thirty, still dragging her feet. She was under-girded with a loaf of bread and an oatmeal box of cookies.

...I had a long letter from Rick. He sent a check to cover the phone bill and groceries. But mostly I appreciated the contents of the letter, an introspective sort of thing questioning his life style and hoping he'd get it all together, sorting the significant from the mundane. He seemed to think I'd arrived at some degree of 'peace of mind.' I must phrase my answer to him carefully.

...got a very special letter from Amy. I wrote back many pages. I hope I chose the pertinent things. I would hate to disillusion her.

...P.J. came with his video cameras and interviewed me for hours at the picnic table about my early years, and the next day did it again.

...Becky came and ran through her song and then I played nearly an hour with Terry and her flute.

...got a note from Patty with a book on modern mysticism: To my Beloved Gramma, Your inspiration will always be alive in me.

As always there were long conversations and games of Scrabble with Lue.

Funny how we struggle so hard to win and then promptly forget who did...She is great to have around and I enjoy our conversations. They are not 'talks' in the usual sense of the word; we are both committed to discipleship and often our talk centers on that, so this morning we discussed troublesome encounters and how to handle them.

The planned-for trip to Israel was cancelled in the wake of one more outbreak of unpleasantness in the Middle East, but there was still Elderhostel. Every fall she signed up for two or three Elderhostels with classes on psychology, religion, fitness, art and nature with side trips to interesting destinations. At the end of them there were always hugs sealing new friendships and adding new names to her list of Christmas letters. She continued to win praise for her poetry recitations – mostly for her ability to memorize them at all. At the end they were all awarded "Master of Youthful Thinking" degrees certificates.

In November, 1991, the last Elderhostel was winding up at the Baptist sponsored Shalom House on Trout Lake in Northern Minnesota when they woke up to one of the worst winter storms in recent history. Roads were closed and the power was out in many areas, "but we are still warm and fed and in the bosom of wonderful people whom we are privileged to fellowship with," she wrote, loving a good adventurous challenge. She bundled up and admired the wintery scene of unblemished snow outside the window. She played oldies for them to sing along, had good one-to-one talks, played games, read her *LIFE* magazine, watched *Driving Miss Daisy*. It was as much fun as the Elderhostel itself.

CHAPTER 19

Crossing Bridges

...better to go in sadness than in pique

If all of this sounds like she was skipping along like a sixteen-year-old, she wasn't, of course. She was easing past her mid-eighties. At the opening of a new journal at the beginning of a new year she wrote this "state of the person" report:

> My health seems to be good for eighty-six years old, probably even very good. I have had, for all the years I can recall, a stomach condition whose main symptom is lots of gas, and there are so many foods that seem to trigger it that it hardly pays to list them. Alka Seltzer and Tagamet seem to work best. This and dry eyes...I try to plan my days around periods of eye use — reading or sewing — separated by periods of housework, shopping etc. That seems to work quite well. My hearing is slightly impaired. I have been doing most of my own work. This week I washed the windows inside and out, climbing the ladder without any shakiness or fear of falling. Also used my new broom to sweep the patio. I need to scrunch the little green plants daring to risk their tiny heads through the gravel. I rather hate to cut them down

after such a brave effort. Made chile for Ruth and me for supper. She brought the baked potatoes.

Years earlier when her legs were really giving her trouble with weakness and claudication, she was diagnosed with high cholesterol and she immediately went on a diet of oat bran and fruit for breakfast. She was never hungry for breakfast, and she put it off later and later until it became "oats and soaps" – oat bran, fruit and *As the World Turns*. She bought Tums in the large economy size.

She was developing cataracts and was sensitive to light, so she took to wearing eye shades like a Dickensian bookkeeper. Only hers were colorful and color coordinated with her outfits.

She signed up again for a trip to Israel the next summer, but in February the trip was scrapped once more when Sadaam Hussein tried to lob Scud missiles into Jerusalem. "I seem destined not to get there." Immediately she filled the gap by signing up to go back to Holden Village.

Every now and then there would be an upheaval at Blue Star – a change of ownership, a precipitous rise in the rent perhaps, new rules – that would send her neighbors who still had wheels on their houses and some who didn't scurrying to other courts. Sometimes it was just the lure of a better, newer community. One such occasion prompted Sue to once again review her situation.

...they are moving to Mountain View I believe along with two other couples going there too. It makes me a little nostalgic, but maybe it is only looking back on more productive days. Appraising it more carefully I find it really no great loss if any. What I cherish mostly is my walk with God, easy home, freedom, adequate means, friends. One really can't take part in many activities and still have time for reading, playing piano and every day chores. I find the ones I have left behind are no more precious than the ones I've hung onto.

I read in *Imprisoned Splendor* with the reading glass — the print is very small — and my eyes feel better this morning. Maybe this is the answer. I must explore that bit of delicious hope. Good night, good music, good reading, good sewing, good day. I also explored a new Beethoven. Doing as you please has its merit.

. . . I skipped bingo and may from now on. So much better things to do at home. Ruth came by for our nightly chat reviewing our day's business.

Much of her focus now was on Epiphany Lutheran, particularly the music. She requested a private talk with Russ, the choir director, who was in charge of all of the music. They had hired an accompanist and introduced guitar music. Was there still a place for her? If there was, if she was called upon to play for choir even just for rehearsals, would she be able to keep up? It was all getting very complicated.

It's certainly different from playing alone. Now I'm trying to be exactly with the choir, the director, and the organ while juggling my pages and keeping my equilibrium and it's not easy. Tonight the fan began blowing my music around. At the end after the Mozart Gloria number, the choir applauded. I need that like I need hugs.

Russ says he has plenty of spots for me but he didn't know how much of a commitment I wanted to make. Neither do I. Do I really want to play for all three services?

She loved the elaborate rituals that developed around the holidays, particularly Easter. They began with Maundy Thursday.

They served a seder meal of herbs, nuts, fruits and horseradish (for the bitter herbs), lamb, carrots and

potatoes. Then they served communion. In rehearsing
for the Easter service music, Gene reminded us of our
responsibility in bringing inspiration to our people. He says
Good Friday is the big day for him because it is so strongly
underscores the enormity of the deed. It's the atoning
sacrifice. We sang "Take My Mother Home" and "All My
Trials Lord."

Wally and Lue drove down that spring, took her on a visit to
Patty's in Los Angeles and then they drove through the National
Parks – Grand Canyon, Zion and Bryce. They hiked some of the
short easy trails, but mostly she waited happily in the car, working
puzzles, enjoying the views and talking to God.

There were weddings that summer. P.J. and Mary were married
and Sue commented on the rather counter-culture nature of the
affair. "…Mary wore a beautiful bright blue vintage 1920s dress,
P.J. wore a suit that Laurie found in a thrift shop and cut down
to fit him. Cara wore a very colorful dress with a great dip in the
back like a tail and some cowboyish shoes with white anklets.
She was very pleased with her 'look.' Polly wore flat black shoes
and tights with a short black pleated skirt and a long white tunic
top. Cute haircut." It was a great romp of a party held in P.J. and
Mary's back yard. All my extended family were there and Irv and
his wife, Brian Ann. It ended with a gully-washing thunderstorm.

In July Wally and Lue hosted a big Rawson family reunion at
their place outside Anoka. Many of the North Dakota family came
with stories and picture albums. The highlight was the collection
of old family movies, most of them taken in Pettibone in the fifties.

In August I rode with Wally, Lue and Mom to Allison's wedding
in Palatine. We went directly to the church, pretty, old fashioned
white clapboard with balconies all around. Allison looked gorgeous in a traditional white flowing gown, and when she first
appeared, looking so much like Claudia, it took my breath away.

The reception at the Country Club was grand and festive. Sue stole the show when she danced the jitterbug with the boys' soccer coach.

At the end of the month Hurricane Andrew whipped across southern Florida and Keeny and Vern left the lake early to help Kristy. She had survived by cowering in the bathroom of her condominium in Miami with her dog while pieces of her home blew off around her and took some of her neighbors' houses away entirely.

In September Sue and Ruth Drost took a Fall Colors bus tour to New England. Her diary reveals more about the accommodations than about the destinations.

Back in Blue Star she continued to monitor her situation.

> We stopped for lunch at Furr's and I went off and left my package. I really must be more careful to check for everything before I move. No harm done, I'll get it next trip in. But I am disappointed in myself. I expect everyone else to deteriorate in their eighties, but I expect better of myself. Horrors, Pride!
>
> ...had one of those fuzzy head episodes with some loss of memory and orientation. I keep wondering if I have a commitment today. I would like to have the day free to give nature a chance to clear my head. It seems good just to stay home and do routine jobs. Ruth came over with baked spuds and broccoli and I made turkey burgers and a fruit plate.

She seemed to be continually plagued by business mistakes – being mis-billed or double billed for things. Not given credit for discounts. She almost always contested them, to the exasperation of those on the other end of the transactions, and almost always she was right.

Marg's kids in San Diego came to assess her (Marg's) situation and finally dispatched Roy to a nursing home where he seldom recognized any of them. He died of pneumonia about two months later. They took Marg back to San Diego to live with Connie. She wasn't there long before she almost burned down the house while Connie was at work, forgetting she had a pan on the stove. And so she was moved to assisted living.

> **JANUARY 27, 1993**   My 87th birthday. It's incredible I've made it this far, active, participating and happy. I played bridge and went to church for bell practice and Bible study. Home to a little cake at Ruth's with the Martins.

By April, Ruth too was going. Sue could tell her memory was going when she said she could not remember the time they had checked on a neighbor and found her dead. "That's something you don't forget." Ruth's children arranged for her to move to a retirement home near them in Salt Lake City.

> I was asked to be the emcee at Ruth's going away party. I told of our friendship and how we shared our evening meals and how we crocheted baby afghans for our great-grandchildren. I gave a couple of recitations, "When I Came Home the Other Night" and "Chums." Next morning I went along to have pancakes with them so I'd have a final precious few moments with them. Finally they were packed up on their way with final goodbyes. Another end of an era perhaps. Who knows what people or events will replace the time we had together. She always said how much I'd strengthened her faith...
> ...got home around three, tired. What else is new? I enjoyed the shelter and quiet of my hut, but I need the radio on to dispel the too, too solid silence.

Back at the lake Gordon and Arlene decided to sell their cottage next door and Wally and Lue bought it. They were more than ready to give up sleeping in the camper. Wally set out on a major remodeling that took much of the summer and became more the center of activities for the younger families that came. They started calling it The Hilton. On June 27 Sue wrote:

A big day in my life history. Sixty-four years since that day I said, "I do," and six that Claude's been gone. It can't be so! And so we take inventory. I look at my speckled, veiny hands and wonder at the work they have done, much of it for others and so indirectly coming back to me like bread cast upon the waters. It all adds up to contentment and fulfillment.

Now I look at the far flung mess in here—three or four sewing centers gradually merge into one as I tidy up and put away much of it. There's a rain coming on, I think – thunder like a grumpy old man announcing his presence.

I cut out my orchid stripe jacket. It needs interfacing. The material I got at Goodwill for less than four dollars is three and half yards, sixty inches wide, so there'll be plenty for a skirt. Still mulling over what the blouse will be. Keeny called and asked if it wouldn't be a good day for serging. It would, so I loaded my machine, work basket and clothes under construction. It was a good cool day and we got quite a lot done.

A big storm came up about nine. It got dark and whipped across the lake which looked black. We stopped our pinochle game to turn out the lights and watch. I headed home at ten or so (after the storm had passed) and had no trouble, but when I was almost to Livingston's there was a big tree across the road. I had to drive around it on a grassy area – a space mysteriously left open for me – and I had no trouble. The lights were out when I got home and Keeny was on the phone to check and see if I made it home.

The years began to run into one another. Thanksgiving at Bonnie's: "…Stephie's Melanie is a sweet baby with two sets of doting grandparents. Lucky babe." "…Melanie is a charming seventeen-month-old," "…found Melanie in Oscar's office cutting Spencer's hair." Elderhostel at United Seminary…Pine River…Ripon, Wisconsin…Crookston. Classes on Journey to Wellness…Moses… Ecology. "…listened to the Clarence Thomas hearings" "…announcer yelling, 'The Twins have won the series!'" "…missed my soaps because the OJ trial is on."

Arlene came by with Dana and asked Sue to play for Dana's wedding. After a few months of deciding what to wear and making it, what to play and practicing it – tucked in with all the other activities of summer – Sue, with Wally and Lue, went to Dana's wedding in Fargo. "The bride was beautiful in her perfectly fitted dress full of lace and beads and puffed sleeves and lacy train. All of Dana's siblings were there and it was good to see them. A good looking bunch. I danced 'The Tennessee Waltz' with Wally."

Her stomach – the relentless, ubiquitous "burps" – continued to plague her. She woke one day in spring 1994 with a searing pain across her back and down her elbows. She took two Tylenol and slept it off. It happened again in the next morning. She thought about going to emergency, but in the end she just alerted her friends in the court.

> Mary said she'd take me into the hospital if I wanted her to, but we sat and talked awhile and decided I'd go home and Les would come by in an hour to check on me. If I was worse I'd take a little suitcase of nighttime needs and we'd go in. That sounded good, so I went home and settled in my chair. Les came by and visited awhile. I took Alka-Seltzer and Tagamet and felt fine when I went to bed. I had a good night and up at seven planning to celebrate by cleaning my oven.

Finally three days later Les took her to emergency. They ruled out a heart attack and recommended a gastroenterologist. I went up to accompany her to the doctor (a "lady" doctor, she noted with a hint of skepticism and then pride). She called it acid reflux, and gave her some sample medication.

Sue had run out of family to make afghans for and turned to making scarves and mittens for the cold climate great-grandkids. That done, she knitted mittens for Vern's and Oscar's golf clubs.

With Ruth gone her friendship with the Martins deepened. Kent drove her to Bible study and movies and they planned special outings to include her. They exchanged meals. "I come to appreciate her [Ruth Martin] more and more as I see her quiet, vital Christianity come through. Ken too gets dearer. We are closer for Ruth's absence, I think." They planned a trip to Utah to visit Ruth Drost and took Sue along.

It became more of a struggle to keep up with the music demands of church. She liked the challenge and discipline of the Bell Choir, but never quite relaxed into the musicality of it. At choir she noted that she was missing the middle page of one number they were singing and failed completely to get the insert with the prayer and readings. "I'm reminded once more that I'm probably too old to be counted on for anything but goofing off. There must be a cut-off someplace short of death. I came home and spent the rest of the day with the Sunday paper, mostly the puzzles."

Disturbing things happened at church that had nothing to do with her. Russ, the choir director, had a serious stroke at Christmas time. He was recovering slowly, but probably would not be back. Then the pastor was asked to resign in a mini-scandal of some sort.

It was the same at Blue Star Court. She watched as illness or circumstance led friend after friend away. "I begin to ponder my own length of stay. Should I stay until I'm unable to function at all? That would be pretty apt to work a hardship on the kids."

I drove up for a visit that Fall and told her that John was agitating to move to a bigger place (bigger than our four hundred square-foot Park Model), and had his eye on a new expanded model that would give us almost a thousand square feet with a guest room. In January when I came up for her birthday visit I was rhapsodizing about the new place and mentioned that we were putting the little one up for sale.

"I think I should buy it," she said.

While it seems perfectly inevitable in hindsight, at the time I was sincerely taken by surprise. I didn't think she would ever CHOOSE to leave Blue Star and her church and everything familiar. She wondered – I wondered – how John would feel having her a half block away. I told her that I would love it, but I would, of course, have to discuss it with John and get back to her.

Rosemary called to say that John thought it was a splendid idea and I told her on the phone that his willingness to have me close strengthened my willingness to do it. He was on the other line and chimed in that he thought it would be "great for all of us" to have me there, and would I like to rent or buy?

A week later my head is full of plans for moving and when I look at the stuff to sort and move I nearly despair. I checked with a dealer to see what my trailer might be worth and they suggested I check with the library. Next week I'm going to Tucson to check out The Voyager (RV Resort) and see if I really could fit into the trailer and the park.

Friends here aren't pleased that I'm leaving. I told them I wanted to be clear that I'm not leaving because I'm not content here. My heart tells me to stay, my head tells me to make plans for wrapping it up. I came home from bridge tired, tired.

I mislaid my purse at church, so there was a little storm of activity before we found it. Now, thankfully, I'm back home just wanting to read and rear back in my chair, but fatigue is spoiling any other plans I might have.

...put a For Sale by Owner sign in the window of the trailer. A fellow came by and asked to show it to a couple. Then he wanted to list it — for $3,000 or whatever he could get. Suddenly I had TWO offers. All at once the impact of really leaving looms, and I'm alternately loving and hating the idea.

...I've started packing. Rose called and all is going well there. They hope to move into their new place about the third of April. We sort of agreed my moving day would be the thirteenth. John is painting the shed that will now be my "studio." I am more excited about my studio hideaway than any spot in the unit itself. I will enjoy getting into serious work on some Mozart sonatas.

...I was struck once more that I am saying goodbye to lots of these people who have been a large part of my life for many years. It's a kind of death. I hope to be back occasionally but probably won't as I get either caught up in the life of The Voyager or old rockin' chair gets me or some of each. Still, far better to leave in sorrow than in pique. I didn't sleep well as I ran through all the stuff I have to pack.

She concluded the sale of her trailer, hired a mover and one by one, emptied drawers and took loads of stuff and clothes to Good Will. She arranged to cash in investments to buy the new place.

I can't believe I'm doing this big transaction nearly all by myself, but of course we all get help from people in positions of service and decision making. What would I have done without Gene [her church friend and financial advisor]? I took two brown bags of food leftovers, my pack of music and my hundred dollar Easter offering and went off to church for what may be my last encounter there. Lots of hugs and kisses and tears.

Rose came and by the end of the day had emptied all the cupboards and sent us scurrying to the donation center with leftovers.

And so it was done. We packed and sorted and dispatched; the U-Haul truck came with its young, strong-backed drivers who loaded up and left; Patty and Stina came in from Los Angeles and helped pile the last of the remains into Whitey (the '86 Ford LTD). As we were about to pull out of Blue Star for the last time, I looked back and saw Patty bolt from the car and pry off the wood carved name plate that read "The Rawson's, Claude and Sue" from the front of the trailer – across from the office and thirty feet from the hall – that had been her winter home for thirty years. She lived there longer than she had lived anywhere in her life, and those years had been her happiest. I asked if it had been difficult (I was expecting traumatic). "No," she said, "I knew it was time. Everything was changing there and it wouldn't be the same if I'd stayed."

When we drove into the Voyager RV Resort in Tucson, the truck was almost unloaded and John was directing the placement of the furniture. We had lunch and sent Sue to bed in our new guest room for a necessary nap.

When I revived they had set up the bed and made it ready for sleeping, unloaded the food into the fridge and arranged the cupboards. Rosie hung up three bags of clothes with remarkable judgment and I began getting used to the new quarters quite quickly. We rearranged a little in the studio and pointed to where John was to hang pictures. Everything fell into place – the music cabinet, the plush chair and hassock, the bookcase. I LIKE the room.

Then she took us all to Luby's cafeteria for dinner and the mood was festive.

The next day was Easter. It was a new sunrise service in the courtyard of her new community – listening to the music, not making it – and she approved of the new non-denominational pastor. We went to a fancy holiday buffet in the foothills, more extravagant than any of us liked much, and then she came home and spent an hour playing her piano in her new studio. Another bridge had been crossed.

CHAPTER 20

The Voyager

...the usual hustle and bustle

Sue settled seamlessly into life at the Voyager. If she had any
regrets about leaving Blue Star she never expressed them to me
or to her journal. In the weeks before she left for the summer we
went on a couple of shopping sprees and she bought a new dinette
set, a stool the exact height to mix her bread, and material for curtains to finish off the Play House (as she decided to call the room
that held the piano). She won high score at bridge three times.

She made her own travel arrangements (using the agent in the
park) and continued to fly out of Phoenix which meant she had to
ride the shuttle from Tucson two hours to get to the plane. For a
little bit more she could fly direct from Tucson, but we could not
persuade her to do that. She knew the Phoenix Sky Harbor Airport
well and seemed to manage fine with her old familiar routine, even
with Humongous.

It was about this time that Lue began the practice of getting
a box of wild baby mallard ducks that would go along and be
installed at the lake. Sue loved having them there. She tried not
to interfere too much in their upbringing, but she couldn't resist
treating them to leftover bread at dusk.

The duckies come swimming full speed when I call them.
They show up out of nowhere with beaks wide open like
ducky smiles and happy little peep-peeps coming from
six throats.

A week later:

One is missing. A pall hangs over the other five and me too.
I feel somehow I should shield them from enemies, but of
course I can't, and they have to learn to survive on their own.
Still I'm always fearful when they aren't directly at hand when
I call. Even when the geese are around they all just seem to be
able to forage together without much fuss. One day one of
them was separated from the others and he cried and cried
out on the edge of the lake by himself. Finally he was reunited
with the others with many contented clucks all around.

By mid-July:

. . . they disappear for days. They have found their wings. All
but Fatso (that little bread hog!) who couldn't get his girth
airborne. What a thrill it must be to discover one has wings.
They always come back to the point to sleep.

They had been gone for several weeks. Then on her walk to the
mailbox one day they called to her, "Quack Quack" all the way
home and waited for their bread handouts. Fatso was not with them.
Summer storms and tornado watches were always part of the seasonal drama along with hot humid days or rainy chilly ones. But in
July that year a gigantic storm took down thousands of trees in the
lake region and many of them landed on cabins and cars and boats.
The National Guard was mobilized to help clear fallen trees off roads
and public driveways. Their lot on Leaf Lake escaped major damage

(one boat was capsized) and so did Keeny and Vern's on Lake Maud, but the power was out for several days and their roads were blocked by fallen trees. The destruction was something to behold.

~

We decided to celebrate her ninetieth birthday during the summer when more of the family could be there. Wally and Lue were called upon once again to play host at their home near Anoka. A notice was placed in the Steele *Ozone* so that any Pettibone people could attend who were of a mind to. There were a few takers. Bonnie came with all of her girls and their kids – seven in all. Duane and Cookie came from Arizona. Scott Gores, his wife and baby girl came from Oklahoma. All of mine came and most of Wally's.

The gathering for Sue's 90th birthday included these thirty family members. Another twenty were unable to attend.

The early comers and the more devout went to church that morning with Wally and Lue; the rest of us gathered and shared pictures and caught up. After the catered buffet we gathered in the living room for a program of honoring and remembering. In the invitation I asked them all to bring their afghans if they could, and we managed to get a stack several feet high and tilting, an impressive cornucopia of color and patterns. Wally started off the program reminding Sue that she had been there through many trials of his life – from 'his borning cry' and the surgery on his leg to his recent heart surgery. "I can only conclude," he concluded, "that you brought me bad luck." Then he got out his mandolin and sang "Mother Machree." Amy and Sydney played a couple of duets on the piano, Amy's Sara, sixteen and gorgeous in her cropped hair and short skirt played a merry number on her trumpet. Terry played "Ave Maria" on the flute. Then Mom got up and recited Browning's "If I forget yet God remembers…" and finished off with "I falter where I firmly trod…" We had not heard the recitations she had been giving to other groups for several years now – not since childhood anyway. I was impressed. She and Wally finished the program singing "Let the Lower Lights Be Burning" in harmony.

> We did quite well, I thought *[referring to the singing]*. I was awash with hugs and "I love you's." I'm so happy to have the assurances from so many of my own. I got many cards with notes of sweet remembrances and wishes. I came home with a suitcase full to process and read. I count my blessings – too many to recall.

This was also the summer she went into battle with the IRS. Since Claude died she had taken her documents to one of the free tax clinics that show up at tax time and they would help her file. In 1994 they told her that she didn't need to file because her income

was too low. So she didn't. Ditto in 1995. Then she got a notice
that she owed back taxes plus a penalty for failing to file. Before
she could get her bearings the penalty was up to $800. She sent
them a check. She enlisted the help of Darold Rath, a Pettibone
boy who was now a CPA. He looked into it and said she probably
owed them $1,400 for each of those years, most of it was penalty,
and he sent her a bill for $500, about standard for professional
services, but it shocked her. Not long afterward she received an
insurance check for minor damage to her trailer in Tucson. It was
for $500, she noticed.

> A day or so later I got dunned ten dollars by the state of
> North Dakota for nonpayment. So I paid it. I will let Darold
> take care of the federal penalty. Still I was depressed in the
> late afternoon again. I don't know if I am allowing this cloud
> of rebuke hanging over me to get to me.

There was more to come. I don't know that she ever consulted
anyone in the family about her dilemma.
The journal recorded the details of life:

> ...went to Medina for Tina's wedding [Frank's granddaughter]
> and was happy to see all Frank's kids – Cara, David,
> Dennis...Wally started singing with the Sons of Norway
> Chorus and we took to calling them "Wally and the
> Norwegians"...Keeny's Jane had a baby girl, Hayley Colleen,
> on October 25, Claudia's and Sydney's birthday. I'll bet
> Garrett is beside himself. Last summer he was talking to her
> on a regular basis...stopped in Pettibone and heard that
> our church had closed for good...got out Humongous and
> he's already half full of clothes and papers...stopped on the
> way out of town to have root canal surgery.

At the Voyager we settled into new habits. She and John would meet at the intersection of Fifth and Mourning Dove and go to the nondenominational church service and the preservice hymn sing at the main hall and then to the restaurant for continental breakfast, taking turns picking up the bill. "I like the order of service, the sermon and the music," she wrote.

Sunday afternoons, as John settled down for a loud, satisfying fix of football, Mom and I went to the movies. Usually I would scan the movie ads and suggest three or four and she would choose. Once she had a choice of her own. She'd read a review and she wanted to see *The Bird Cage* with Robin Williams. I was a little baffled – and curious. When we came out she said, "Did you know it was all about homosexuals?" Well, yes. "Well, it was interesting – and pretty funny," she said. The next week we saw *Braveheart* because it won the Academy Award, but we both found it way too violent for our liking. Then we saw *Titanic* and we thought we'd never warm up again.

The IRS saga went on. They continued to send notices of penalties and claimed they had not received the $800 she sent. She made copies of the cancelled check and sent it to them. She called the IRS and talked to a guy, explaining the whole sad tale. He thought she could appeal and said he would look into it. She never heard from him again.

Monday nights we played partners bridge and sometimes took top prize. Usually we ended up somewhere around 3,000 to 4,000 points. One memorable night we had wonderful cards and could do no wrong, bidding and making slams. We ended up with 7,790 points and became legendary in the bridge circles. The scorecard was taped in her journal and I remembered it well.

Thursdays we went shopping. This involved going to three different supermarkets to get their specials. The "loss leader" snare never worked on her, she just picked up the bargains and left. I would fill my cart and head for the checkout. If there was one line longer than the rest I could usually find her at the front of it, carefully going through her coupons and digging out the appropriate check book (she had three and kept them bound together with a rubber band in her purse). Then we would go to lunch, usually sharing an order. We tried a new place every week, just for the adventure of it.

I always went to the vegetarian potluck at the Voyager and she went along – nothing's more vegetarian than dark bread. John didn't like potlucks at all, or she might have gone with him to the regular one. She always took two loaves of fresh, warm dark bread and her fame spread. She once tried to engage the group in a sing-along, but it didn't work.

I encouraged her to try yoga and to learn mah jongg, but she resisted. Her mornings centered on Chuck Swindoll's broadcast on the Christian station. Two or three times a week we shared the evening meal much as she and Ruth Drost had done. Frequently the three of us went out to Luby's cafeteria or Tony Roma's for ribs or to the restaurant in the Voyager.

John checked on her almost daily to bring her mail and see if she needed something fixed or errands run. She was lavish with her thanks and he loved doing it.

Her stomach problems got worse; sometimes she was hardly able to sleep at all. We took her to John's geriatrician, Dr. Gallagher (Sue persisted in referring to him as Dr. Shenanigan). He suspected it was more than acid reflux and sent her for tests. It was *H. pylori*, a bacterial infection often confused with ulcers. For a week or so she was on a strict regimen of medications, some to be taken with food, some without, strictly on schedule. There was much improvement and relief, but the everyday burps continued. In all her years at Apache Junction, she had never had a regular doctor. When Dr. Gallagher/Shenanigan asked what prescription medications she was on and found out there were none, he could hardly believe it.

She continued going to Bonnie's for Thanksgiving, riding the shuttle to Phoenix to start the flight. She developed a disarming technique for ensuring help, picking out a likely looking burly passenger she would say, "When it comes time to board would you look out for me a little?" Invariably he would be glad to and went out of his way to get her settled, and often seemed pleased with himself over his good deed. Almost always she engaged her seatmates and shared stories. Often they ended up exchanging addresses and sending Christmas cards. Some were un-engageable. That was always a disappointment, a waste of a good airplane trip, in her world. Increasingly it got to be a very long, tiring trip with the shuttle rides at both ends and often a layover in the middle. She was, after all, in her nineties.

That first Christmas Sue was asked to play for the Christmas carol sing-along in the hall. She accepted and practiced and marked her books for the favorite songs. It would have been fine if she'd been allowed to call out the carols and march through her books of music, but the guy leading the sing-along was taking requests from the audience. They called out requests, sometimes many at once and she couldn't always hear. Up on the stage she fumbled through the books while the audience waited and the leader rolled his eyes. I wanted to kill him. I got up to help her when he finally called an end to it. She didn't discuss it, but she was uncharacteristically quiet on the way home. In her journal she called it "A FIASCO!"

On New Year's Day, 1996, my cousin Connie called from San Diego to tell me Marg had died. She was ninety-two. Mom and I took her car and made the eight-hour drive across the desert to San Diego. She drove for about a hundred miles of it. We sang all the way, as I remember, all the hymns we could think of with as many of the verses as we could conjure up. For her that was most of them. We sang in harmony. We sang the golden oldies from the twenties and thirties and the World War II songs from the forties and my songs from the fifties. By the time we were up to the Beatles we were hoarse and almost to the turnoff to Connie's.

At the service at the cemetery, the pastor (who didn't know any of them) recalled how Margaret loved to play the piano for her family. I was puzzled. I'd never heard Marg play the piano or even heard that she did. I looked at Mom who looked back with the same puzzled look – and perhaps a little umbrage. Marg got in one last poke.

> Marg didn't look much like herself. It's just as well. It's when they look like the ones you remember that it triggers grief. I could only feel relief that her vigil was over at last. It was good to see her kids and grands and great grands. Nice family. No one seemed devastated. Connie seemed the most moved and George hovered over her gently as she viewed the body. We were both touched by that. We stopped in El Centro for breakfast on the way home. Oatmeal soothed the ragin' in my belly and it was a pretty comfortable drive. I drove a hundred miles or so and Rose took us into Tucson.

Later that month we celebrated her real ninetieth birthday and they gave her special recognition in church. Ruth and Kent Martin came down for the day. Arlene came for a week's visit and one of those days Kelly (Arlene's daughter) flew in from Vegas for the day. She was gorgeous and sophisticated and good company. Arlene beamed.

When Sue moved to Tucson, Stephanie wrote to say she had a colleague here, an ophthalmologist she had worked with in New Orleans, Barry Kusman. We went to consult him about Mom's cataracts. He was delighted to hear about Stephanie's family and scheduled Mom for surgery on one eye.

I was conscious through the whole thing. I could feel him sewing and clipping the eye ball. It felt like tender loving care and I was content, just a brief stab of light pain at the end and Barry was there to say, "How are you, Sweetie?" They brought me coffee and doughnuts and I dressed and we left. Rosie watched the whole thing on a monitor in the waiting room. Barry called that night to find out how I was doing.

John's daughter Kathy lived in Windsor, England, around the corner from the Queen. She and Nick had their first baby, Robert Dylan (Nick was an ardent fan of Bob Dylan) on Kathy's birthday in February. So in March we flew out to see our English grandbaby. Our Wisconsin friends, Wes and Jane Ostlund were planning a trip west so we persuaded them to come to Tucson and stay in our place – and incidentally keep an eye out for Mom. It all went swimmingly. They even took her up to Blue Star for a reunion.

At tax time Sue scouted around for some free help with her taxes, and so she made the acquaintance of Jay Rose. Jay was not pretty. Half of his face and one eye were disfigured from some surgery or accident, but he had long ago made peace with it and so did everyone else. He was outgoing and generous with his time and very conscientious. He took the stack of papers she had accumulated and went home to make sense of them. It was Jay who found the letter from the IRS saying they had given her erroneous information, and Jay who laid out the evidence for her appeal.

Spring brought the usual migration, Mother's Day was amply celebrated and Wally and Lue were packing for the upcoming Memorial Day weekend and Sue's summer at the lake. Sue wrote:

The usual hustle and bustle and confusion as suitcases, coolers, baskets and boxes are set out for loading. That plus a box of ducklings. How cunning they are. Kitty sensed the panic of the occasion and hid under the bed and paid no attention to our pleading. It took awhile to find her when we were ready to leave...the ducks are getting a curl in their tails. At dusk we put the food inside their house that Wally made and say 'chip-chip-chip' and they come running in for the night...

...watched with horror what was happening on Tiananmen Square...the operated eye continues to fog up occasionally, and the thought of losing my sight is staggering. I prayed nightly and it cleared up some.

4TH OF JULY 1996   Darold came by and picked up the letters for the IRS problem. It looks as if the problem could be solved soon. Dare I hope? It's been hanging over me like a dark cloud for a year.

...celebrated the July birthdays — Lue turned sixty-five and Keeny sixty-seven. They say you don't feel old until you see your kids getting old. Now even the grandkids are showing their age...

In August, Mom, Keeny and Vern, Wally and Lue drove to Minneapolis for my surprise sixtieth birthday party. John gave my girls a check and told them to plan it. I'm a wonderful candidate for a surprise party because I never suspect a thing. I thought we were just having a picnic at Lake Harriet with the kids. When we walked over the hill and saw the banner and a huge group gathered, I was still thinking, "Oh look, someone's having a party." Then the faces came into focus — Polly was there, Mom and Keeny, even Dudley from the old comedy club days.

Her bridge buddies were there and Dudley Riggs, who said, "Rosemary was the real humorist in the family." Others came up wanting "to meet Rosemary's mother." Polly flew in from Vail just for the party. So we ate the catered lunch that Cara ordered and John paid for. Cara and her Jim were flying out the next day to meet his family in Alaska, so things look serious.

In September Darold wrote a letter and accused the IRS of harassing her and the letters stopped.

Wally retired and they began to think about leaving their Minneapolis/Anoka place. They decided on Detroit Lakes. Leaf Lake wasn't appropriate for a permanent year-around home (even though some people were building them). They found their new home three miles outside of Detroit Lakes on State Highway 34.

> The Anoka house sold in a flurry. The new house looks
> like something out of *Better Homes and Gardens* with plants
> indoors and out, beautifully landscaped outside, multi levels
> inside and a three car garage.

Sue went again to the Eldershostel in Crookston at Saint Benedict; the classes were on Lake Agassiz, music and tai chi. This would be her last Elderhostel.

In December the IRS finally settled. "The gal who did the paperwork said she was sorry they'd caused me so much trouble. The $380 I had coming had dwindled to $39." But it would be another year before they quit withholding money from her annuity with the Lutheran Bible Institute. In April, 1997, she got a refund check for $781. "I hope 1997 isn't another round of perpetual aggravation. Darold seems to think they've got it right now."

> ...played a Mozart for the offertory for church services.
> Several people stopped me in the street afterward to express
> their appreciation ...went with Jay to the Marshall Home for
> Men and played for them ...went to a fiddlers' event at the
> hall and the guy from across the street asked me to dance

"The Waltz You Saved for Me"... listened to Chuck Swindoll,
listening intently, nodding assent... down sick with the flu for
three days, then Rosie got it... had surgery on my other eye...

Sue learned that Jay Rose shared her birthday and that year she
found the perfect card for him. It featured a cowboy flashing his
bare buns and hanging his just-laundered boxers on the clothesline
attached to his horse. "Birthdays are like underwear," it read, "You
got to do them once a year whether they need it or not." It tickled
her enough to record it in her journal.

With her cataract surgery complete Sue was once again able to
do fine needlework. She came across an old instruction book for
tatting and remembered that she had long ago enjoyed making the
delicate lacy trim and doilies. She knew that nobody used doilies
anymore, but still, the art of making lace... She bought a tatting
shuttle and some #80 thread and practiced. The best ones she
blocked on white paper and sprayed with starch to stiffen them.
She showed her handwork to family and friends and, of course,
they ooed and aahed.

Everyone who got an afghan now got a doily. Anyone who did
her a favor got a doily. After she had her second cataract surgery
she brought Dr. Kusman a doily. "I explained to him that I wasn't
assuming he *wanted* a tatted doily, but it was a token of what I was
able to do after he fixed my eyes."

I planned to have my doily framed. On one of our shopping outings we stopped at the frame shop and there was some discussion
about the matting, the color, the size and how it would be mounted,
whether or not the glass should be raised to give it a three dimen-
sional effect. The framer was a guy with a gray ponytail and a bit
of a paunch and he seemed genuinely engaged in the whole project.
When we went to pick up the finished project she brought him a
doily. He seemed pleased. Mine still hangs in the guest room and
I still enjoy it. She won a blue ribbon at the Pima County Fair for

her doilies and another for the crocheted baby afghan. The baby afghan won a purple ribbon for Best in Class as well. There was one other entrant in the tatting category. That entrant was ninety-six.

When she ran out of the usual recipients she made tiny keepsake doilies for seven great-granddaughters. She sent off Jill's baby afghan with doilies for The Guys to be left in Allison's safe keeping until such time as they might have wives who would value them. That left only P.J. and Reid to be doilied. It was getting harder to find tatting yarn. "They are cute as little ducks in the early stages of their creation and I marvel that I've made so many and I'm still not bored with them." By November 1997, she noted, she had made over forty.

Her Thanksgiving trip to Florida was a long ordeal of one darn thing after another. It snowed, the plane was delayed and she missed the connecting flight, she almost got on the wrong plane, she got home fourteen hours later exhausted and reevaluating her circumstances. But a week later, when Patty called to invite her to Seattle for Christmas (Patty pointed out that they had the basics: a piano, a violin, a Scrabble board, a pinochle deck and a private room) she accepted in a heartbeat.

Seattle was snowy and slushy, but inside it was cozy and filled with music and seasonal cheer. A break in the weather allowed them to go out to lunch at The Needle. The flights home were delayed by the weather, but the kids stayed with her and they played pinochle in the Seattle airport waiting for the weather to clear and connecting flights to be rearranged. At home at last she celebrated the New Year with popcorn and Walter Cronkite hosting the Vienna Orchestra on NPR. "What a blessing it is to have a good home with shelter and food."

On her ninety-second birthday she wrote:

> . . . one more milestone. In times past all that seemed to
> be expected of someone this old was that they be as little

trouble as possible until they mercifully slipped away. Not quite so with me. I try to have some course to my life, achieving some goals each day. Chuck Swindoll comes on the radio at nine weekdays and if I carelessly fail to tune in I am distressed. I generally do my tatting while I listen. Then I have my International Coffee with four Tums for calcium, write a letter or pay bills or send a donation. I've been doing exercises again of late. I am grateful that it isn't physically difficult for me. Last year it would have been harder. Then I go over to the Play House for an hour or so to work on the piano. By then it's time for my breakfast of oat bran or bear mush. Then it's nearly time for my afternoon soaps *[soap operas]* during which I generally doze off. There's always some sort of tidying up to do. I get the PBS News Hour with Jim Lehrer. If there's nothing good on PBS I turn on public radio to have with my newspaper. I'm trying to finish three or four books and establish some system to my reading. I've almost finished McCourt's *Angela's Ashes, Life after Death* and *Prayer* by Stedman (one of Swindoll's offerings). Still, I persevere...

One of the things that puzzled me about the journals was her habit of recording every compliment and accolade she received. It suggested an emotional neediness I did not notice in her daily encounters. Then I came across this explanation:

I got a copy of my medical record where Dr. Gallagher refers to me as "a delightful eighty-nine-year-old woman." I report these neat little indulgences to my journal so I can enjoy them later without annoying my friends.

The years spun on as she recorded the details of her own and family events. Wally and Lue celebrated their forty-five years together with a big party and Sue wrote and presented a comic history of their marriage; we went to Chicago for Jill's wedding; Arlene had a bad car accident, totaling her car, and she arranged to buy Sue's Whitey that had pretty much sat in the carport since she moved to Tucson.

Sue left early one year to attend the wedding of Jessie (Rick's daughter) and Chris in Texas – the first of the great-grands to marry. A year later she went again to see their new baby, Shelby Sue, her first great-great-grandchild and namesake. Word came that Ruth Drost had died.

On turning ninety-three she wrote: "I have better endurance than I had a couple of years ago. I can walk to play bridge or to the mailbox [about a city block] with only one or two pauses to rest my legs and back. I go to the Play House almost daily to play. People tell me they hear me playing as they go past and enjoy it." She recalled and recorded entire bridge hands. She was reading Scott Peck and Jon Kabat Zinn.

> ...we went to the zoo and walked...bought a $33 roll of stamps...went to hear the Struthers Jazz Band. They were very good, I guess, but jazz puts so many extraneous notes in its music I lose the melody.

On the flight back to Minnesota she sat with a congenial couple who brought out a small travel version of Scrabble. She beat them soundly.

That spring a dog got into the baby duck pen and killed nine of the fifteen babies. They gave away the rest of them and reluctantly "we went out of the duck raising business."

> I have a pretty full calendar for an old woman: Sunday, read for church; Monday, all day ALCW Women's Retreat; Tuesday, bridge; Wednesday, ALCW closing reading;

Thursday, X-rays in the afternoon, theatre in evening; Friday, Crazy Daze sales in Detroit Lakes.

She was interviewed for a feature in the Becker County *Record* for a couple of hours and when the reporter left she remembered, "I forgot to tell her of my love affair with poetry and my history of sharing dark bread."

CHAPTER 21

Getting Home

...weeks slip by

In August 1999 Wally came out to the lake to take care of some chores as the summer wound down. Sue was in her trailer nursing a cup of coffee and finishing up a game of Yahtzee with herself. There was an old tree on the far side of the compound that had to come down. He'd taken down trees before, and he knew the dangers. He was maneuvering it into position when it gave way. It caught him diagonally, crushing his left shoulder and collarbone, twisting and breaking his right ankle and causing internal injuries to his brain, lungs and heart. It was a neighbor who heard him groaning and rushed to his aid and then to Sue's trailer.

> He knocked at the door saying "Wally's had a heart attack. Call 911 right away." Between us we got it done. Then I went to his side rubbing his terribly painful back and took off his shoe. He was conscious all the while. The ambulance arrived soon after, and the medics took him in to St. Mary's emergency. I called Lue at the Elks where she was playing bridge. I called Keeny and Vern and they arrived at the hospital about the same time I did. Then the interminably

315

long wait for things to get sorted out. They found the broken ankle right away. He was given morphine to take care of his multiple injuries. I stayed overnight with Lue. Terry arrived in the middle of the night; Rick, Patty and Tony came the next morning. The next day they took him to Fargo all hooked up with tubes.

Leaving the lake was confused and chaotic while others pulled in the boats and drained the pipes, chores that Wally usually did. Sue decided to move in with Lue so she wouldn't be at the lake alone. "...hard to believe it's the last night here for the year and maybe forever. But first I have to clean the oven and the fridge before Ted drains the pipes."

After a few scary days Wally stabilized and came home to sit – hurting and frustrated, but grateful to be alive – in a recliner while Lue waited on him. Then she went out and cut the grass and righted the mailbox that a highway crew knocked down.

He slowly recovered, determined to do the jobs he had always done. The doctor said there was nerve damage in the shoulder and he would probably never recover the use of his left arm. It was very weak and he couldn't raise it above the shoulder. After a few months of frustrating disability, Wally declared he 'couldn't live like this' and they went to a specialist in nerve damage. The specialist said there was a fifty percent chance a graft procedure might work, but why not wait a bit longer? At home, with Lue's help, he continued to exercise the muscles. And they prayed. When he went back a month or so later, X-rays showed the nerves were beginning to grow again. The doctors were amazed at his tenacity. By summer he was functioning pretty well.

Sue continued to drive, mostly back and forth to Keeny and Vern's. More and more she got rides to bridge and shopping. She went to get her driver's license renewed and passed the eye test.

My friend nearly flipped when she heard I'd got my drivers license renewed. She exclaimed over and over how GREAT it was, but I presume was secretly horrified to think of me out on the road. I could have assured her I would be selective and discreet about times and distances. Actually I feel quite comfortable behind the wheel.

But later she wrote:

I drove home from Wally's *[maybe twenty miles]* about midnight. I shouldn't do that, I decided. Too many miscues in driving. It was very dark.

As Keeny and Vern prepared to leave for the season:

I went to the Gores to eat up a couple of little pizzas left from Garrett and Hayley's visits and Keeny baked a berry pie. Everything was beautifully prepared. Then there was bridge and Shanghai and margaritas — lovely togetherness which leaves us a bit sad at our pending goodbyes. I am increasingly reminded that each lovely moment may very well be the last by the sheer rightness of things in God's plans for this world and His children in it. I have been blessed in hundreds of ways through the years and I guess I can trust Him to see me through the final ones too.

Polly had begun her quest to walk around the world. By the time we headed back to Arizona she had walked from Vail, Colorado, to Flagstaff, Arizona, and we were to meet up with her there and walk with her for a couple of days. For me it turned out to be a couple of weeks; she needed someone to drive the support van until the new driver got there. Polly wrote a journal almost every day, documenting her progress, and we followed it on her website. I printed the journals and sent them on to Mom. In November she wrote: "A new log arrived from Polly. The walk goes on (in New Zealand now) and she is meeting more key people for the cause *[breast cancer]*. She has gone through Auckland and is on her way again."

John Jr. and Dianne and their kids, Abbie and Dan came for Christmas, along with John's sister Sue from Santa Fe. Yes, there were seven for Christmas: two were named John Rawson and two were named Sue Rawson. It smacked of a lack of imagination.

It was lovely to have family for Christmas again. We drove around the city looking at lights and to Tubac and the ruins of the Tumacacori Mission where the soft light of luminarias set a quiet, spiritual Christmas mood. Abbie and Dianne got up early Christmas Day and went to the traditional mariachi mass at St. Augustine Cathedral for a little local Christmas experience.

Sixteen-year-old Abbie admired the crocheted cap Sue was making, so Sue started one for her. We had a taco night and a sticky caramel roll morning. They brought gifts for everyone, including a collection of classical CDs for Sue, and when they discovered she had no CD player they bought her one of those too. She was, she said, quite humbled. John Sr. gave her a batch of hand-written gift certificates, tasks to be completed as needed – washing windows, sweeping the carport, errands. She gave him gift cards to Luby's.

John asked Sue to give the blessing for Christmas dinner and she did:

> *Thou art the way the truth and the life. Without the way there is no going, without the truth there is no knowing, without the life there is no living. Lord show us the way that we may know the truth which shall set us free and we would lay hold of eternal life.*

Then we sang the table prayer, "be present at our table Lord...." We gathered later in the Play House to sing Christmas carols.

"... finished Abbie's cap the next day. That ugly yarn turned into a rather charming little cap. She looked as cute as a bug in it."

They flew home and we all settled down to watch and await with some trepidation the arrival of the year 2000.

※

I don't know exactly how or when or who decided, but that spring they began to look for a permanent place for her in Minnesota. For years we had watched with increasing unease as she flew back and forth and to Florida for Thanksgiving, none of us brave or wise or foolhardy enough to say, "Enough, already!" She shouldn't be alone at the lake for days at a time, and she really shouldn't be driving. The first signs of spidery, quavery handwriting appeared in the journals. I think it was Vern who first discovered the Lincoln Park Senior Apartments being planned next to the nursing facility and hospital in Detroit Lakes. He put her name on the waiting list, just in case.

In Tucson, too, there were some small signs of decline, but nothing specific. We went back and forth a little less. We sponsored the flowers for church for her ninety-fifth birthday. "It was a wonderful church service. I felt little twinges that my time here is limited," she wrote. She was having more trouble hearing at movies and on television, but not a lot. She mentioned several times she wished she had a best friend here, a peer like Ruth maybe. But she had no peers, she was ninety-five. She had admirers. She was an icon.

> I have periods of depression, but they are gratefully rather short and always in the late afternoons and usually have dissipated with supper and the news. My evenings are fine. When I get to worrying over something I remember Jon Kabat Zinn: "At the deepest level there is no giver, no gift

and no recipient — only the universe rearranging itself." I'm
signed up for bridge, but I felt depressed and burpy and
only wanted to put my head under my wing (poor thing).
I considered calling to cancel, but I took the Tylenol I was
supposed to have taken last night and some Alka-Seltzer and
went back to bed. An hour later I was more interested in the
bridge idea and got up and dressed.

John and I were ready to stop the migration back and forth
ourselves, ready to give up the cabin in Wisconsin. I was more
than ready to leave the Voyager and so was John, but I told him I
would not leave the Voyager as long as Mom was there. But secretly
I began to scope out neighborhoods in the city.

Somewhere along the line it was decided. There was resignation
as she prepared to leave this time.

APRIL 1, 2001   I left the 2001 journal and the others with
Rosemary, for what it's worth (not much). I've been making
slow progress getting everything ready to throw out or pass
on to donation centers, and put large amounts of junk into
assorted boxes to be loaded into a rental U-Haul to tote
to D.L., pretty much permanently. Wally and Lue arrived in
their camper pickup as per plan. They are camped over in
the temporary section. We gathered at Rosie and John's for
lasagna and played a couple of rubbers of bridge. But we were
all tired and soon gave up and went to bed. Wally picked up
the U-Haul and it seems small to me. I may have to leave the
green sofa but I won't fuss about that. I'm leaving GOBS of
clothes [I took forty-three blouses to Pio Decimo; she had made all of
them]. It feels like abandoning your dog. Most of my clothes
are older than most dogs. The final goodbyes at church and
with Rose and John were painful, clinging and difficult.

It was one of the saddest days of my life. I still treasure the winters we spent together in Tucson. I tried to imagine what it was like for her to cross the border into New Mexico, knowing she was leaving Arizona for the last time. Many – maybe most – of the happiest times of her life were spent here, and for the first time, I think, she was not looking forward to the future.

The journals that summer were alternately hopeful and discouraged. She never quite settled at the lake, the two bedroom apartment at the Lincoln Park facility was not quite ready, but in time she was invited for a tour and started to move in. Keeny made the curtains. It was probably the nicest place Sue had ever lived.

> It's as nice as I anticipated. I've started a list of things to get for it. It has only a shower, not a bath. But it has a seat, so I may adjust to it easier than I first thought. In my spare moments I am visualizing tables and lamps. The piano sits placidly dominating the room. I was planning to break in my new mattress and spend my first night in the new digs, but then discovered that I had no nightie or toothbrush. Besides feeling dumb I was feeling sort of abandoned, so I called Lue and Wally and had them take me back to the lake. I just have this uneasy sense of being uprooted. I found two hundred dollars tucked in books when I filled the bookcase. I forgot I'd put it there for safekeeping.
>
> More people have moved in. It looks like we might have two tables of bridge. Patty gave me a new book of musical classics; I can't wait to dig in. I get a little nostalgic when I see people in their RVs heading south and west.

It never quite seemed like home. In September Wally, Lue and Sue started on a road trip that would take them to Chicago (with a stop at Allison's to see the Leones), Cincinnati and North Carolina to see Bonnie and Oscar. Bonnie could no longer travel. They were on the road when they heard about the attack on the Twin Towers in New York on September 11.

> Rosemary called. I'd been eager for news of Polly who was walking in Malaysia on 9/11 and is now in Thailand and getting honored guest treatment.

Back in Detroit Lakes Sue fell into depression. She watched cable news for hours at a time and thought her building was being infiltrated – by what I'm not sure. Soon she was spending most of her time back with Wally and Lue. Wally called one night and said, "Mother wanted me to call the girls. She thinks she's dying." I don't know what we said beyond, "I love you. Please get over this." I couldn't imagine 'Sue' and 'depressed' in the same sentence. She did come out of it and Wallys moved her to a one-bedroom apartment in the assisted living facility next door, the fourth time they'd moved her that year. Wally and Lue really earned their angel's wings that year.

> I have no appetite. Dear Mary came in and gave me a shower. I was fearful if I tried it alone I'd have trouble, all bare naked and helpless. She was kind and understanding. I went to exercises and did well with the challenge. I played a bit on the piano in the dining room – badly. If I don't improve it won't pay to move mine [from the apartment]. May God guide us through these important decisions … trying to psych myself into being hungry. Pills leave me drowsy and it's easier just to fall asleep. On Saturday I went out to Wally's and made two batches of chokecherry jelly.

There is one entry in April, one in May:

I get more sluggish about doing my journal, my days are so
similar. People complain about the weather. I just enjoy my
comfortable digs and my shut-in-ness. The doctor says he
doesn't quite believe I had depression, said I wasn't the type.
My "keeping" a journal is sort of a joke; the weeks sort of
slip by.

Her handwriting was getting more crimped and scratchy. She
wrote that she'd had a slight stroke and lost her speech for a few
minutes. They sent her to the hospital for tests and wanted to put
her in the nursing home – Wally said she wasn't ready for that
and Keeny and Lue arranged to do more care giving. She started
a couple of snowflake doilies but she made mistakes and ended
up throwing them away. The first anniversary of 9/11 brought it
all back – "it hasn't lost any of its horror." Fall goodbyes to Keeny
and Vern grew more intense, all of them assuming they would be
the last. People in her facility died or went to the nursing home.
She complained that it was hard to maintain a foursome to play
bridge – they kept dying.

In July 2003 she made a doily for a young couple getting married – "possibly the closest to flawless as any I've made. Time goes
by mostly pleasantly."

In October, 2003, Polly walked into Detroit Lakes, only a slight
detour on her walk around the world which was almost complete.
It had been the plan all along that she would walk there and Sue
and the whole family would walk with her for this little stretch.
John and I came from Tucson, the other kids from Minneapolis.
All of us, including Mom, wore our GlobalWalk t-shirts and posed
for pictures at the Lakeside Pavilion. The Lions Club provided
pizza for everyone. Sue was taking some of her last steps carefully
and with assistance. Cara's son Eamon was taking his first. He was
eleven months old.

Polly's GlobalWalk brought her to Detroit Lakes where four generations of the family met to walk with her. From the left standing: Laurie, Polly, Sue, Rosemary; in front Cara and her children, Eamon and Rose.

Almost a year later she wrote:

> Lue, Wally, Keeny and Vern are packing up to go to Vail to welcome Polly as she completes her walk around the world. She continues to write in her journal as she completes the last steps of that journey.

It was the last journal entry.

At the end of February the next winter she had an "episode," just a steady weakening until she was admitted to the hospital. "The doctor says she is bleeding internally and is too weak to tolerate the necessary treatment," Wally wrote in an email to the family.

We assumed the worst. Wally, anticipating that if she died her bank accounts would be frozen, informed us (his sisters) that he had taken money out of the account and made tentative funeral plans. Arlene came to keep vigil, taking turns with Wally and Lue. Gradually Sue responded. Two weeks later Wally wrote, "My observation now is that Grandma has stabilized. Each day she is a little stronger and talks more and even, maybe, makes a little more sense. Relax everyone, she may outlive us all!"

We exhaled. She was released from the hospital to the nursing home and Wallys cleared out her apartment in assisted living.

The next winter we gathered for the celebration of her one hundredth birthday. The staff did a lovely job of setting it up. Patty brought her a tiara. A dozen or so people came halfway across the state from Pettibone, all of them from my generation – the kids that boarded with us, the ones who took piano lessons. Sue knew them all and recalled memories from their past acquaintance. Grandchildren and great-grandchildren provided the music. I gave a retrospective of her life that concluded with this:

"Now we are here to celebrate the last one hundred years – a remarkable number. By my reckoning that's 36,525

Sue at 100

days, marching by one after the other. Some of them good, some of them bad. Some of them VERY good (When Wally came back from Korea unscathed). Some of them very, very bad (The day we lost Claudia). And most of them probably a little of each.

"I don't know what she might say she has learned in all this time, but I know what she has taught – by sharing and by example: To love music. And poetry. Be tolerant – go easy on people, they're trying to do the best they can. Try new things, don't fear change – embrace it! Keep busy. Be useful. Don't complain. Don't gossip. If you're not sure, err on the side of curiosity and possibility, not caution. Be generous – with your time, your money and your talents. Love the Lord with all your heart, with all your soul, with all your mind – and your neighbor as yourself. Always look forward."

Goodbyes were particularly hard this time. One last enveloping hug. She was so small and frail by now it was like hugging my child. "I adore you, you know," she said. "I know, I know." I got to the end of the hall and turned and came back one more time.

She endured the nursing home for most of another year, sometimes remarkably lucid, sometimes delusional.

In October she broke a hip. Doctors said that she would have to have surgery or the pain would be unbearable. The chances of her surviving the surgery were not great, but she did. The staff tried to get her to do the rehabilitation exercises, but she resisted. She was exhausted and in pain. She wanted nothing more than to go to bed. To go. Wally sent daily emails on her status, and finally to say that her care had been taken over by the hospice team. Arlene came again. Wally wrote, "We are sitting with her twenty-four hours now in shifts, Lue, Arlene and I. She struggles to talk but I don't get much of it. I told her we were a bad match because she can't talk and I can't hear. It got a faint smile out of her." The next day she stirred enough to say, "I hope this doesn't take long."

Before I could fly across the country and drive across the state she was gone. At the end it was Arlene keeping vigil, loyal to the end. They were all waiting in the room when I arrived an hour later in case I wanted to see her. She was an abandoned shell, the chrysalis that remains when the butterfly has flown. There was no sign of my generous, funny, courageous, loving mom.

At the funeral Keeny and I went for one last goodbye before they closed the casket. "I wonder what secrets she took with her," she said. I wonder, too. They weren't *all* revealed in that bushel and a half of journals that awaited me.

Pettibone 2013

Pettibone celebrated its Centennial birthday in 2010 and the ones who stayed threw a grand party for the ones who had left and came back for the occasion. Nancy Morlock, a granddaughter of Zana Kaczmarski, Pettibone's celebrity artist, put together the Centennial book of family histories, so Nancy was the one I called on to find out how my hometown looked at age 100. That day the population of Pettibone was 66. She knew because she counted them, something I used to do when it was more like 120.

I remember the first postcard photos of Pettibone with just a house or two poking out of the flat prairie. Today the aerial photo shows a substantial cluster of trees hiding the houses, many of them aging and empty. The railroad tracks were removed by 1999; the depot was torn down years ago. Our little Evangelical Lutheran Church closed and was sold. The grain elevator burned in 1984; the white clapboard school in 1971. The last class to graduate from Pettibone High School was 1995 with four graduates. It included Paul DeKrey, the grandson of the Paul DeKrey who graduated with Sue and Margaret in the first class in 1923.

That fall the Pettibone School joined with Tuttle. Pettibone had the elementary school and Tuttle had grades seven through twelve. By 2007 there weren't enough kids to keep that arrangement going and now the dozen or so kids from Pettibone go to Medina or Steele, both about forty miles away. The Post Office and its rural delivery service are still hanging on, but there are rumblings of cutting back the hours.

Still, there are several thriving businesses. The two bars and the café do well. There aren't many farmers left. The Standard Oil Agency closed after Dad left and the Farmers Union takes care of the few remaining. Arena Manufacturing, which does welding and iron works, is a new industry in town and a family in Pingree contracts with local farmers who have irrigation systems to raise potatoes.

"Pettibone is nothing like it used to be. There are so few young people left, we are mostly an area of oldies," Nancy says. "I live in Petersville Township, just north of town. In the whole thirty-six square miles of the township there are only seventeen of us living here and only two are kids. The township north of us has only three people." In 1920 the population of Kidder County was 7,798; in 2010 it was 2,435.

The Conservation Reserve Program took a lot of the land out of production, ostensibly for conservation reasons, which consequently raised the rents making it doubly difficult for young farmers to get started. Even the ones that wanted to stay found they couldn't.

"We still have a very nice community building *[the new hall that replaced the old one of my childhood]*. Our Savior's Lutheran is the only remaining church and that has very few members left. It's become the community church; all the funerals are held there," she says.

But in one hopeful sign, a set of triplets was born just before Thanksgiving 2012.

The Legacy

...every least loving act or thought

S ue's life was not so extraordinary. Every life is a story, after all. But it was well-documented. It shows how seemingly small decisions can have far-reaching effects. What prompted her Pop to buy the piano that defined so much of her life? What if it really had been repossessed? What if Claude had returned home in time to make that deposit the day before the bank failed? It might have meant the difference between staying in Pettibone or following Margaret's family west. What sparked her love of travel? It began with the honeymoon trip to the Black Hills and led to the bold family road trip to Yellowstone Park in 1940, the eye-opening trips to California and the life changing trip to Europe with Claudia and Giulio. Her friendship with Helen Vogel and the summer of enlightenment with Dexter Marsh led to her study of Christian philosophy which was distilled in her sermonette to the ALCW in 1981: "that every least loving act or thought diminishes by that amount the sin and sorrow of the world." From then on this premise guided her every day.

We continue to enjoy her rich legacy of music; half a dozen or so grandchildren have been, at one time or another, professional musicians. Two of her sons-in-law, Vern and John, continued baking her famous dark bread. I still make it on John's birthday every year. I miss her chokecherry jelly. We tend to be a family of cat lovers as she was. I play Words with Friends, an on-line version of Scrabble, with Lue and Keeny, my daughters and nieces.

In December, 2006, when her estate was settled, I wrote this letter to my children:

> *Dear Kids,*
>
> *I happily pass on your share of Grandma's inheritance.*
>
> *Grandma and Grandpa worked hard when working hard was physical. He drove that red gas truck over dreadful dirt roads in all kinds of North Dakota weather. She took in boarders and gave music lessons and gardened. You know the stories.*
>
> *It is astonishing to me that even though Grandpa probably never made more than $5,000 a year in all the years he worked, he left her an estate of about $150,000.*
>
> *When he died, she lived on Social Security and his savvy investments. She spent it on travel, education and music and gave away a lot of it to charity. She lived almost twenty years more, that last year and a half in a nursing home, and still left over $100,000 to her kids — none of whom really need it.*
>
> *So you see what a legacy of frugality and generosity you have in your hands. I know you will use it in ways that would make her smile.*

As of this writing (2013) Sue has sixty-five living descendants. Wally died in 2009; Bonnie in 2011. None of them live in North Dakota. Most of them still have an afghan and a tatted doily.

ACKNOWLEDGMENTS

No project like this comes off without a lot of help from one's friends. They are numerous, but special thanks and appreciation go out to these:

Thanks first to my mom, Sue Rawson, for leaving me the raw materials and the challenge of bringing it off, and most of all for trusting me with some of the most intimate details of her life.

To my daughter, Polly Letofsky, who showed me that it could be done, by keeping on keeping on, and pointed a way through the labyrinth when I was stuck.

To Maxine Fifer who transcribed the early tapes and the Europe journal.

To Sally Cushman and Maureen Kopach who volunteered to be the first non-family readers and had the courage to tell me what didn't work.

To Mary C. Canavan, my copy editor and proofreader, who can spot a typo at twenty paces.

To Carol White, the designer, who made it look like a real book.

To Shannon McBride, neighbor and friend, who produced the family tree and the map of Kidder County, North Dakota.

To my son, P.J. Letofsky, who digitized all the photos and brought some old ones back from the dead.

To my sisters, Lue Rawson, (Colleen) Keeny Gores and Arlene Flanders, who knew Sue as long as I did, sometimes more intimately, who were quick to answer my emails asking for such inane details as "Do you remember what car they were driving when…?"

And to my nieces Allison Voehringer, Jane McDaniel, Stephanie Griffin and Sydney Lenit, who provided a needed perspective from the next generation.

To my daughters Cara and Laurie Letofsky who encouraged me to write about my own childhood growing up in Pettibone.

To the State Library of North Dakota and the Pima County Library in Tucson who found resources and statistics I couldn't find on my own.

To Hazel Stuart and Elaine Luehr who put together the first, remarkably complete history of Pettibone for the Golden Jubilee in 1960.

To Ann Low, the young diarist from Kensal, ND, whose *Dust Bowl Diary* provided ballast for my own thin descriptions drawn from family lore.

And last of all, my thanks and appreciation to Eighty and Miss Puss, my furry family, who kept me company, napping nearby while I clicked away at odd hours, provided a welcome diversion when I was stuck and never failed to remind me when it was time to take a break.

And my sincere apologies to the Families for the things I didn't get quite right.